Essentials of

Political Science

Samuel A. Johnson, Ph.D.

FORMER PROFESSOR OF HISTORY AND GOVERNMENT,
HARRIS TEACHERS COLLEGE

FORMER LECTURER IN POLITICAL SCIENCE,
WASHINGTON UNIVERSITY

FORMER LECTURER IN GOVERNMENT,
ST. LOUIS UNIVERSITY

BARRON'S EDUCATIONAL SERIES, INC.

WOODBURY, NEW YORK

THIS SURVEY OF POLITICAL SCIENCE undertakes to present, briefly and simply, the essential material in this broad field of knowledge. Every effort has been made to avoid technicalities and confusing details. When it is necessary to use technical terms, they are clearly defined, and all terms, about which there might be any question of meaning, are defined in a glossary.

To pinpoint the generalized material of the text, sketches of the governments of the major powers are appended, along with "thumbnail" sketches of sixty other governments.

This little book can stand alone as a simple textbook in political science, but it will also be useful to supplement and clarify larger and more involved textbooks in the field. It is hoped, also, that many readers other than students will find it interesting and instructive.

I wish to express my gratitude to my wife, Winifred Feder Johnson, not only for general helpfulness and encouragement, but also for very specific and highly valuable assistance in proofreading and in the preparation of bibliography and index.

Samuel A. Johnson

PETERBOROUGH, NEW HAMPSHIRE

CONTENTS

1

Political Science and Its Language

Political science is one of the group of studies or
fields of knowledge that are commonly called
the social sciences. Besides economics and sociology,
the group includes anthropology and social psy-
chology, as well as other disciplines that may
be considered branches or offshoots of one of the
major fields.

History is usually included, although it differs from the other fields in that it is concerned mainly with time relationships while the others seek to analyze the present scene. All of the other social sciences borrow from history to provide perspective.

Are These Sciences? Some scholars object to calling these fields of knowledge sciences. They define a science as a body of knowledge which is so exact that "laws" can be deduced which will always hold. On the basis of these "laws," it is possible to predict exactly what will happen in any given situation. The chemist, for example, can predict exactly what chemical changes will occur if certain chemicals are combined in specified proportions under specified conditions of heat and atmospheric pressure. The physicist, without measuring, knows the exact speed and force of falling bodies, and he knows that a meter-length pendulum always beats seconds. The astronomer can calculate the orbit and speed of planets and predict exactly when one will appear in a certain position in the sky.

The social sciences are not "exact" sciences in this sense. It may be noted, however, that some of the physical sciences are not as exact as they were once thought to be. Nuclear studies have changed many of the old concepts in physics, and the discoveries of Einstein and others have shown up significant inaccuracies in Newton's so-called "law of gravitation," or more accurately, law of matter and motion. Economics does, indeed, deduce some "economic laws," such as the law of supply and demand, but these will not hold with the certainty of the laws of chemistry.

The reason is simple enough. The raw material of the social sciences is human beings, and human beings are always unpredictable. The social sciences, by definition, are dealing with human relationships. The social scientist can determine, largely by drawing on past experience as recorded in history, that people will tend to react to certain situations in certain ways, but many factors, such as emotions, prejudices, traditions, propaganda, and training, may modify or nullify the trend in given situations. Certainly these trends or tendencies are not exact laws, and the social scientist has no scientific basis for prediction. He can only set forth principles which are helpful in understanding situations and solving problems.

Nevertheless, on two scores, these fields of knowledge may properly be regarded as sciences. One is the etymology of the word. Science is simply the Anglicized form of the Latin word *scientia,* which means knowledge. It can be applied to any systematic body of knowledge, and the dictionary so defines it. The social sciences are certainly systematic bodies of knowledge. The other basis for regarding these subjects as sciences is that they use scientific methods of research, analysis, and deduction.

The Study of Government.

The Study of Government. Political science may be defined briefly as the study of government. Our word political comes from the Greek word *polis,* which means a city state—the only kind of state the ancient Greeks knew. Hence it means pertaining to the state, or to government which is the main business of the state. In colloquial usage, we are apt to associate the word political with partisanship and the conduct of elections. These are, indeed, political activities, but the term has much broader meaning. It includes anything and everything pertaining to government: form, structure, functions, and policies. Principles of political science, as a subject of study, deals with government in general rather than descriptions of particular governments. There may be some question as to whether the factual statements and generalizations it includes may properly be called principles, but we use that term for want of a better one.

Relation to Other Fields of Knowledge.

In some degree, political science is related to all the other social sciences, including history. Indeed, history is its closest relative, since it draws heavily on the information provided by historical research. Many scholars have begun their careers as historians and changed over into political scientists. History gives political science its third dimension: depth. It provides perspective for comparing and evaluating features of present day government by showing how these have developed out of the past.

Political science, sociology, and economics are all concerned with people grouped into communities or societies. They overlap heavily, and the difference is mainly a matter of emphasis. Sociology is concerned with government in such matters as social control and social legislation. Political science, in turn, recognizes that social structure is the basis of government. A scheme of government that is well adapted to one type of society may be entirely unworkable in a different social structure. For example, democratic government can work only in a democratic society. Moreover, much of the business of modern government is coping with social problems.

The relationship of political science to economics is even closer. The kind of government a country has is always entwined with the country's economic system. An ever growing proportion of the activities of all governments deal with economic matters. Governments have always exercised some control over the economic processes and, in the twentieth century, that control has grown by leaps and bounds. In a country like the Soviet Union, it is well nigh complete, and even in the democratic countries unrestrained *laissez faire* has had to yield to more and more government regulation and control of business. So the economist is always concerned with government and the political scientist with economics.

Philosophy might appear to be a totally unrelated field, but some aspects of it tie in with government. All governments are based on some particular political philosophy, and a part of the function of the political scientist is to analyze, compare, and evaluate various philosophical doctrines of government. Indeed, political philosophy has become a subdivision of political science.

Approaches.   There are several ways to approach the study of political science, but they are not mutually exclusive. Most modern studies involve several of them. The oldest approach historically is the philosophical or theoretical. Plato and Aristotle philosophised about government, and philosophers and theoreticians ever since have expounded their pet theories of what government ought to be and how it ought to function. In the Middle Ages, theologians spun their theories of the nature of the state and its proper relationship to the Deity and the Church. Strictly speaking, this theorizing is not political science at all, but the political scientist must take account of some of these theories and note the extent to which they have influenced actual government.

Modern political scientists began with the descriptive approach. They simply described, as objectively as they could, either particular governments or forms and institutions of government. From this it was an easy and inevitable step to the analytical approach. Starting with descriptive material, and drawing on political history for perspective, the analytical political scientist analyzes, compares, and evaluates different forms and institutions of government. In the process, he deduces some generalizations which may be called principles of political science.

A recent trend, an offshoot of the analytical approach, may be called the statistical approach. Those who approach the subject in this way gather great quantities of statistics about particular phases of government. They usually publish their figures grouped and classified into tables, sometimes visualized in diagrammatic charts, assuming that the trends indicated are self-evident, and leaving the reader to draw his own conclusions. These statistics are valuable, and analytical political scientists make extensive use of them as summaries of information. In this little book we shall not adhere rigidly to any one approach, but shall draw on all of them.

THE LANGUAGE OF POLITICAL SCIENCE

Its Own Terminology. To some extent, political science, like every other field of learning, has a language all its own. For the most part, we can avoid the use of technical terms. But there are a few common words that are used in political science with distinctive meanings that need to be defined.

State. The state, with its attributes and institutions, is the chief concern of political science, and it uses the term with a very definite meaning. In this sense, a state may be defined as a relatively large group of people inhabiting a more or less definite area of land, possessing sovereignty, and living under a government that is generally obeyed at home and recognized abroad. The number of people may vary from the less than a thousand permanent residents of the State of Vatican City to the hundreds of millions of residents of a country like India or China, but there must be enough people to maintain an independent government. The area of a state may vary from the slightly more than a hundred acres of Vatican City to the vast stretches of the Soviet Union. We say the area may be more or less definite, in that disputed boundaries will not invalidate a country's claim to statehood, but there must be some territory of which the state has undisputed possession.

We shall discuss the meaning of sovereingty presently but, for the moment, we may think of it as complete independence. In this sense, sovereignty is an indispensable attribute of a state. There may be a large group of people, even running into millions, inhabiting a definite territory and living under an effective government, but unless the country is completely independent of any government outside itself, it is not a state. It may be any one of several kinds of dependencies, a unit of a federal union, or even what is inaccurately called a "part sovereign state," but it is not a state in the political science sense of that word.

In the United States and some other federal unions the component units are called states, although they do not fit this definition. The reason, at least in our case, is purely historical. There was a brief period between the winning of independence and the adoption of the Constitution when the original thirteen were true states, possessing full sovereignty. At that time they very properly called themselves states, and the usage continued after they had merged into a federal union. For international purposes at least, it is the United States which is a state in the true meaning of the term. In some places, notably the Union of South Africa and some Latin American countries, the main divisions are called states, even though the country is not a federal union. These are states in name only.

Nation.   The term nation is often confused with state, even in such official usage as the name of the United Nations. The countries that are members of the United Nations may or may not be nations, but, with a couple of minor exceptions (two of the "republics" of the Soviet Union), they are all states. Strictly speaking, a nation is a sociological rather than a political grouping. It may be defined as a relatively large group of people, inhabiting a more or less definite area, and having enough in common to consider themselves a distinctive people. Attempts have been made to specify the things the people of a nation must have in common, such as language, race, religion, and common history, but no one of these is essential. There are bi-lingual nations, such as Belgium and Canada, and at least one tri-lingual nation, Switzerland. All nations are racially mixed and in some, such as the United States, racial diversity is marked. Certainly religious uniformity is no longer essential, if it ever was. Probably some measure of common historical background is necessary, but it is sometimes very remote. Actually, it is a feeling of unity that makes a people a nation, and various factors may contribute to that feeling of unity. In the United States we usually refer to the country as a whole as the nation in contrast to the separate states. This is convenient and it is unobjectionable for ordinary purposes, but in reality it is the American people who are a nation and not their governmental arrangements.

The Nation State. If the people of a nation do not have a state of their own they normally aspire to have one. Thus the Poles, though divided for a century among Prussia (later Germany), Austria, and Russia, considered themselves a nation and longed for the revival of a Polish state. Most commonly today the nation and the state coincide fairly well. This combination we call a nation state or a national state. It is this fact that has led to the confusion of terms. A national state may contain a sizable minority who do not consider themselves a part of the nation; they may even consider themselves a part of a nation which has a neighboring state to which they would like to belong. But in most cases, the overwhelming majority are of the nation whose name the state bears.

Sovereignty. Sovereignty has two aspects: external and internal. In the external relations of a state, sovereignty means complete independence of any governmental authority outside the state. This implies certain inherent sovereign powers, such as the power to wage war, the power to enter into treaties, and the power to punish certain internationally recognized offenses committed on the high seas, such as piracy. Of course the sovereign state is not quite free to do absolutely as it pleases. It limits its freedom of action by treaty commitments, but entering into the treaty was in it itself a sovereign act. In general, a state will usually obey the rules of international law, but these rules can not be enforced by any superior authority. If a state commits an act of aggression against another state, it risks war, and in this atomic age that can be a powerful deterrent. But the sovereign state recognizes no government other than its own as having legal authority over it.

Internally, sovereignty means the complete right to rule. This does not usually mean that the government of the sovereign state has absolute power, because its powers are usually restricted by a constitution. Somewhere in the state, though, this absolute authority exists. In the old absolute monarchies (of which there are still a few) the monarch held complete sovereignty; only his conscience or the fear of revolution restrained his exercise of power. In an oligarchy the sovereignty belongs to a compartively small minority of the population. In totalitarian states, sovereignty rests, at least for all practical purposes, with a political party. In Free World countries, though, sovereignty belongs to the whole people. Through the sovereign process of constitution making, they grant certain powers to their government and reserve others to themselves. Some, but not all, of these reserved powers are listed in a bill of rights or similar document as things which the government is forbidden to do.

Some scholars are arguing that the concept of sovereignty must change or is already changing. Many would assign a larger role to international law and international institutions in curbing the freedom of action of the individual state. As for internal sovereignty, a viewpoint is being advanced called the pluralistic doctrine. The prevailing view has always been that sovereignty is indivisible, although the powers of sovereignty are certainly divided in a federal system. The pluralist, however, rejects the whole concept of the indivisibility of sovereignty and holds that internal sovereignty, the right to rule, is divided among several institutions, such as government, the church, business, social customs and mores, and perhaps others. Certainly these various institutions play large parts in controlling the life and actions of individuals and, in some cases, the life of the people as a whole. It is really only a matter of semantics whether we consider this situation a division of sovereignty, or merely say that there are many influences outside sovereignty which partly control our lives.

Government. It is probably futile to try to define government. Most of us understand it sufficiently well, even though there is no fully satisfactory definition of the word. One difficulty is that it is used with various shades of meaning. In Great Britain, for example, the government means the ministry which is responsible politically to Parliament and through Parliament to the people. Perhaps for our purposes we may say that government is the institutions and their personnel which make and administer the laws and manage such public affairs as are entrusted to their care. Government in this meaning is the chief subject matter of political science.

People. In its workaday meaning of persons, *people* is one of our most used words. It is only when we have the term *the people* in a constitutional or governmental context that the word presents problems. When our constitution begins, "We the people of the United States . . . ," it is using the word people to mean a body politic, or group of people organized into a political community for the purpose of government. When the body politic is that of a sovereign state, people becomes synonymous with citizenry, or the total of all the citizens. In some situations, *the people* may include those non-citizens who are permanent residents of the state and are accorded some of the civil rights, but when we speak of sovereignty belonging to *the people,* the term includes only the citizens. In expressions like "government by the people" and "responsibility to the people," the meaning is more restricted. It then means only those citizens who can participate in government through their right to vote. Suffrage requirements vary from state to state, and even among parts of a state if it is a federal union, but there are always restrictions which deny the vote to some of the citizens. To vote, the citizen must always have reached a specified age, must usually have maintained the same residence for a required period of time, and must sometimes have a minimum of education, own a certain amount of property, or pay stipulated taxes. For practical purposes, the meaning is even narrower. *The people* who choose officials and decide issues are not all of those who can vote, but only those who do. It is not even as simple as this, though. Persons who can not vote may sometimes exert influence on government through participation in public opinion and pressure group activity. When they do, they must be considered part of *the people* so far as these activities are concerned.

POLITICAL PHILOSOPHY

Theories of the Origin of the State.   There is no need, in a brief survey of this kind, to go through the numerous political philosophies that have been advanced by thinkers from Plato's day to our own. Later it may be necessary to touch briefly on a few of them. For introductory purposes, it is enough to glance at several theories of the origin of the state and hence of its fundamental nature.

Divine Right.   One of the oldest theories, held almost universally in ancient and medieval times, is called somewhat inaccurately the divine right theory. This theory holds that some supernatural will (God in the thinking of medieval Europe) created the state, selected its ruler through some sign of divine favor, and granted this ruler sovereignty, the right to rule, as the representative of divine will. Thus the ruler was held to be infallible, because he spoke with the voice of God. In the middle ages, both kings and popes were accepted as God's agents on earth, and many a bitter controversy raged over which spoke with the higher authority. In early modern times, this doctrine, then called "Divine Right of Kings," was used to uphold the claims of absolute monarchy. After the downfall of Napoleon, the theory was secularized into the doctrine of legitimacy, which held that the head of the historic or traditional ruling family was the only legitimate ruler and was endowed with full sovereignty by natural law. Today, except in such underdeveloped countries as Ethiopia and Saudi Arabia, no one believes in divine right or even its watered down form of legitimacy. Nevertheless the doctrine has left clearly discernible influences on the governmental institutions of some very modern states, such as Great Britain.

Social Contract. Glimmerings of the social contract theory can be found in the writings of some medieval scholars, but as a clear cut doctrine it dates from the latter half of the seventeenth century when two main versions of it appeared. Both versions held that mankind originally existed in a "state of nature," without law or government other than "natural law." Views differed as to whether this "state of nature" was good or bad. All agreed, though, that the people of a group or area entered into a solemn "social compact," binding on their descendants forever, by which they created a state. The individual gave up some of his personal liberty in exchange for security and the benefits of law and order. Then the people of the state, in some unexplained manner, chose a ruler and gave him authority to govern. In the version of the English philosopher, Thomas Hobbes, the people, by this "social compact," had vested sovereignty forever in a line of rulers, so that the King was the beneficiary of the compact, not a party to it, and revolution against him was a violation of the compact itself. Thus Hobbes used the doctrine to denounce the Puritan Revolution and to uphold the authority of the Stuart kings.

A generation later, another Englishman, John Locke, postulated a second step. When the people had formed the state by the "social compact," they entered into a "social contract" with a ruler and his heirs. Thus the King was a party to this contract and was bound by it to rule honestly and justly. Should he fail to do so, he broke his contract and so released his people from their obligation of allegiance; they were then justified in overthrowing him. Locke expounded his theory to justify the Revolution of 1688 against James II. This Lockian version, as elaborated by the French *philosophes*, became the philosophical basis for the American and French Revolutions. Thomas Jefferson used it as the justification of the Declaration of Independence.

In modern times, bodies politic and even states have been created in this way. The earliest known example was in the colony of Plymouth in New England when, by the Mayflower Compact, the Pilgrims agreed to "associate themselves together into a civil body politic." The arrangement became so common in the settlement of early New England that a general name for it developed. When a group would go out from an already settled area to launch a new settlement or "plantation," they would adopt a "plantation covenant" along the lines of the Mayflower Compact. In 1639, three towns on the Connecticut River merged into a single colony by adopting "The Fundamental Orders of Connecticut." Although intended only as a temporary substitute for a colonial charter until one could be obtained, this document was the first written constitution in the world's history drawn up by representatives of the people who were to live under it.

As with divine right, no one today believes that primitive states originated in a social contract. Out of the idea, however, grew our concept of government by the consent of the governed which is the philosophical basis of government throughout the Free World.

Patriarchy. Another theory once widely held, with Scripture quoted to prove it, was the patriarchal theory. According to this view, the early state grew out of an expansion of the family. The oldest and most direct descendant of the original father of the family became the partriarch or ruler of the clan and, as the clan expanded into a tribe, he became the chief or king. In some parts of the world, especially the Middle East, there are indications that the primitive states originated in this way, but from the outset the "family" were not all blood relatives but only a group who lived or migrated together. However, this certainly was not the universal origin of the state.

Power. In the latter half of the nineteenth century, the explanation most favored was the power or "strong man" theory. According to this view, in a primitive group of savages the man who was the strongest in will or in physical strength would impose his rule on other members of the group and so become its chief. As the group expanded by conquering and absorbing other groups, its chief developed into the king of a primitive state. In some instances, this probably happened, but we can not be sure it happened everywhere. At any rate, out of this theory has grown the doctrine, still widely held, that fundamentally the state rests on power or force, and that sovereignty is based on this power or force.

Evolution. Today most students of the subject accept some form of the evolutionary theory. It is also called the "Topsy" theory, from the character Topsy in *Uncle Tom's Cabin* who said that she never was born, just growed. Probably the earliest beginnings of governmental organization came about in various ways: sometimes patriarchy, sometimes power, and sometimes by a priest of a nature cult imposing his rule on the devotees as a representative of the god (a rudimentary form of divine right). Whatever its earliest beginnings, the state as we know it evolved in keeping with circumstances and environmental surroundings. Nevertheless, we must take account of the older and now largely discarded theories because each of them, through historical development, has left its influence on at least some modern states.

TEST YOURSELF-QUIZ

Without referring back to the text, check the answer or completion in each question that you think is right. Then turn to answers on page 236 and see how well you have done.

1. Political science may be defined as the study of:
( ) a. How to get elected to office.
(X) b. Maneuvering for advantage in public or private affairs.

( ) c. Everything about government.
( ) d. Political parties.

2. Some people object to calling political science, economics and sociology sciences because:
( ) a. They do not use scientific methods of research.
(✗) b. They are not "exact."
( ) c. They do not deal with the physical world.
( ) d. They do not produce new inventions.

3. Political science is related most closely to:
( ) a. History.
(✗) b. Sociology.
( ) c. Economics.
( ) d. Philosophy.

4. The most distinguishing feature of a state is:
( ) a. Land.
( ) b. People.
(✗) c. Government.
( ) d. Sovereignty.

5. A nation is:
( ) a. The whole country as distinct from its parts.
( ) b. All the people who speak the same language.
(✗) c. A large group of people in a certain area who have a distinctive sense of unity.
( ) d. The same as a state.

6. The theory of the origin of the state that has had the most influence in shaping society and government in Free World countries is:
( ) a. Divine right.
( ) b. Social contract.
( ) c. Patriarchy.
( ) d. Force.

7. For most purposes, the term "the people," when used in connection with government, means:
( ) a. All the inhabitants of a country.
( ) b. All citizens of a country.

( ) c. Persons who have the right to vote.
( ) d. Persons who do vote.

8. A nation state is a country in which:
( ) a. All the people speak the same language.
( ) b. Most of the people think of themselves as belonging to the
same nation.
( ) c. There is no minority group which considers itself as belonging to a different nation.
( ) d. Sovereignty belongs to the people.

SUGGESTIONS FOR DISCUSSION

1. Are the social sciences really sciences? Why or why not?
2. Clarify the relationship of political science to the other social sciences.
3. Evaluate the good and bad points of the various approaches to the
study of political science.
4. Distinguish internal and external sovereignty.
5. Discuss and evaluate the pluralist theory of sovereignty.
6. What is the distinction between a state and a nation?
7. In what ways are theories of the origin of the state important?
8. How do you think a knowledge of political science can be useful?

BIBLIOGRAPHY

Cowling, M., *The Nature and Limits of Political Science* (London and
New York, 1963).
Hobhouse, L. T., *The Metaphysical Theory of the State* (New York,
1962).
Laski, H. J., *Introduction to Politics* (New York, 1962).
Lowie, R. H., *The Origin of the State* (New York, 1962).
MacIver, R. M., *The Modern State* (Fair Lawn, N. J., 1964).
Roucek, J. S., Ed., *Classics in Political Science* (Ames, Iowa, 1964).
Runciman, W. G., *Social Science and Political Theory* (London and
New York, 1963).
Schieder, T., *The State and Society in Our Times* (Camden, N. J.,
1962).

2

The State and Its Sovereignty

A state consists of four elements: people, territory, government, and sovereignty. We have already considered the meaning of these terms, but we must now look at them in a little more detail, and we must consider them jointly in their relation to each other.

People. The first essential of a state is people: those who govern and those who are governed. The number of people may vary from a few hundred to hundreds of millions. There are several small states in the world with populations of only a few thousand each, but the typical state numbers its people in millions. A considerable proportion, normally an overwhelming majority, of these people must be citizens; that is, they must be full members of the body politic of the state. What proportion of these people have the right to participate in government by voting or being elected to office varies from state to state. In an absolute monarchy, only the king and perhaps the higher nobility have such rights. Still, all who owe allegiance to the state or its ruler are considered members of the political community as citizens or subjects.

Territory. Every state must possess territory over which it exercises full control. The area may vary from a mere pinpoint on the map to the greater part of a continent. There is always some block of territory, large or small, which is the "homeland" of the state, but there may be disconnected areas, sometimes larger than the homeland and separated by great distances, which are also a part of the territory of the state. In some cases, boundaries may be undefined or in dispute, but there must be some area that is the undisputed territory of the state. It does not follow that all other states must recognize this territory of a state. For example, all of the territory of the State of Israel is claimed by surrounding Arab states. However the Arabs can not deny that Israel exercises effective control over this territory, and Israel's possession of it is recognized by most states of the world.

Government. Every state must have a government which is generally obeyed by the people of the state and which is able to enforce its authority under all normal conditions. This government must be recognized by some other states, though not necessarily by all other states. Normally this government will be "legitimate," either because of its long existence or because it has been set up by established constitutional process. "Legitimacy," however, is not necessary to statehood. A government may recently have been set up by revolution or *coup d'état*, but if it is generally obeyed, can enforce its claim to authority, and gains the recognition of at least a few foreign governments, it qualifies as the government of the state.

Nor is there any standard form of government. In fact, no two governments are exactly alike. It can be an absolute monarchy, a constitutional monarchy, any of several kinds of republic, or any of the numerous forms of dictatorship. So long as it meets the requirements of being generally obeyed, enforcing its authority, and having some measure of foreign recognition, it is the government of the state.

Sovereignty. Presently we shall discuss a bit more fully the changing concepts of sovereignty, but at this point there is little to add to what has already been said. However sovereignty is conceived, it is an absolutely essential element of a state. A community may have all the other characteristics of statehood, even including autonomy in government (which means that it has its own government which manages most governmental affairs), but, unless it has full sovereignty, it is not a state.

UNITARY AND FEDERAL STATES

Classification of Governments and States. Governments are classified on several bases and later we may have occasion to consider some of these classifications. States themselves, though, are classified only into unitary and federal.

Unitary States. A unitary state is one in which all the sovereign powers that any government within the state may exercise are concentrated at one level of government. There may be divisions—provinces, counties, cities, or others—which have a high degree of local self government. Some of them may even have autonomy, including the right to adopt and amend their own constitutions or charters. In every case, however, final authority over the divisions rests with the central government. Administration may be centralized, as in France, or decentralized, as in Great Britain.

Federal States. A federal state is one in which such powers of sovereignty as may be exercised are divided between two (or among more than two) levels of government: a central government and governments of the component units. These powers are apportioned in some manner by the constitution of the country. In the United States, the Constitution grants certain sovereign powers to the central government and reserves all others to the so-called states. In Canada, certain powers are granted to the provinces, and all others reserved to the Dominion. Each level exercises its powers independently of control by government at the other level, though both levels are subject to the constitution of the country. The typical federal state or federal union has two levels of government, but there can be three or even more.

Russia, for example, is one of the republics of the Union of Socialist Soviet Republics, but it also has a federal organization within itself.

The component units of a federal state are known by different names in different countries. In our country they are called states, although they are not true states in the political science sense of the word. In Canada they are called provinces, though they do not fit the definition of a province either. In Germany they are called *Länder* or lands; in the Soviet Union, republics; in Switzerland, cantons. It goes without saying that the powers of external sovereignty must always belong to the central government. These include the power to conduct foreign relations, the power to make war, and the power to make treaties. The powers of internal sovereignty may be apportioned in any manner, but normally the central government will have powers to deal with matters that concern the whole country, with matters of more local concern given to the component units. The component units have their own divisions which may have extensive powers of self-government, but these divisions have no sovereign authority of their own.

Quasi-Federal States. There are a number of countries that appear superficially to be federal unions. Their component units adopt and amend their own constitutions and normally conduct government at their level with little or no interference from the central authority. The catch is that there is a constitutional provision by which the central government may, at least in specified circumstances, overrule the governments of the component units. Thus in the Union of South Africa the central Parliament may, whenever it decides that the national interest requires it, overrule any legislation by the parliaments of the "states." In several Latin American republics, the central government, having declared a "state of seige" (or as we should say, a state of emergency), can suspend the government of a state or province and appoint a "federal intervenor" to rule as agent of the central government. Even in the Federal Republic of Germany (West

Germany) the central government may, in certain circumstances, veto acts of the *Länder*.

These states, which appear to be federal but do not quite measure up, are called quasi-federal states. The older political scientists regarded them as merely decentralized unitary states, but it would seem better to consider them something between federal and unitary, some of them leaning more in one direction, some the other. In fact, even in such old, well established federal unions as the United States and Canada, there is an ever growing tendency for the central government to find ways to exercise control over the component units. Perhaps these are evolving from true federal to quasi-federal states.

CHANGING CONCEPTS OF SOVEREIGNTY

Present Trend. We noted earlier that some scholars are saying that the concept of sovereignty must change or is already changing. Others still adhere rigidly to the old viewpoint, but the advocates of change would seem to have the wave of the future on their side. The old view of absolutes, absolute independence and absolute right to rule, just do not fit the facts of today's world. The change has not developed far enough to warrant a new definition, but the old idea of the absolute character of sovereignty is obviously losing ground.

Internal Sovereignty. Without taking the pluralists too seriously, the state, even in the realm of internal sovereignty, is restrained in its freedom of action by something more than its own constitution. External pressures are exerted in matters that the state would formerly have considered strictly its domestic affairs, such as race relations and religious freedom, to a degree that sometimes proves irresistible. There has developed what may be called a world conscience and an almost universal belief in human rights. These often serve to restrain a state in its treatment of its own citizens. The development of traditions, which transcend and even overrule formal constitutions, weaken the absolute character of the state's internal sovereignty.

External Sovereignty. External sovereignty has lost even more of its absolute character. A growing respect for international law leads even major powers to observe its rules, sometimes to their own disadvantage, even though they could be compelled to do so only by defeat in war. International organizations, especially the United Nations, exert pressures that bring changes in policy of even the strongest powers, and can usually impose their will almost completely on weaker states. The force of world public opinion is becoming an ever more powerful force in controlling the action of sovereign states. Finally, the fear of atomic destruction has become a far more powerful deterrent than the fear of old-fashioned war ever was in restraining the freedom of action of even the strongest powers.

Relativity of Sovereignty. We must continue to use the old definition of sovereignty until a new one emerges, but in our thinking we must realize that sovereignty is relative rather than absolute. In theory, a state is completely independent and has complete right to rule, but in practice it must defer to influences and pressures that restrain its freedom of action.

Who Is Sovereign? The question "who is sovereign" is largely an academic one and need not detain us long. In an absolute monarchy, of which few survive, the monarch is sovereign and his people are his subjects, having no rights that he is bound to respect. In modern constitutional monarchies, such as Great Britain and the Scandinavian countries, the monarch is still sometimes called the sovereign, but he is sovereign in name only; he has few if any of the powers of sovereignty. In the Fascist and Nazi totalitarian states, the state itself, as an organism or institution, was regarded as sovereign. Its people might be called citizens, but actually they were subjects of this organic state and, for all practical purposes, of the dictator or party oligarchy which controlled it. In all Free World countries, the theory is that the people are sovereign, but, as we have already seen, there is some difficulty in determining just which people really share in the exercise of this sovereignty. All that really matters is that sovereignty must exist somewhere within the state.

SO-CALLED "PART SOVEREIGN STATES"

Meaning. The expression "part-sovereign state" is really a contradiction in terms. By definition, a state is fully sovereign and any community which is not can not properly be called a state at all. Still the expression is widely used and is applied to various types of communities which fall just short of true statehood.

Component Units of a Federal Union. One of these types is a component unit of a federal union. Such a unit may be called a state, as in the United States, or it may be called something else. It possesses extensive powers of internal sovereignty which it exercises free of control by the central government. Normally such a unit will have none of the powers of external sovereignty. It carries on no foreign relations and can not enter into treaties or make war. A theoretical exception is found in the member republics of the Soviet Union, two of which are represented in the United Nations Assembly. Actually, the strict control by the central organization of the Communist Party makes this pretense of external sovereignty meaningless.

Autonomous Dependencies. Another type of so-called part-sovereign state is the autonomous dependency. These communities usually enjoy complete internal self-government, often including the privilege of adopting and amending their own constitutions, though token approval by the mother country is sometimes required. Their foreign relations are conducted by the mother country. Even in internal matters, though, the government of the mother country has the power, although it may seldom use it, to override the acts of the dependency government and even to legislate for the dependency directly. The members of the French Union have a status something like this. True, the constitution of the Fifth Republic guarantees them against interference in their internal affairs by the French government, but the President of the Republic, acting as head of the Union, can interfere. A better illustration is found in the British dominions as they were before World War I. Their internal self-government was so complete that the government in London absolutely never interfered. Even so, the British Parliament had authority to legislate for the dominions, so they could not be said to possess internal sovereignty. Thus, strictly speaking, the autonomous dependency is not even part-sovereign, as is a member of a federal union, but for some purposes it is sometimes treated as a state. Thus the British dominions were permitted to become charter members of the League of Nations.

Lands in Transition. Dependencies that are definitely in the process of becoming independent states represent a third type. Technically the former ruling power has not yet relinquished its sovereignty over them, but it has set a date for doing so and permits them to act as though they were fully independent. At the close of World War II, India and the Philippines were in this situation. Britain and the United States respectively had made definite promises of independence, had permitted these future states to adopt constitutions, set up governments and to act independently. All that remained to be done was the formal transfer of sovereignty. While in this situation, both of these countries were permitted to take part in the San Francisco Conference that drafted the Charter of the United Nations and to become charter members of that organization.

Others. This is not a complete list of the types of communities that may be called part-sovereign states, but these types illustrate the meaning of the term. Perhaps quasi-state would be a better name, since they are communities that, to some extent,

look and act like states, but fail to qualify as true states because
they do not possess full sovereignty.

DEPENDENCIES AND COLONIES

Varieties of Dependencies. A dependency may be defined
as any land with its people which owes allegiance to a state of
which it is not an integral part. There are so many kinds of
dependencies that we can glance at only a few of the most common varieties. Some of them are ruled completely by the country
to which they belong. Some have an amount of self-government
varying from a mere modicum to full autonomy. Some do not
belong to the country that rules them, but are held in trust
from the United Nations with the avowed aim of preparing them
for independence.

Colonies. The word colony is sometimes used as inter-
changeable with dependency, all of the dependencies of a country being referred to as its colonies. In the British Empire, the
term colony (actually the full term is Crown colony) has a special
legal meaning referring to a particular governmental relationship
between the colony and the mother country. In the very strict
sense, a colony is an area, normally with a separate local government, in which the predominant element of the population
(though not necessarily a numerical majority) are transplanted
from the mother country. Thus the thirteen colonies which, when
they gained independence, formed the United States, were
colonies in this strict sense of the term. Most of the colonists or
their ancestors had actually migrated to America from England.
The word is also used to mean a sizable group of people from
one country who have migrated into another sovereign state
where they retain many of the characteristics of their old nationality (usually including language) and have not been fully
assimiliated into the population of their new home. This meaning
of colony has significance in sociology, but not in political science.

Colonies (except the British ones) do not have a standardized governmental relationship to their mother country. The ancient Greek colonies were independent from the outset, though they usually maintained close commercial relations with the mother city state. At the other extreme, in the eighteenth century the American colonies of all European countries except Britain were governed arbitrarily by officers sent out by the government of the mother country. For the past century, the tendency has been for most "colonial powers" (countries that have dependencies) to grant ever increasing self-government to most of their dependencies, but especially to those that are true colonies, and in many cases to grant them independence.

Annexed Territories. In the past, states have sometimes annexed territories, either contiguous or non-contiguous. Annexation has usually come about in one of three ways: conquest, cession by another sovereign state, or seizure of an undeveloped area over which no other state had established its rule. At first, the annexed territory was governed arbitrarily by the annexing state, and in some cases this situation has continued to the present. In other cases, especially if the annexed territory was contiguous, it has, after a transition period of being governed as a dependency, been absorbed fully into the annexing state and is no longer considered annexed territory. With the single exception of Algeria, which the French undertook unsuccessfully to incorporate into France proper, non-contiguous annexed territories were all ruled as dependencies, sometimes with more or less self-government, either down to the present or until they were lost in war or given independence.

Protectorates. A protectorate is a former state which nominally retains its sovereignty but which has bound itself by treaty, usually imposed by force or threat of force, to accept the guidance and virtual control of another sovereign state. Protectorates are usually, but not necessarily, monarchies. The native monarch is retained and goes through the motions of ruling. The protecting state, though, maintains a high commissioner or other officer in the protectorate who dictates every official act of the monarch. This has been found to be an effective device for ruling backward dependencies since it does not arouse in the people of the protectorate a strong resentment against foreign rule.

Semi-Protectorates and Protected States. Although these terms do not mean quite the same thing, they are used almost interchangeably to designate what might be called a type of "part-sovereign state." Like the protectorate, they nominally retain full sovereignty, but have bound themselves by treaty to accept limited control by a stronger state in exchange for protection. The difference lies in the word *limited.* Under normal conditions, the country is governed by its own government, usually a republic in form, though in its foreign relations it is usually restrained from making certain treaty commitments or making loans in any foreign country except the protecting one. But in time of crisis, either from threat of attack by another state or a break-down of law and order in the protected country, the protecting state has the right to send in armed forces and take control until the danger passes. In some cases, the protecting state may take over the government completely. In other cases, it may use its troops only to preserve order or take over financial administration. This was the relationship that existed between the United States and Cuba under the "Platt Amendment" treaty from 1902 to 1933. Normally the semi-protectorate or protected state is accepted as a state internationally. It may join any international organizations, such as the United Nations, or enter into any treaty that does not conflict with its commitments to the protecting state.

Occupied Territories. An occupied territory is any area that is occupied by armed forces of a foreign state. This situation, normally intended to be temporary, may come about in various ways. If a state is defeated in war, all or part of its territory may be occupied by the victor or victors pending a peace settlement. Sometimes a stronger state may intervene in a weaker one and occupy all or part of its territory. Again, a state may seize and occupy disputed territory that is claimed by another state. Occasionally an international organization like the United Nations or the Organization of American States, uses troops supplied by some of its member states to occupy an area for the purpose of restoring or preserving order, or to stop local fighting. Examples are the U. N. occupation of areas in the Middle East to prevent a revival of the war between Israel and her Arab neighbors, and the U. N. occupation of the Congo to stop a devastating civil war.

If the occupied area is disputed territory, conquered territory which is to be annexed, or a state or part of a state in which government has broken down, the occupying state or states will administer it through military government. This may vary from giving the commander of the occupation forces governing authority, subject always to orders from his home government, to such elaborate arrangements as were set up in Germany after World War II, presided over by Military officers, but staffed with civilian administrators. In other cases, the old government is allowed to continue to function subject to some direction and a veto of its actions by the commander of the occupation forces. In Austria and Japan, after World War II, the occupation commanders (four of them jointly in the case of Austria) directed the creation of such native governments which continued to function under the supervision of the occupation authorities until treaties restored the full independence of these countries. In general, we may think of an occupied territory as a temporary dependency.

League Mandates and U. N. Trust Territories. After World War I, Germany and Turkey were stripped of all of their dependencies and most of these became League of Nations mandates. Each was assigned by the peace treaty to a member state of the League of Nations that was called the mandatory power. In a few cases of very backward areas, the mandatory state was permitted to annex the territory as a direct dependency. In most cases, though, it was responsible to the League for the administration of the mandated territory and was to govern it with a view to preparing it for independence. By the time of World War II, many of these, especially former Turkish dependencies in the Middle East, had become independent states.

After World War II, Italy and Japan were stripped of their possessions. Ethiopia was immediately restored to independence, but the four major Allies were given authority to dispose of the other Italian possessions. After several years of failure to agree, the Big Four turned the matter over to the United Nations Assembly. The Assembly gave independence to Libya, but set up temporary international administrations in the other former Italian dependencies.

In the Far East, Formosa was returned to China and Korea was divided for occupation between the Soviet Union and the United States. The remaining Japanese possessions, along with the surviving League mandates, were made United Nations trust territories. Each was assigned for administration to a member state of the United Nations. The arrangement differs from the old League mandate system chiefly in that the trustee state is more fully responsible to the United Nations than the mandatory power was to the League. It must make annual reports to the U. N. Trusteeship Council and this Council may order inspections at any time to find out whether or not the trust territory is being administered according to United Nations rules and principles. Thus, they are essentially joint dependencies of the United Nations, but are administered by the trustee state much as though they were its own dependencies except that the trustee is answerable to the U. N. for its treatment of the trust territory.

Internationally Administered Lands. From time to time areas, usually small, have been administered by international councils, usually set up by such organizations as the League of Nations or the United Nations. The arrangement is ordinarily temporary, though sometimes it is intended to be permanent. The scheme has been resorted to, mainly, in situations where one state had a valid claim to the area, but the interests of another state were vitally involved. For example, after World War I, the city of Danzig in the Polish Corridor was placed under League of Nations rule because, while the inhabitants were Germans and preferred to be a part of Germany, the Poles needed to use the city as a seaport. At the same time, the Saar Valley was placed under League administration. The people were Germans and always had been, but France demanded the coal mines as war indemnity, claiming that they were essential to French economy. Some time after World War II, some of the Italian colonies were placed under United Nations administration because there was no suitable country to whom they might be assigned as a mandate. The arrangement has seldom lasted very long and has never worked satisfactorily, but while it has lasted the area has been a dependency of an international organization.

TEST-YOURSELF QUIZ

Without referring back to the text, check the answer or completion in each question that you think is right. Then turn to answers on page 236 and see how well you have done.

1. For most purposes in political science, states are classified into:
( ) a. Unitary and federal.
( ) b. National and multi-national.
( ) c. Sovereign and part-sovereign.
( ) d. Monarchies, dictatorships and republics.

2. Internal sovereignty means:
( ) a. Dictatorial power in the government.
( ) b. Complete right to rule.
( ) c. Protection of all human rights.
( ) d. The will of the people is supreme.

3. External sovereignty means that a country:
( ) a. May do absolutely as it pleases.
( ) b. Is legally independent of any government outside itself.
( ) c. Is recognized as independent by other countries.
( ) d. Is not legally bound by its treaties.

4. Which of these would not be called a part-sovereign state?
( ) a. A component unit of a federal union.
( ) b. An autonomous dependency.
( ) c. A country that is being given independence and is fully self-governing.
( ) d. A colony that is ruled almost completely by the mother country.

5. To be the government of a sovereign state, a government must be:
( ) a. In complete control of all the territory claimed by the state.
( ) b. Accepted as "legitimate" by all the people of the state.
( ) c. Recognized by some foreign governments.
( ) d. Recognized by all foreign governments.

6. A federal state (or federal union) is a country in which:
( ) a. The people are of different nationalities or races.
( ) b. All sovereign powers which may be exercised are divided between two (or among more that two) levels of government.
( ) c. Some powers are "reserved to the people."
( ) d. Divisions of the country are self-governing, but may be overruled by the central government.

7. To qualify as a state territorially, a country must have:
( ) a. Control of all the territory it claims.
( ) b. Territory of millions of square miles.
( ) c. Some territory over which it has complete control.
( ) d. No disputed boundaries.

8. Which of these would not be classed as dependencies?
( ) a. A partly self-governing colony.
( ) b. A protectorate.
( ) c. A United Nations trust territory.
( ) d. Annexed territory which is governed as part of the annexing country.

SUGGESTIONS FOR DISCUSSION

1. What is meant by saying that legitimacy is not necessary to statehood?

2. Distinguish unitary, federal and quasi-federal states.
3. How is the concept of sovereignty changing?
4. How and why is the term "part-sovereign state" self-contradictory?
5. What characteristics must a government have to be the government of a state?
6. What territory is necessary for an area to be a state?
7. Compare the meaning of the terms "colony" and "dependency."
8. Distinguish between a "protectorate" and a "semi-protectorate" or "protected state."

BIBLIOGRAPHY

Bennett, W. H., *American Theories of Federalism* (University, Ala., 1964).

Center of the Study of Democratic Institutions, *Two Faces of Federalism* (Santa Barbara, Cal., 1961).

Ebenstein, W., *Today's Isms: Communism, Fascism, Capitalism, Socialism* (Englewood Cliffs, N. J., 1961).

Lovenstein, M., *Capitalism, Communism, Socialism* (Minneapolis, 1962).

Peterson, W. C., *The Welfare State in France* (Lincoln, Neb., 1960).

Schumpeter, J. A., *Capitalism, Socialism and Democracy* (New York, 1962).

Wells, R. H., *The States in West German Federalism* (New York, 1961).

Wheare, K. C., *Federal Government* (Fair Lawn, N. J., 4th ed., 1963).

3

Ideology

An ideology may be defined as a doctrine or set of doctrines which is accepted as the basis of government and largely determines the character of government. All states of the Free World follow the ideology of democracy. Mussolini and Hitler had slightly different versions of fascistic doctrine. The Soviet Union holds to the ideology usually called Communism.

Ideology in History. The term ideology is comparatively new, but the fact is as old as history. The Middle Eastern states of ancient times, Babylonia, Egypt and others, accepted the doctrine of a god-king as their basis of government. Some of the Greek city states, such as Athens, had an early version of the ideology of democracy, while others, such as Sparta, based their government and social structure on militarism. The early Romans developed the concept of the state as *res publica* (public affairs) from which we get our word republic. From the tenth to the thirteenth century, feudalism was the ideology of western Europe, along with being the social, economic, and military system of the time. The king was the vassal of God. The seventeenth and eighteenth centuries were a time of conflict, sometimes in the form of violent revolution, between the ideologies of natural rights and divine right of kings. For our purpose, though, we need concern ourselves only with very recent and contemporary ideologies.

TOTALITARIANISM

Meaning of Totalitarianism. Rather than being an ideology in itself, totalitarianism is a class of ideologies. Presently we shall have a look at some of its principal varieties. They differ in theoretical basis and in concepts of the structure and operation of government. They do, however, all have certain features in common. They all hold to the doctrine of total government; that is, government which controls, or at least claims the right to control, all phases of the life of the people it governs. Such a government may have a constitution which purports to guarantee certain civil rights, but in practice there is no personal liberty as that term is understood in the Free World. There is no effective protection against arbitrary arrest and imprisonment, no assurance of a fair trial, and no security against government interference in private life, even in such matters as religion. Another common feature of all totalitarian regimes is that they are irresponsible. There is no orderly way, such as free elections, in which they may be compelled to respond to the will of the people. There may be a formality of elections, but the voter is given no freedom of choice and so can not use his ballot to hold his government responsible.

Forms of Totalitarianism. Absolute monarchy is a form of totalitarianism. So, too, is military dictatorship. More important in the present century are such forms as Italian Fascism, German Nazism, and Communism.

Fascism. Mussolini named his movement Fascism from the old Roman *fascis,* a battle axe tied in a bundle of rods which was carried before Roman magistrates as a symbol of authority. Thus the name implies that Fascism was authoritarian as well as totalitarian. The authority in this case was the state itself, which was conceived, not as the body of citizens acting collectively, but as a living organism and an end in itself. The citizen stood in much the same relation to the state that a body cell has to the organism of which it is a part. Such cells may differ according to the biological functions they perform, but they have no individuality and no existence apart from the organism. Similarly the citizen of a Fascist state had no individuality and no rights of his own; he was to find his "fulfillment" in performing faithfully, for the benefit and glory of the state, the functions that might be assigned to him. We need not go into the structure of Mussolini's state. It was, of course, a dictatorship, nominally of the Fascist Party, but actually of Mussolini as *duce* or leader, both of the party and of the state. The only ameliorating feature was that Mussolini did not carry his theory to its logical conclusion and life under him did not become unbearable until he came under the domination of Hitler.

Nazism. There is no question that Hitler got his original idea for a totalitarian state from Mussolini. As he developed his National Socialism, however, it came to differ from Fascism in several important particulars. One of the most important of these differences lay in the personality of the leader (*Führer* in German). Mussolini was a politican and something of a bluff. Hitler was a fanatic and a ruthless tyrant. Another difference was that in National Socialism, or Nazism as it was usually called, the supreme entity was not the state but the German nation. Hitler expounded a rabid racism which found its most horrible expression in the torture and massacre of Jews, but which was also taken as justification for conquering any non-German people and exploiting them for the benefit of Germans. Germans were the master race and were destined to rule the world through the German *Führer*. But Germans had no individual rights of their own and were to find their "fulfillment" in serving the *Führer* in any role assigned them in the building of this greater Germany.

Other Fascistic States. With help from both Mussolini and Hitler, Franco succeeded in overthrowing the Spanish Republic and creating a regime modeled on that of Mussolini. In Spain the regime was called Falangist and Franco called himself the *cau-*

dillo, Spanish word for leader. Franco still continues to rule Spain, but after the collapse of the Fascist and Nazi regimes he began to veer away from fascistic ideology. For a time Peron in Argentina and Vargas in Brazil set up regimes that were clearly fascistic in character. There is still a weak neo-fascist movement in Italy, but the outcome of World War II put an end to wide acceptance of any form of fascistic ideology.

Communism. If the Second World War virtually eliminated fascistic totalitarianism as a force in the world, it gave a new impetus to the type of totalitarianism usually called Communism. It is not true communism or even socialism, although the rulers of the Soviet Union, Red China, and other so-called "Communist countries" call their regimes socialist and call their organization the Communist Party, maintaining that their ultimate goal is pure communism. Real communism would mean a fully cooperative society, without formal government (Marx talked about the "withering away of the state"), with no property of any kind, without a money economy, in which each member would produce according to his ability and consume according to his needs. This has never existed (and probably never can exist) except in closely knit religious organizations in which devotion to some particular religious faith overshadowed the normal human instincts. The ideology which Communists embrace may better be called, to use their own name for it, Marxism-Leninism.

Marxism-Leninism. We can not go into all the doctrines of Karl Marx, about most of which he was far from clear in his writings. In general, he proposed public ownership of all means of production and the operation of these for the sole benefit of the workers. He did not specify a particular form of government or spell out his idea of economic arrangements. He failed to indicate who was to manage the publically operated economy. Except for his demand that the whole economy be operated for the benefit of the workers, he expressed no thoughts on such subjects as civil liberties and human rights. Essentially, Marx was negative, protesting against capitalism as he knew it in the England of the mid-nineteenth century.

Nevertheless, protest groups throughout Europe picked up the Marxian label and organized Socialist Parties. Most of these demanded the nationalization or government ownership of industry, but they differed among themselves on how to bring this about, how the nationalized industries should be managed, and what type of government would be suitable for a Socialist state. In Russia, where the movement had to operate as a secret conspiracy and hold its meetings outside the country, the Socialists split into two hostile factions. The Bolshevik (majority) group, headed by Lenin, called itself Communist; it stood for seizure of power by force and violence, and the creation of a "dictatorship of the proletariat" to run the country until true communism could be achieved. The Menshevik (minority) group called itself Social Democrat and stood for the use of peaceful political means to achieve nationalization and other reforms.

The collapse of the Tsarist regime in World War I and the failure of Russian moderates to establish an effective government opened the way for Lenin and his Bolsheviks to return from exile and seize power. Lenin became the dictator of the Russian Empire which he renamed the Union of Socialist Soviet Republics. He quoted Marxian phrases as his justification, but he found little in the teachings of Marx that could be applied to a backward country like Russia with almost no industry and with most of its population illiterate peasants. So he set about to formulate an ideology and government scheme of his own, and this became known as Marxism-Leninism. While Stalin was dictator, he added some facets of his own, and the ideology was called Marxism-Leninism-Stalinism. Since his death, most of his additions and the name Stalinism have been dropped, at least in the Soviet Union. The rift that has developed between Russian and Chinese Communism stems in part from clashes of national interest between the two countries, partly from the ambition of Mao Tsetung to be recognized as the world leader of Communism, but mainly from the fact that Khrushchev was adopting a practical policy in dealing with the Free World while Mao sticks to the hard Stalinist line.

Marxism-Leninism accepts the Marxian thesis that a foreordained course of history makes a world victory of Marxism inevitable. The inevitability of history is to be helped along, though, by governments that follow the system. In pushing for this "world revolution," the old "bourgeois" morality is discarded on the ground that the end justifies the means. Deceit, intrigue, and violence are held to be fully justified to achieve the end.

Like other forms of totalitarianism, Marxism-Leninism holds that government should be absolute and irresponsible. This is regarded as necessary in order to revolutionize the economic and social structure. It differs from fascistic totalitarianism, however, in that the supreme authority is neither the state itself nor a particular nation, but the Communist Party, which is the infallible interpreter of Marxism. The absolute authority of government may be exercised by a personal dictator, such as Stalin or Mao Tse-tung, or by a party oligarchy as in the Soviet Union at the present time. All industry and business are operated by the state, which is controlled completely by the Party. Party membership is rigidly restricted and party members are an elite class with special privileges. Personal liberty is tolerated only to the extent that it does not interfere with the designs of the Communist Party. Labor is required to be organized into party-controlled unions, but it has no collective bargaining and no right to strike. In this ideology the state is only the instrument of the Communist Party, and all aspects of life are subject to control by the state.

DEMOCRACY

Meaning. The ideology of the Free World is usually called democracy, although this is a somewhat inaccurate use of the term. Literally, democracy means rule by the people, but direct rule by the people can exist only on a very small scale. What we commonly call democracy is representative government based on the authority of the people, who are able to hold their government responsible through free elections. It does not imply a particular economic system, though most democratic countries allow a large measure of free enterprise.

As an ideology, democracy regards the state as the citizens acting collectively for purposes of government. It always guarantees extensive civil rights to its citizens and uses the authority of government to enforce these rights. It holds that the individual should have all the personal liberty that is consistent with a well ordered society. It always insists that government be responsible to the people and that the voters have the means to hold government responsible through free elections. While necessarily imposing some restrictions on suffrage, democracy implies that most adult citizens shall have the right to vote. It also requires enough freedom of political actions so that there can always be at least two contending political parties.

Democratic Government.   Within these broad bounds, there is no standard pattern of democratic government. There are several principal forms, each of which has a number of variations. Later we shall have occasion to look at some of these. When all is said, the essential characteristic of the democratic ideology is that the state exists for its citizens in contrast with totalitarianism which holds that the citizens exist for the state.

NATIONALISM

Not a True Ideology.   Strictly speaking, nationalism is not an ideology in the same sense as totalitarianism and democracy. Among a given people, it may coexist with either of these. However, it is such a potent force in guiding the thinking and determining the actions of people in many countries that it seems desirable to discuss it under the broad heading of ideology.

An Emotional Condition. Nationalism may be defined simply as devotion to one's nation or nationality, although it takes many forms and has many diverse manifestations. It differs from a true ideology in that it is basically an emotional condition, a matter of feeling. People may, of course, develop great devotion to an ideology, but the ideology itself is rational, rather than emotional; it is constructed through a process of reasoning, however faulty the reasoning may be.

Patriotism. In its simplest form, nationalism is almost synonymous with patriotism, especially if the patriotism (loyalty or devotion to one's state) is to a national state. Patriotism may vary in kind from the utterly uncritical, the "my country right or wrong" viewpoint, to the highly critical which is always demanding improvements and reforms. It may also vary in degree from a mere passive loyalty to an intense emotionalism which easily spills over into some form of hypernationalism. A modern state could hardly exist without the patriotism of its citizens.

Hypernationalism. Hypernationalism means exaggerated or excessive nationalism, and it takes a number of forms. Indeed, on its emotional side, Nazism was an extreme form of hypernationalism. A relatively mild form that was formerly prevalent in many countries was anti-foreignism. The people were not only hostile to foreigners in their midst, but were antagonistic to all foreign countries. In the United States, this feeling has, on several occasions, mushroomed into major "nativist" movements, most notably the "Know Nothing" Party of the 1850's and the Ku Klux Klan of the 1920's. Developments since World War II have largely dissipated this sentiment in most of the Free World.

Somewhat more extreme is the form commonly called "jingoism." This is an aggressive nationalism. It is a feeling that one's country should blatantly demand whatever it wants internationally and should use open threats of force to obtain it. People who feel this way are usually extremely voluble in expressing their feelings. Closely related to "jingoism" is imperialism, which in turn takes many forms. Imperialism is not a feeling, but a national policy, though it is usually supported by a feeling of "jingoism." It is a policy of gaining control over other lands or people by force, threat of force, or intrigue. Communists call all capitalist countries imperialist, but actually the major Communist states are the only really imperialist countries in the world today. Also closely related to "jingoism" is militarism. This is both a situation in which the military establishment is treated as the most important institution of the state, with great deference paid to military men whose higher officers play a dominant role in shaping government policy, and an attitude which supports this situation. This attitude often expresses itself as "jingoism."

Irredentism. The term *irredentism* comes from the Italian phrase *Italia irredenta* (unredeemed Italy). From the formation of the Italian state to World War I, Italians regarded the area around Trent in the Alps and the Istrian Peninsula as properly Italian although they were ruled by Austria. Italian sentiment demanded that these districts, which they called "unredeemed Italy," be redeemed and annexed. From this, irredentism has come to mean a feeling in any country which regards territory held by another state as an unredeemed part of the country and demands that it be acquired. Thus, from 1871 to 1918, the French considered Alsace-Lorraine as unredeemed France. It is nationalism applied to a territorial situation.

Desire for Independence. When the people of an area come to regard themselves as a nation or a nationality, but are under the rule of a state of another nationality, their nationalism almost invariably takes the form of a desire for independence. Thus for more than a century Irish nationalism meant the desire of the Irish people for independence from Britain. It is this brand of nationalism which has prompted the clamor for independence among the peoples of Africa and Southeast Asia in recent decades. With this emotion running so strong, often breaking out in acts of violence, the people concerned seldom make a rational evaluation of their qualifications (or lack of them) to maintain an independent state. As a consequence, many of the new nations which have been granted independence in recent years are finding themselves in very serious trouble.

In the past, there have been several cases in which the people who developed a strong feeling of nationality were broken into fragments. Thus, from medieval times until about a century ago, Germany consisted of a large number of independent states which, in the eighteenth and nineteenth centuries, varied in size and importance from major powers like Prussia to mere pinpoints on the map. Italy was similarly divided, with most of the little states ruled by foreigners. The Poles were partitioned among Austria, Prussia (later Germany), and Russia. Some of the Balkan peoples were partitioned in a similar fashion. In these situations, nationalism takes the form of a desire for unification, plus independence if the component fragments do not already have it. The people want a national state.

Anti-Colonialism.   Closely akin to this type of nationalism is anti-colonialism. This is both a doctrine, the belief that no people should be held in unwilling subjection to any other people or state, and a feeling. The feeling of anti-colonialism, tied in with a desire for independence, is apt to be most intense among people who are themselves being held as dependencies. However, in recent decades, the achieving of independence has not dissipated the feeling. Practically all of the newly independent national states are constantly pushing anti-colonialism in the United Nations and in their diplomacy. The major Communist states, although practicing colonialism of the worst sort, have made anti-colonialism a part of their propaganda. Thus, it is one of the strongest forces at work in international relations today.

TEST-YOURSELF QUIZ

Without referring back to the text, check the answer or completion in each question that you think is right. Then turn to answers on page 236 and see how well you have done.

1. Which of the following is not totalitarianism?
( ) a. Absolute monarchy.
( ) b. Military dictatorship?
( ) c. Marxism-Leninism.
( ) d. Strong government with free elections.

2. Which of these forms of totalitarianism holds (or held) that the supreme reality, to which all else must be subordinated, is the nation?
( ) a. Fascism.
( ) b. Nazism.
( ) c. Communism.
( ) d. Military dictatorship.

3. Which of these is not a characteristic of democratic ideology?
( ) a. Responsible government.
( ) b. Protected civil rights.
( ) c. Unrestricted suffrage for all adults.
( ) d. Representative government.

4. "Jingoism" is synonymous with:
( ) a. Patriotism.
( ) b. Aggressive hypernationalism.
( ) c. Irredentism.
( ) d. Anti-colonialism.

5. Democracy, as an ideology, is almost synonymous with:
( ) a. Responsible government.
( ) b. The free enterprise system.
( ) c. Desire for world peace.
( ) d. Universal education.

6. All forms of nationalism involve:
( ) a. Devotion to one's national state (actual or prospective).
( ) b. Imperialistic ambitions against other peoples.
( ) c. Militarism.
( ) d. Unwillingness to cooperate with other countries.

7. Militarism means:
( ) a. A strong policy of national defense.
( ) b. Drafting young men into the armed forces.

( ) c. Subordinating civil life and civil authority to military domination.

( ) d. A policy of imperialism.

8. Nationalism creates international problems and may erupt into violence when:

( ) a. It takes the form of hypernationalism.

( ) b. Subject or divided people demand an independent national state.

( ) c. It is identified with a particular ideology.

( ) d. It takes the form of anti-foreignism.

SUGGESTIONS FOR DISCUSSION

1. Discuss the term "ideology" to make sure you understand its meaning.
2. What are the common features of all forms of totalitarianism?
3. What were the distinguishing differences between Fascism and Nazism?
4. Distinguish between the real meaning of the word communism and its meaning as the name of a present-day ideology.
5. How does Marxism-Leninism differ from other forms of socialism?
6. What is the essential point of contrast between totalitarianism and democracy?
7. How does nationalism differ from a true ideology?
8. Compare the various forms of nationalism.

BIBLIOGRAPHY

American Universities Field Staff, *Expectant Peoples* (New York, 1963).

Arendt, H., *The Origins of Totalitarianism* (London, 1961).

Colegrove, K. W., *Democracy* versus *Communism* (Princeton, N. J., 1961).

Dallin. A., and others, *Diversity in International Communism* (New York, 1963).

Daniels, R. V., *The Nature of Communism* (New York, 1962).

Dux, D., Ed., *Ideology in Conflict* (Princeton, N. J., 1963).

Ebenstein, W., *Two Ways of Life* (New York, 1962).

Friedrich, C. J., and Brzezinski, Z. K., *Totalitarian Dictatorship and Autocracy* (New York, 1961).

Goldrich, D., *Radical Nationalism* (Lansing, Mich., 1962).

Grimes, A. P., and Horwitz, R. H., Eds., *Modern Political Ideologies* (New York, 1959).

Hoover, J. E., *A Study of Communism* (New York, 1963).

Jarman, T. L., *Democracy and World Conflict, 1868-1962* (London, 1963).

Lane, R. E., *Political Ideology* (New York, 1963).

Marcuse, H., *Soviet Marxism* (New York, 1961).

Meyer, A. G., *Marxism* (Lansing, Mich., 1963).

Royal Institute of International Affairs, *Nationalism, New Impression* (London, 1963).

Schlesinger, A. M., *The Vital Center, the Politics of Freedom* (Boston, 1962).

Sigmund, P. E., Ed., *The Ideologies of the Developing Nations* (New York, 1963).

4

Constitutions and Constitutional Principles

> *To find a definition broad enough to fit all varieties, we can only say that a constitution is a body of superior law or of long established customs which governs a government. Every state has a constitution of some sort. It may be a single document, such as the Constitution of the United States which declares itself to be the "supreme law of the land," or it may be, like the British constitution, an accumulation of customs, traditions, and acts of Parliament, which determine how government shall be carried on.*

Even an absolute monarchy, though it may not admit the fact, has a constitution of sorts. It always has a set of rules, crystalized by long tradition, that govern the succession to the throne, prescribe the machinery of government, and at least in some measure determine what the monarch can and can not do. Moreover, it is not only sovereign states that have constitutions. Divisions and subdivisions also have their constitutions. These may be developed as custom, enacted as legislation by the central government, or adopted by the people of the community itself. Thus, the charter of a city is actually the constitution of the city whether granted by the state or adopted by the city under home rule.

Classification of Constitutions. Constitutions may be classified on several different bases. The old traditional classification was into written and unwritten, with the American and British constitutions cited as typical examples. Actually, though, this classification has never been valid. While the British constitution is not embodied in a single document, most of it is written down somewhere: in charters of kings, in acts of Parliament, or in learned commentaries on customs and traditions. On the other hand, while the Constitution of the United States is a written document, much of our actual working constitution is embodied only in customs, traditions, and precedents.

A more valid classification is into granted, enacted, and evolved. A granted constitution is one which, without conveying sovereignty, is granted by a sovereign authority. A century ago many states had constitutions granted by their monarchs, and the constitutions of divisions of states are often granted by the state of which the community is a part. Legally the sovereign authority which grants a constitution can revoke it, and in the past many constitutions granted by monarchs have been revoked. In a few cases, though, notably the *Statuto* of the old Kingdom of Italy, the granted constitution acquired such sanctity that no monarch would dare to tamper with it without the approval of representatives of the people.

An enacted constitution is one that is drawn up by a deliberative body representing the people of a state and adopted by a direct or indirect vote of the people. In some instances the constitution is drafted by the regular legislative body, but the more common practice is to have a constitutional convention or constituent assembly called for the purpose. Ratification may be by especially elected local bodies, by the regular legislative bodies of divisions (especially in a federal union), or by popular referendum. Each country has its own procedure. This may be embodied in an old constitution which is to be supplanted, or it may only be prescribed by tradition and custom. However it is done, though, a constitution of this class is regarded as an enactment of the people acting in their sovereign capacity through regular legal procedures.

An evolved constitution is one that has developed step by step over a long period of time. It is essentially an accumulation of traditions and customs, though parts of it may be embodied in statutes, charters, or other legal documents. The British constitution is the best example of this. It has been evolving from old Anglo-Saxon customs, with new developments from time to time to meet changing historic conditions, for more than a thousand years. Major English constitutional developments down to the eighteenth century are taken over into our constitutional system in the United States.

Constitutions are sometimes classified into flexible and rigid. This is hardly a valid basis for classification, though, because these terms are relative. No constitution is absolutely rigid. Even if there is no provision for amendment, ways are found to bring about change. On the other hand, few constitutions are so flexible that they can be changed without procedures that are more difficult than ordinary legislation. That of Britain is the one notable exception. Constitutions differ in their degree of flexibility, but they can hardly be grouped into classes on this basis.

A classification that is rarely made, but which has both validity and pertinence, is into old and new. Without laboring the point as to how old old is, it is an easily observed fact that constitutions which have been in effect for several generations acquire characteristics of stability, adaptability, and authority which newly adopted constitutions lack. Thus the Constitution of the United States, the oldest enacted national constitution in the world, stands as a tower of strength after a century and two thirds of operation, while many a country has seen its constitution, adopted laboriously only a few years before, "suspended" or swept away at the whim of a "strong man."

Constitutional Systems.   Actually, the difference between Britain's evolved constitution and what we have in the United States is more apparent than real. Like other countries with "old" constitutions, we have developed what may be called our constitutional system or working constitution. It consists of four elements. 1. The Constitution of the United States which provides the structure of government and is supreme law—as far as it goes. 2. Certain acts of Congress which we may call constituent statutes. These do not differ in form from ordinary legislation, but in effect they elaborate or add to the Constitution. Thus, our system of courts was set up by acts of Congress and all of our federal administrative machinery has been created by Congressional enactment. 3. A body of customs, traditions, usages, and precedents which we sometimes call our unwritten constitution. The President's Cabinet exists only by custom and tradition, and our actual method of choosing our President (in contrast with the now almost meaningless procedure of choice by electors appointed by the states as prescribed in the Constitution), is to be found in our unwritten constitution. 4. Finally, an immense body of constitutional interpretation, chiefly by the courts but also by Congress and the Presidents, which reads new meanings into old constitutional provisions. When we look closely at Britain's constitutional system, we find the same elements, with only a difference in emphasis. There is no single document corresponding to the Constitution of the United States, but there are several great historic documents, such as Magna Carta and the Bill of Rights, which stand above ordinary law. Constituent statutes, or constitutional laws as the British call them, play a larger part than in our system because, unlike Congress, Parliament is unrestricted in enacting them. Most of the major features of the British constitution have been embodied in acts of Parliament. Traditions and customs likewise are more important than with us, particularly those dealing with what is called the prerogative of the Crown. These are historic powers of the monarch, now exercised by ministers responsible to Parliament. On the other hand, interpretation is less important than in our scheme of things because there is no basic document like our Constitution to interpret. However, both the ministers and the courts do interpret constitutional laws in applying them to current situations.

SOURCES OF CONSTITUTIONS

Enacted Constitutions. In discussing the sources of constitutions we must limit ourselves largely to enacted constitutions. The sources of an evolved constitution are all found in historic developments. A granted constitution may draw on any sources the granting authority sees fit. But when a constitutional convention or constituent assembly sets about to draft a constitution, where do the members get the material that goes into it? They may draw on any one or combination of several sources.

Ideology. In some cases a constitution may be drafted to embody a particular ideology, especially in totalitarian governments. The individual or group drafting the document may introduce variations in detail or draw some provisions from constitutions of non-totalitarian states, but the whole purport of the constitution is to provide a governmental arrangement that will conform to the accepted ideology.

Other Constitutions. When a state or one of its divisions is adopting a new constitution to replace an older one, it will usually draw heavily on the constitution that is being supplanted, often taking over many of its provisions intact. Normally it will make only minor changes in the structure of government. In many cases, too, a newly independent state will draw most of the features of its constitution from that of an older state. Thus, the original constitutions of most of the Latin American republics copied most of the features of the Constitution of the United States, and many constitutions in Western Europe have drawn heavily on the British constitution and on many features of the various constitutions of France.

Political Philosophy. The ideas of outstanding political philosophers, such as John Locke, frequently influence constitution makers. This is not quite the same as an ideology as a constitutional source because, with a few exceptions like Hegel and Marx, these thinkers did not crystalize their views into distinct ideologies. Political philosophy is never the only source of a constitution, but it may be important along with others.

History. Usually the best source upon which constitution makers can draw is the history and past experience of their own people. Only by basing a constitution on the background of the people can the drafters be reasonably sure that it will fit the needs and capacities of the people who are to live under it. The Constitution of the United States is an outstanding example of this. Although it embodied the prevailing political philosophy of the time when it was written, almost all of its provisions, except for matters of detail, were drawn from the history and experience of the people. The reverse side of the picture is illustrated by the Latin Americans. Copying the institutions of the United States when they lacked the experience and traditions to make these work, they found their governments breaking down and lapsing into dictatorships.

WHAT CONSTITUTIONS CONTAIN

Great Variation. Some constitutions are long; some are short. Some go into great detail; others limit themselves to generalities. Different styles of wording are followed, as well as different schemes of dividing the material covered into articles, sections, and clauses. However, there are certain things that a constitution must contain, and some other things that are frequently found in one.

Enacting Clause. To be valid, a constitution must contain an enacting clause. This is a statement that the constitution is enacted (or ordained or adopted) by or under the power of the sovereign authority of the state. This clause is usually included in the preamble. The preamble, with which a constitution normally opens, may be very long, summarizing the political philosophy on which the constitution is based, or it may be very short, but it must contain an enacting clause. Thus, the Constitution of the United States begins, "We the people of the United States . . . do ordain and establish this Constitution. . . ."

Framework of Government. An enacted constitution always (and a granted constitution usually) sets forth a framework of government providing for executive, legislative, judicial, and sometimes administrative institutions with procedure for choosing their personnel. This framework may be somewhat skeletal, as in the Constitution of the United States, or spelled out in great detail as in many of our "state" constitutions and the constitutions of most countries of Western Europe. Either way, it provides for the structure of government.

Grant or Restriction of Powers. A constitution must either, like the Constitution of the United States, grant powers to the various organs of government or, like our "state" constitutions, assume that the government has all powers not prohibited and impose restrictions on those powers. The constitution of a federal union must also set up a basis for apportioning powers between the federal government and the governments of the component units. Sometimes a constitution will both grant and restrict powers of the same level of government, but this is done only for clarification.

Bill of Rights. Actually coming under the heading of restriction of powers, but usually placed in a separate category, are guarantees of the civil liberties of citizens. In English speaking countries we usually call these guarantees a bill of rights, from the original English prototype. The French have their Declaration of the Rights of Man, which has been taken over by several other countries. These guarantees may be scattered through the constitution or grouped into a separate article or section as is usually done in our "state" constitutions. The Constitution of the United States guaranteed several individual rights in the original document, but many more were added by the first nine amendments and the fourteenth amendment. The constitution of the Fifth French Republic, without enumerating rights, merely states that the old Declaration of the Rights of Man is still in effect.

The constitutions of all Free World states contain such guarantees of civil rights and provide, through the courts or otherwise, for their enforcement. The constitutions of some totalitarian states also contain such guarantees but, since no effective means of enforcement is provided, this is little more than a meaningless gesture.

Provision for Amendment. An enacted constitution should always provide procedures for amendment. Most of them do. In the few cases where such provision has been omitted, ways have been found to make changes anyway. We shall have more to say about this very shortly.

Legislative Material. Most enacted constitutions contain what we may call legislative material. This is material which, instead of regulating government, regulates individuals like ordinary legislation. Practically all political scientists agree that this material does not belong in a constitution but should be left to legislative enactment. Still there is almost always pressure to write legislative provisions into a constitution, probably because advocates of a proposal feel that if they can get it into the constitution it is more apt to be permanent than if passed as an ordinary law.

FLEXIBILITY

Need for Change. No individual or group has ever had the wisdom to draft a constitution that will work unchanged generation after generation. Probably no one ever will because times and conditions change and constitutions must be altered to meet the changing needs. For this reason, all constitutions should, and most of them do, contain provisions for amendment.

Provisions for Formal Change. Provisions for amending or formally changing a constitution vary widely from one state to another. In some cases this may be done by the legislative body alone, provided it votes the amendment by a specified majority or by following some special procedure. In the Third French Republic, the two chambers of Parliament could amend the constitution if they met jointly at Versailles (instead of Paris) as a National Assembly. Probably the most common procedure is for the amendment to be proposed by the legislative body (usually requiring some special majority such as two-thirds, three-fourths, or an "absolute" majority) and then for it to be ratified by a popular vote. In France (Fifth Republic) the President may also propose amendments and submit them to the voters. In some of our American "states," amendments may also be proposed by an initiative petition. In federal unions, it is usual for amendments to the federal constitution to be proposed by the federal legislative body and ratified by the legislatures of a required proportion of the component units. Thus, in the United States, Congress may propose amendments by a two-thirds vote of each house and they must be ratified by the legislatures of three fourths of the "states," or, if Congress so specifies, by conventions in three fourths of the states. Some constitutions also have provisions for the calling of a constitutional convention or constituent assembly for extensive revision of the constitution or the drafting of a completely new one. The work of such a special body usually requires the same process of ratification as single amendments.

Informal Change. Besides formal change by amendment or revision, constitutions may be changed in effect by several informal means. Probably the most common is official reinterpretation of existing provisions. Thus, in the United States, the power of Congress to regulate interstate commerce has been expanded by reinterpretation from its original simple meaning to a grant of broad powers to regulate business, labor, purity of food, and many other things. Another means of changing the effect of constitutional provisions is by legislation; that is, by the enactment of what we have called constituent statutes, which have the effect of adding to or modifying the constitution without either changing it formally or violating it. Finally, the longer a constitution remains in effect, the more it will grow and change by precedents being set which develop into customs and traditions. Thus, while we still go through the motions of following the constitutional provision that the states choose electors and the electors choose the President, custom and tradition decree that the political parties shall nominate candidates in their national conventions and that the voters choose the President from among these candidates. Comparable changes take place in any country where a constitution remains in effect for a long time.

Another comparable but somewhat different development has taken place in France, which has experienced a number of irregular changes in regime during the past century and a half. The French have come up with what might be called an informal super-constitution which prescribes what shall be done when a regime collapses or is overthrown. A self-appointed provisional government is set up, usually consisting of a council, which governs until constitutional order can be restored. This provisional government has a constituent assembly elected, which takes over government until a new constitution can be drafted and ratified by a popular vote. The constituent assembly then holds elections under the new constitution, calls the newly elected parliament into session, and turns over the government to the newly created regime. Something very much like this has developed in several Latin American countries, and some other European countries have followed the French procedure.

Revolutionary Change. Finally, constitutions are sometimes changed by revolutionary means, either a full-blown revolution or a *coup d'état.* In political science, revolution means any change in the structure or personnel of a government by illegal or unconstitutional means, whether or not the change is brought about by violence. Once the revolution has succeeded, the new regime with its constitution is usually accepted by the country involved and recognized diplomatically by foreign countries, thus giving it the stamp of legitimacy.

ATTITUDES AND ENFORCEMENT

How Good is a Constitution? It is obvious that a constitution is good if it works; not good if it does not. Its workability will depend in large part on how well suited it is to the needs of the people who are to live under it. It also depends on how well the constitution is enforced. Adequate enforcement machinery is important but, in the last analysis, enforcement depends on the attitude of public officials and of the people toward the constitution. It may be true in the United States, as Chief Justice Hughes is alleged to have said, that the Constitution is what the judges say it is, but the words of the fictitious Mr. Dooley are equally true, at least over a long span of time, the "the Supreme Court follows the illiction returns." It is the attitude of the American people toward our Constitution that gives that document its strength and stability.

Attitudes. Attitudes toward constitutions vary from the American one of regarding the document as almost sacrosanct to the opposite extreme of considering a constitution little more than a propaganda document. In most countries with stable government the attitude falls somewhere between these extremes. Only the British approach the Americans in their veneration for their constitution but, since most of it is informal and almost any part of it can be changed by a simple act of Parliament, even the

British can not regard their constitution as "the supreme law of the land."

Enforcement. Constitutional enforcement is an American concept which developed through an evolutionary process. The roots of it go back to colonial days when the Judicial Committee of the Privy Council in England could overrule a colonial law which it found to be in conflict with the charter of the colony or the constitutional laws of England. From this beginning, we have developed "judicial review" into almost complete power of the courts to interpret and enforce the Constitution, with the Supreme Court having the final word. A Supreme Court decision on a point of constitutionality can be overruled only by amending the Constitution. This American system of enforcement has been copied in many other countries, mainly in Latin America, but how effective it is depends on the attitude of the people and their public officials. Several of the post-World War II constitutions of Western Europe provide for special constitutional courts, apart from the regular courts, to interpret and enforce the constitution. It is too soon to tell whether this arrangement will work out as well as our American scheme.

In the nature of things, there can be no real enforcement machinery for the British constitution. The House of Commons can enforce compliance by the monarch and the ministers, but Parliament itself is bound only by custom and tradition and the consciences of its members. Perhaps we might add political enforcement because the attitude of the British public is such that the voters would refuse to reelect any member of Parliament who voted against established constitutional principles.

In totalitarian states and other dictatorships there can be no real enforcement of the constitution. In form, there may be enforcement machinery, but this machinery is controlled by the dictator or the "party." In fact, a dictator will usually, either through some slim pretense of legality or by outright decree, either suspend the constitution or replace it with one of his own making which puts all power in his hands.

CONSTITUTIONAL PRINCIPLES

Principles of Constitution Making. Drawing both on past experience as recorded in history and on observation of what works and what does not, political scientists have been able to formulate a few principles which they believe should govern the making of enacted constitutions. With rare exceptions, the more closely a constitution follows these principles the better it works in operation.

Background of the People. The most important of these principles is that the constitution should be based on the background of the people. It should be devised to fit their customs, traditions, and habits of life, as well as their political experience and their economic and social conditions. If a constitution sets up institutions and procedures with which the people are not familiar, which they do not understand and for which their training and experience do not fit them, it will be next to impossible to make the constitution function successfully, however excellent it may be in other respects.

Brevity. While a constitution should not sacrifice other desirable features for brevity, it should be as brief as is consistent with completeness and clarity. As far as possible, it should limit itself to general provisions and avoid including details which might prove unworkable or may soon get out of date. The more a constitution spells out details of government arrangements, the sooner it will need to be changed. The Constitution of the United States is a good example of what a constitution should be in this respect. Partly because it limits itself to general provisions (except in regard to the electoral college, which has never worked as planned), it is as vital as ever after nearly two hundred years in

operation. One of the longest and most detailed enacted constitutions in history was that of the first German republic adopted
shortly after World War I. It never worked well and Hitler was
able to overthrow it completely. True, there were other factors
involved. It did not fit the background of the German people.
But its excessive length and excess of detail added to its unwork-
ability.

Clarity. It is of great importance that a constitution be so
worded that its meaning is clear. Direct, simple language is always to be preferred to involved statements, rhetorical flourishes,
or high sounding legalistic terminology. Lack of clarity may not
only lead to prolonged litigation, but it can sometimes make the
difference between success and failure of the constitution.

Elasticity. Every constitution should set up procedures for
orderly change by amendment or revision. Some measure of
elasticity is absolutely essential. The amending process should
not be so easy as to invite frequent tampering, but neither should
it be so difficult as to prevent needed change. Only the British
have been able to get along with a constitution so elastic that it
can be changed by an ordinary act of legislation.

Enforcement Procedure. The view that a constitution
should set up procedures for its own enforcement is a comparatively new one, but it is gaining in favor. Most of the newer constitutions of Western Europe have created special agencies for
this purpose. No scheme is foolproof. Judicial review by the regular courts works reasonably well in the United States, but not
elsewhere. For some countries the constitutional court may be the
answer. Other countries may need to devise a still different arrangement. It would appear to be a sound principle, though, that
there should be some organ of government that is independent
of direct control by the political branches which is given final
authority in interpreting and enforcing the constitution.

Extraneous Material. It would seem obvious that a constitution should contain no extraneous material. Still, constitution makers are always tempted to inflate the document with platitudinous statements and provisions which have no direct bearing on the structure, powers, or operation of government. Some of this may be harmless, except as it tends to becloud the meaning of other provisions. However, the widespread tendency to clutter a constitution with legislation is objectionable for several reasons. Probably the least serious objection is that it blurs the distinction between constitutional law and ordinary law. Another objection is that, by unduly enlarging the size of the document, the inclusion of legislative matter makes it more difficult to pick out and apply the provisions that properly belong in a constitution. Most serious of all is the fact that, by its very nature, legislation requires frequent change. It may prove unworkable from the beginning. Changing conditions may render it inadequate. Public attitude toward it may change. The more of this there is in a constitution, the more frequently the document will need to be amended. Over a period of time, amendments may be piled on amendments until the result is utterly confusing.

For the most part, the Constitution of the United States has avoided the fallacy of including legislation. One significant lapse illustrates the unwisdom of writing law into the constitution. This was the eighteenth amendment. If public sentiment demanded national prohibition, the amendment should merely have empowered Congress to pass a prohibition law. Instead, the amendment stated: ". . . the manufacture, sale, or transportation of intoxicating liquors . . . is hereby prohibited." That was legislation. Had the prohibition law been only an act of Congress, repeal would have been a simple matter of Congressional action when public sentiment changed. The power to prohibit would have remained, but Congress would have been under no compulsion to use it. As it was, it was necessary to go through the ordeal of securing the adoption of the twenty-first amendment to repeal the eighteenth.

TEST-YOURSELF QUIZ

Without referring back to the text, check the answer or completion in each question that you think is right. Then turn to answers on page 236 and see how well you have done.

1. A constitution must always be:
( ) a. Granted to the people by a ruler.
( ) b. The supreme law of a sovereign state.
( ) c. A body of superior law or custom which governs a government.
( ) d. A single written document.

2. The most significant way in which the British constitution differs from the American constitutional system is:
( ) a. It is unwritten.
( ) b. Custom and tradition play a larger part.
( ) c. It provides for a monarchy instead of a republic.
( ) d. It is not "the supreme law of the land."

3. Which of these classifications of constitutions is the least significant?
( ) a. Written and unwritten.
( ) b. Granted, evolved and enacted.
( ) c. Flexible and rigid.
( ) d. Old and new.

4. Which of these sources is most important in drafting a constitution?
( ) a. Ideology.
( ) b. Other constitutions.
( ) c. Political philosophy.
( ) d. History of the people to be governed.

5. Without which of these items will an enacted constitution not be legally binding?
( ) a. Enacting clause.
( ) b. Framework of government.
( ) c. Bill of rights.
( ) d. Provision for amendment.

6. Which of these items, usually found in a constitution, would be better omitted?

( ) a. Grant or restriction of powers.
( ) b. Bill of rights.
( ) c. Provision for amendment.
( ) d. Legislative material.

7. Which of these ways of changing constitutions becomes more and more prevalent as a constitution grows older?
( ) a. Formal amendment.
( ) b. Legislation.
( ) c. Growth of custom and tradition.
( ) d. Revolution.

8. Which of these is most effective in enforcing a constitution?
( ) a. Enforcement by the courts.
( ) b. Political enforcement.
( ) c. Deep respect for the constitution.
( ) d. A totalitarian government.

SUGGESTIONS FOR DISCUSSION

1. In what sense is it true that every state has a constitution of some sort?
2. What is wrong with classifying constitutions into written and unwritten?
3. Try to clarify the meaning of the term "constitutional system."
4. Evaluate the various sources of constitutions. Why will they differ in different situations?
5. Why must an enacted constitution contain an enacting clause?
6. Why must a constitution either grant or restrict powers?
7. How flexible should a constitution be?
8. In what ways are constitutions enforced?

BIBLIOGRAPHY

Adams, J. C., and Barile, P., *The Government of Republican Italy* (Boston, 1961).
Andrews, W. G., *Constitutions and Constitutionalism* (Princeton, N. J., 1961).

Bombwall, K. R., and Bhandari, D. R., *Major Contemporary Constitutional Systems* (Ambala, India, 1958).

Godfrey, E. D., *The Government of France* (New York, 1963).

Harvey, J., and Bather, L., *The British Constitution* (London, 1963).

Heidenheimer, A. J., *The Governments of Germany* (New York, 1961).

Mehdi, M. J., *Constitutionalism: Western and Middle Eastern* (San Francisco, 1963).

Pickles, D. M., *The Fifth Republic* (New York, 1962).

Rossiter, C. L., *Constitutional Dictatorship* (New York, 1963).

Spiro, H. J., *Government by Constitution* (New York, 1959).

Strong, C. F., *A History of Modern Political Constitutions* (New York, 1963).

Strong, C. F., *Modern Political Constitutions* (London, 1958).

Wilson, W., *Constitutional Government in the United States* (New York, 1961).

5

The Citizen and His Rights

*Citizenship is a legal relationship of an individual
to a political or governmental community. A
citizen may be defined as a full member of a
body politic having all the rights and obligations
which go with such membership. This body politic may or may not be that of a sovereign state.
It may be the body politic of a division or subdivision of the state, or even of a dependency.
In our country we are citizens of our town or city,
our county, our "state," and of the United States.*

Who are Citizens? A citizen need not be an adult enjoying political rights. A child, if born under conditions stipulated by
law, is a citizen from the instant of his birth. A convicted felon is
usually deprived of his political rights, but does not lose his
citizenship. Until recent decades, women were not permitted to
vote or hold office, but they were always citizens. Anyone is a
citizen who meets the requirements set up by law to qualify as a
citizen.

OTHER RELATIONSHIPS

Non-Citizens. Other than being a citizen, there are several
relationships which a person may have to the sovereign state in

63

which he lives or happens to be. It may help to clarify these to
put them into the form of an outline.

Legal Relationships of Individual to State.
    A. National.
        1. Citizen.
        2. Subject.
        3. Denizen.
    B. Alien.
    C. Stateless person.

Nationals. A national may be defined only as any person
for whom a sovereign state is responsible in international relations. The term is sometimes defined as any person who owes allegiance to a particular state, but it may also include persons, such
as denizens, who do not owe allegiance, but for whom the state is
responsible in its dealings with other states. A national may be a
citizen, a subject, or a denizen.

Subjects. A subject, properly speaking, is a person who
lives in a state or one of its dependencies, who is subject to the
laws and the sovereign authority of the state, but does not enjoy
the status of citizenship. At present, the only subjects of the
United States are the natives of a few small islands in the Pacific.
Formerly, though, the Puerto Ricans (until they were given
United States citizenship in 1917) and the Filipinos (until they
received independence) stood in this relationship. Inhabitants of
dependencies are normally subjects of the state to which they
belong. In some countries which retain the forms of monarchy,
the people are referred to as "subjects" of the monarch, even
though they are really citizens. In Great Britain, the term "British subject" has a broader meaning. It includes both citizens of
the United Kingdom and citizens of those Commonwealth nations which accept the titular sovereignty of the Queen.

Denizens. The literal meaning of denizen is inhabitant, but as a legal term it means a person who is a native of the territory of a sovereign state, and for whom the state is responsible internationally, but who is not fully subject to the authority of the state and does not owe it allegiance. A good example is found in the American Indians before they were given United States citizenship. They had their own tribal or "national" governments, with which the government of the United States carried on wars and made treaties. These tribal governments, however, had no standing with foreign states, and the United States government was responsible for the Indians in any international situation. Natives of dependencies of European states have sometimes stood in the same relationship.

Aliens. An alien is a national of one state who is in the territory or under the jurisdiction of another state. He may be in the host state as a permanent resident or only on a temporary basis. As a matter of international courtesy, aliens who are nationals of a friendly state are usually accorded the basic civil rights, though there may be restrictions on their right to hold property or to engage in some occupations. In time of war, an alien who is a national of the enemy country, called an alien enemy or enemy alien, has no rights which the host country is bound to respect. His property may be seized and he may be interned in a concentration camp. However, he usually will not be treated too badly if there is no evidence that he has personally plotted against the security of the host country. Usually an alien is eligible for naturalization in his adopted country, but there is never a compulsory requirement that he become naturalized.

Stateless Persons. It sometimes happens, through some combination of circumstances, that an individual will find himself without a legal nationality. He has lost the nationality of his birth and has failed to acquire another. Such individuals are known as stateless persons. The laws of most countries, including our own, do not recognize statelessness, but the situation exists none-the-less. Such an individual is literally a man (or woman) without a country.

SOURCES OF CITIZENSHIP

Various Sources. A person may have citizenship in his state from any one of several sources: birth, naturalization or, sometimes, marriage. Again an outline may be helpful.

Sources of Citizenship.

A. Birth.
 1. *Jus soli.*
 2. *Jus sanguinis.*
B. Naturalization.
 1. Individual.
  a. By special act.
  b. Under general law.
 2. Group.
C. Marriage.

Citizenship by Birth: Jus Soli. *Jus soli* means law of the soil. Under this rule, followed in most countries, a person is a citizen of the country in which he is born. The fourteenth amendment to the Constitution of the United States declares, "All persons born . . . in the United States and subject to the jurisdiction thereof are citizens of the United States. . . ." While some countries impose restrictions as to race or ancestry, it is the common rule that a person is born a citizen of his native country. Such persons are known as native-born citizens.

Citizenship by Birth: Jus Sanguinis. *Jus sanguinis* means law of blood. Under this rule, a person would take the nationality of his parents, regardless of his place of birth. Under Roman law, the son of a Roman citizen was himself a Roman citizen, wherever he might be born. Most modern countries apply the rule, with many limitations and restrictions, to permit children born to their citizens outside the country to have the citizenship of the parents without going through naturalization. Usually, upon reaching the age of adulthood as defined by the law of the country or countries concerned, such a person must make a choice of citizenship, either by some specific act or by implication from his place of residence. Even for the United States, the conditions imposed are too involved to be discussed here. A citizen under either the *jus soli* or the *jus sanguinis* is a natural-born citizen.

Individual Naturalization: Special Act. Practically all modern countries permit an alien to acquire citizenship by naturalization. An individual alien may be granted citizenship by a special act of government. In the United States this means a special act of Congress. In such a case, the individual himself need do nothing to acquire citizenship. Such special grants of citizenship are rare, however, and most individual naturalization takes place under general laws.

Individual Naturalization: General Laws. Almost all countries have general laws under which an alien, who meets specified eligibility requirements, may become a naturalized citizen. The eligibility requirements vary, of course, but usually include legal entry into the country, a minimum age, and freedom from criminal record. In the United States, the applicant must also prove that he is not associated with any subversive organization or ideology. In most countries, there is special administrative machinery to administer naturalization. In the United States, it is administered by the courts. Procedure varies also. Usually the applicant must have lived in the country a minimum length of time (five years in the United States except for such favored persons as members of the armed services and wives or husbands of citizens), must apply for naturalization, and must undergo an examination on his qualifications. For the most part, a naturalized citizen enjoys the same rights and privileges as a natural-born citizen. However, he may be deprived of his citizenship more readily and he may not receive diplomatic protection if he returns to his native country and gets into trouble with its government. In the United States, he can never be eligible to become President or Vice President.

Group Naturalization. Group naturalization is always by some special action of government. This usually means an act of the legislative body, though in some countries it may be done by executive decree. It means the conferring of citizenship on a large group or classification of persons, usually, but not necessarily, the inhabitants of acquired territory. Thus, the United States, by acts of Congress, has conferred citizenship on all legal residents, or most of them, of all major areas we have acquired since independence. Sometimes the recipients of such a grant of citizenship may be an indigenous group. In 1924, Congress gave citizenship to all native-born Indians who had not already qualified under earlier special legislation. After the Civil War, citizenship was given to the former slaves by constitutional amendment, the fourteenth.

Citizenship by Marriage. It was formerly the law in all countries, and still is in most of them, that a married woman automatically acquires the citizenship of her husband. Thus, if a British woman marries a French citizen, she also becomes a citizen of France without any action on her part. In 1922, the United States changed the law to the effect that American citizenship is not affected by marital status. This causes some complications, and is one of the ways in which a person may become stateless. Thus, if an Italian woman marries an American, she loses her Italian citizenship, but does not acquire citizenship in the United States. The procedure of naturalization is simplified for her somewhat, but she still must go through naturalization to become an American citizen.

LOSS OF CITIZENSHIP

Expatriation. Expatriation, which most countries now permit, means the voluntary renunciation of one citizenship in order to acquire another through the process of naturalization. Hence, we may think of it as naturalization in reverse. No state, however, permits one of its citizens to renounce his citizenship except to become a citizen of another state. When, some years ago, a man declared that he was renouncing his American citizenship to become a "citizen of the world," it had no legal effect whatever.

Implied Renunciation. In some situations, the law implies that a citizen has renounced his citizenship by some act which indicates loyalty to another sovereign. Under the law of most countries, a citizen who enters the armed forces of another country and takes an oath of allegiance to that country is, by so doing, renouncing his citizenship. This may not bring him citizenship of the country in whose forces he is serving; it may only make him stateless. To avoid this, many countries now excuse foreign volunteers in their armed services from the oath of allegiance.

Again, courts in some countries, including some in the United States, hold that when a citizen is convicted of spying for a foreign power, or engaging in conspiracy or subversion on behalf of a foreign power, he has indicated by his acts that he has transferred his allegiance and so may be deprived of his citizenship. In legal theory, a native-born citizen can lose his citizenship only by renouncing it voluntarily, but in these situations voluntary renunciation is implied.

Forfeiture. A naturalized or *jus sanguinis* citizen may forfeit his citizenship by illegal acts. A naturalized citizen will always forfeit his citizenship if it can be shown that he obtained it fraudulently. When the naturalized citizen is convicted of this or other specified offenses, the court may impose loss of citizenship as part of the penalty. This may be, but is not necessarily, followed by deportation to his native country.

A *jus sanguinis* potential citizen forfeits his claim to citizenship in the other country than the one in which he lives if, upon reaching his majority, he fails to make a proper declaration of choice. Once he has established his citizenship, he will forfeit it if he goes to the other country and does things which he could do legally only as a citizen of that country, such as voting or applying to its government for a passport.

Married Women.   In most countries, a woman marrying a foreigner loses her citizenship in her native country and acquires the citizenship of her husband. As we have noted, United States law permits an American woman to retain her citizenship when she marries a foreigner, even though the law of her husband's country gives her his citizenship. However, she can not be a citizen of two countries at once (Uruguay is the only country that permits dual citizenship), so she must make a choice. Unless, as few brides do, she takes the trouble to go before a proper official and declare her choice, she will be judged by her acts. So long as she does nothing in her husband's country which she can do legally only as a citizen of that country, she remains an American citizen. But if she votes in her husband's country, applies for a passport there, takes a government job open only to citizens, or does various other things, it is implied that she has chosen her husband's citizenship and renounced her citizenship in the United. States. She can regain it only by naturalization.

RIGHTS OF CITIZENS

Civil Rights.   The rights that are characteristic of citizenship are such civil rights as the particular country confers. These vary somewhat from one country to another, and in totalitarian states they may be almost meaningless, but such as they are, they are the earmark of the citizen. A civil right may be defined as a right, other than political, which is given by law. It may be in the constitution, in a separate constitutional document like the English Bill of Rights or the French Declaration of the Rights of Man, or it may be an ordinary legislative enactment. It is always a *legal* right, which normally is enforceable in the courts. Some civil rights may be granted to non-citizens, but all of the civil rights belong to every citizen.

In the Free World countries, the civil rights include the ordinary personal liberties, protection of property rights, and protection against arbitrary arrest or imprisonment. In common law countries, they include "due process of law," which we may think of as the right of an individual to defend himself or his interests by legal process in trials in court and hearings before administrative bodies. The Constitution of the United States and most of our "state" constitutions spell out due process in detailed procedural rights such as trial by jury, the right to be represented by counsel (a lawyer), the right to subpoena witnesses, the right not to be compelled to testify against one's self, and many others.

Political Rights. In addition to the civil rights, the adult citizen who can meet specified qualifications normally enjoys political rights, which mean the rights to vote, to participate in political campaigns, and to hold office. Strictly speaking, political rights are not rights at all, but are privileges given by the state to such of its citizens (and rarely to some category of non-citizens) who may be expected to exercise them in the best interests of the country. There are always requirements of age, residence, freedom from criminal record, and sanity. There may also be requirements of literacy, tax paying, or even religious affiliation. There are still a few places with racial requirements. South Africa restricts drastically the political rights of non-whites, and in Liberia only Negroes can vote. Like civil rights, political rights are given by law, but unlike them they are given selectively and not to all citizens.

Natural or Human Rights.   There is a large but ill-defined group of so-called rights which, at least in free countries, most people enjoy, but which are not conferred by law and are not legally enforceable. They rest, rather, on a moral basis. In earlier times, they were called natural rights, and were believed to have been ordained by the Creator. In the Declaration of Independence, Jefferson wrote: "We hold these truths to be self-evident, that all men are created equal, that they are endowed by their Creator with certain unalienable Rights, that among these are Life, Liberty and the Pursuit of Happiness." In our time, we call them human rights. It would be impossible to formulate a complete list because we can believe in anything as a human right. Several years ago, a commission of the United Nations formulated a "Universal Declaration of Human Rights," but it contained only items on which delegations of many diverse nations could agree. Anyway, it was only a statement of ideals, with no legally binding force. When there is general concensus on a human right, it is generally respected, but if it is infringed, there is no legal redress. A human right becomes a civil right only when it is enacted into law.

OBLIGATIONS OF CITIZENS

Enforceable Obligations.   Although we tend to lose sight of the fact, citizenship involves obligations as well as rights. The most obvious obligation is to obey the law, and violations of law are always punishable. If a citizen dislikes a law, he may work through political and legal channels to have it changed, but while it is law his duty is to obey it. Some other obligations are also legally enforceable, such as the obligation to military service and jury service. For the most part, though, the observance of these obligations is left to the conscience of the citizen.

The "Good Citizen."   By the term "good citizen" we usually mean the individual who tries, to the best of his ability, to live up to his obligations as a citizen. He must, himself, be the judge of what these obligations are, but there are some things that they certainly include. One is to keep himself informed on public issues and to take an intelligent part in the formation of public opinion for the guidance of his government. Voting, if he is eligible, is usually considered to be an obligation. However, voting, to be meaningful, must be intelligent. This means that the voter, rather than voting in response to pressures or on the basis of his prejudices, tries honestly to evaluate candidates and issues and votes according to his best judgment as to what is good for the country or the community. Good citizenship also means respect for the rights of others and a willingness to serve voluntarily in any capacity that will benefit one's community or country. In a word, the "good citizen" is one who takes the obligations of citizenship seriously.

TEST-YOURSELF QUIZ

Without referring back to the text, check the answer or completion in each question that you think is right. Then turn to answers on page 236 and see how well you have done.

1. A citizen is:
( ) a. An adult inhabitant of a country.
( ) b. A full member of any body politic.
( ) c. An inhabitant who has the right to vote.
( ) d. Any person "born or naturalized" in a country.

2. A "national" of a country may be any of these except:
( ) a. Citizen.
( ) b. Subject.
( ) c. Denizen.
( ) d. Alien.

3. Usually, a naturalized citizen is more apt than a natural born citizen to lose his citizenship by:
( ) a. Expatriation.
( ) b. Implied renunciation.

( ) c. Forfeiture.
( ) d. Marriage.

4. The only one of these things that can not make a person stateless is:
( ) a. Expatriation.
( ) b. Marriage.
( ) c. A *jus sanquinis* citizen failing to meet legal requirements.
( ) d. Forfeiture.

5. Every citizen of a sovereign state, except totalitarian states, has, by law:
( ) a. Civil rights.
( ) b. Political rights.
( ) c. Human rights.
( ) d. Moral rights.

6. In all Free World countries, civil rights include:
( ) a. "Due process of law."
( ) b. Protection against arbitrary arrest or imprisonment.
( ) c. Trial by jury.
( ) d. The right to vote.

7. A human right becomes a civil right when:
( ) a. It is generally accepted by public opinion.
( ) b. It is enacted into law.
( ) c. Most people enjoy it in "free" countries.
( ) d. It is included in the United Nations "Universal Declaration of Human Rights."

8. The enforceable obligations of a citizen include all but one of these. Which one?
( ) a. Obey the law.
( ) b. Work only through political and legal channels to change a law.
( ) c. Military service if required.
( ) d. Vote if eligible.

SUGGESTIONS FOR DISCUSSION

1. Just what is a citizen? Can a person be a citizen of something other than a sovereign state?

2. What, other than a citizen, might an inhabitant of a country be?
3. Compare the various ways in which a person may have or get citizenship in a country.
4. In most countries, how may a citizen lose his citizenship?
5. Compare the effect of marriage on citizenship in the United States and in most other countries.
6. What is a "stateless person"? Discuss some of the ways in which a person may become stateless.
7. Compare individual and group naturalization in their various forms.
8. Distinguish clearly: civil rights, political rights and "human" or "natural" rights. How may a human right become a civil right?

BIBLIOGRAPHY

Appleby, P. H., *Citizens as Sovereigns* (Syracuse, N. Y., 1961).
Borer, M. I. C., *Citizenship: Its Rights and Responsibilities* (New York, 1962).
Brogan, D. W., *Citizenship Today* (Chapel Hill, N. C., 1961).
Cranston, M. W., *What are Human Rights?* (New York, 1963).
Davis, G., *The World is My Country* (New York, 1961).
Douglas, W. O., *The Anatomy of Liberty* (New York, 1963).
Hayek, F. A., *Constitution of Liberty* (Chicago, 1960).
Levy, L. W., *Legacy of Suppression* (Cambridge, Mass., 1960).
Meiklejohn, A., *Political Freedom* (New York, 1960).
Muller, H. J., *Issues of Freedom* (New York, 1960).
Rienow, R., *The Citizen and His Government* (Boston, 1963).

6

Government and Its Functions

The extent of the powers of a government depends mainly on the functions that government is to perform, and this in turn depends on the theory which that particular country follows. We shall discuss this matter very shortly. It is obvious, however, that whatever functions are assigned to a government, it must have, by constitutional grant or otherwise, the powers needed to perform those functions.

We can not list all the possible powers of government or even mention all of the classifications of powers, but it is desirable to glance at the principal categories based on the source of power.

Arbitrary Power. Arbitrary power is found today only in the few remaining absolute monarchies and in personal dictatorships. In these, the monarch or dictator is the sole judge of his own power, and he may do anything that is physically possible. He is, himself, the source of power. Something approaching this situation may be found in totalitarian states, but even they have constitutions which, in form if not in fact, grant and restrict the powers of government.

Sovereign Powers. Sovereign powers may be defined as powers which the government of a state, or a unit of a federal union, may exercise independently of control by any other government. These powers derive from sovereignty, but are not the same thing. They are not unlimited. They are granted by the sovereign in a constitution, and are subject to constitutional restrictions. In a unitary state, the sovereign powers are all the powers which the central government possesses. In a federal union, it is sometimes a question whether such controls as the central government may hold over the units, especially through its courts, infringe the sovereign powers of the units. If it is a real federal union, though, the units have some sovereign powers with which the federal authorities can not interfere.

Delegated Powers. In federal unions, we often use the term "delegated powers" to mean the sovereign powers granted or "delegated" by the constitution to one level of government as distinct from the "reserved powers" of the other level of government. Here, however, we are distinguishing delegated powers from sovereign powers. In this meaning, delegated powers are powers which the government of a sovereign state gives to its divisions, sub-divisions, or dependencies. They are exercised only with the consent of the granting government and subject to its control or even veto. Thus, in the United States, counties, towns, and cities have extensive powers of self-government, but these powers are given by the "state," and may be overruled by "state" authority.

Police Power. There is one category of sovereign power which deserves special mention. It is called the police power. It is roughly equivalent to what is often called "general welfare power" and may be defined as the power to make and enforce any laws that may be deemed necessary or expedient to safeguard the health, morals, or general well-being of the people. In a unitary state this poses no problem, but in federal unions it sometimes causes complications. It was the intention of the authors of the Constitution of the United States to reserve the police power to the "states" exclusively. However, the time came when problems of this nature became too big and complex to be handled by the individual "states," and federal action seemed necessary.

THEORIES OF THE FUNCTIONS OF GOVERNMENT

Traditional Functions. There are certain things that the governments of sovereign states always have done and still do. These may be called the traditional functions of government. They include such things as maintaining order, defining and punishing crimes, and the settling of disputes among their citizens or subjects. They almost always maintain a military force to defend their realms against attack and to suppress revolts and rebellions. They issue money and prescribe standards of weights and measures. They raise funds by taxation and other means to meet their operating expenses. Beyond these traditional functions, however, governments do a wide variety of things, and theories have developed from time to time as to what the proper functions of government are. For the most part, these theories relate to the relation of government to economic processes and the social order.

Mercantilism. We need not concern ourselves with ancient and medieval theories of government function. From the beginning of the modern era through the eighteenth century, the countries of Western Europe followed the mercantile theory or mercantilism. Believing that only gold and silver are real wealth, governments regulated economic activities, especially foreign trade, very rigidly with a view to bringing the precious metals into their country. They sought to export more than they imported so that the difference would have to be paid for in gold and silver. They called this a favorable balance of trade, a term we still use. Different countries applied it differently. Spain and Portugal used it mainly to exploit their colonies. In France, the government paid subsidies and granted privileges to stimulate new industries in order to have more to export. In Britain, where the industrial revolution started early, the government was concerned mainly with the profits of business. Since the colonial trade was highly profitable, few mercantilist restrictions were placed on the colonies, but stern measures were taken to exclude foreigners from their colonial trade. Today we no longer use the term *mercantilism,* and we no longer believe that gold and silver are the only real wealth, but in the modified form of economic nationalism, mercantilism is still a potent force. Governments today still follow many of the old mercantilist practices, especially in the regulation of foreign trade.

Laissez Faire. With the beginning of the industrial revolution, a new theory arose called *laissez faire,* also spelled *laisser faire.* Literally it means "leave be," but the usual free translation is "let alone." According to this theory, governments should limit their activities to the traditional functions, keeping their hands off the economic processes completely and leaving the control of economic matters to the free play of such economic forces as supply and demand, with unrestricted competition. The term *laissez faire* was coined by a group of French economists, called the Physiocrats, late in the eighteenth century, but it was popularized by the Scottish economist Adam Smith in his book, *The Wealth of Nations,* published in the same year as the American Declaration of Independence. Smith was protesting against mercantilism. He objected especially to restrictions on international trade, such as protective tariff. He believed that the wealth of nations—all nations—would be increased if each country would produce only what it could produce most economically and would trade freely with other countries which could produce other commodities to better advantage. During the nineteenth century, practically all business people professed faith in the doctrine, but most of them had some mental reservations. They wanted no government regulation of their business, but they insisted on tariff protection and were often seeking government subsidies in one form or another.

Today we seldom hear the term *laissez faire,* and probably few people believe that it would be possible under present-day conditions. Even so, many still hold it as an ideal and wish to keep government regulation and control at an absolute minimum.

Socialism. It is difficult to define socialism because different people use the word to mean different things. To Russians, it means totalitarian state capitalism. To people who lean strongly to the *laissez faire* ideal, any government participation in the economic process is socialism. To most people who call themselves socialists, the term implies some measure of "nationalization" or government operation of industry. The word "socialism" was first used, at least in the English language, by the British mill owner and philanthropist Robert Owen. In a book, *A New View of Society,* he used the word *socialism* to describe the scheme of cooperative workers communities which he advocated. A generation later, the economic philosopher John Stuart Mill adopted the term. In his book, *Principles of Political Economy,* published in 1848, he used it to describe his ideal of "the greatest good to the greatest number." Both these men were fully committed to the free enterprise system, merely favoring government action to bring about what they considered a fairer distribution of the benefits.

For the past century, socialism has been associated with the doctrines of Karl Marx. We can not, in this brief space, undertake a real analysis of Marxism. He began by interpreting history as a record of the exploitation of the masses by the classes, with luxury for the privileged few and misery for the many. As time moved on, one order of society had become outworn and had given way to another, which in turn had had its span and had broken down. Thus the slave economy of the ancient world had given way to feudalism. Feudalism had run its course and been replaced by capitalism. Now capitalism was ready to give way to socialism. This Marxian socialism was to be a classless society in which everyone would be a worker, and production would be for the common good of all. The capitalist class, with private investment and the private ownership of industry, would be eliminated. All industry would be run by and for the workers. Marx was not clear how this was to be done, but his followers have usually interpreted it to mean that all industry should be operated by government, and that the working class should control the government.

In Free World countries, Socialist parties, which usually call themselves "Social Democratic" parties, are for democracy and against totalitarianism. They usually advocate the nationalization of basic industries and the operation of these industries, not for profit, but to provide a maximum of goods and services at a minimum price. Few, if any, Free World Socialists favor the entire elimination of private enterprise and they are usually willing to cooperate with other parties, through coalition cabinets, in supporting "welfare state" programs.

The Russians have produced their own version of Marxian socialism under the name of Communism, a version which has been taken over by all so-called Communist countries. In its literal meaning, communism would eliminate all property and all buying and selling. Everything would be owned in common. Each would work according to his ability and receive according to his needs. Obviously this does not exist in the Soviet Union. The government operates all business and industry, but operates them for profit. People work for wages, and buy what they have the money to buy—if it is available. Workers are "exploited" far worse than in capitalistic countries. Their wages are set by the government; they can not bargain collectively and they can not strike. They work longer hours for a smaller return than workers in any other industrialized country. Karl Marx would hardly recognize this as the socialism he preached.

Perhaps the nearest we can come to summarizing the socialist theory of the functions of government, at least as the theory is held in Free World countries, is to say that, according to socialism, it is the function of government to see that goods and service are made available to the consumer at reasonable cost; that whenever, because of the basic character of the industry or for some other reason, private enterprise fails to meet this condition, it is within the proper sphere of government to take over and operate these industries. Obviously, the line between the socialist theory and the "welfare state" theory is hazy.

Welfare State.   The welfare state theory of the functions of government differs from the socialist theory in two significant particulars. First, it owes nothing to Marxist doctrine. Second, it seeks to preserve the essential features of a capitalist free enterprise economy. It sanctions the government's engaging in economic projects only to supplement private enterprise, or in extreme situations where private enterprise is unable or unwilling to undertake projects that are needed for the public welfare. There are two aspects of it which have different backgrounds. One aspect is the extensive regulation of private enterprise by government. This differs from the old mercantilist regulation in that its goal is the protection of the welfare of workers and consumers, rather than enhancing the profits of producers or accumulating wealth in the country regardless of how that wealth is distributed. Such regulation came about step-by-step in Great Britain during the nineteenth century, and the United States began to turn to it in the early 1900's. Most industrialized countries outside the Communist group now practice such regulation, some of them with socialist or mercantilist overtones. The other aspect of the welfare state theory is that government should engage directly in activities to promote the well-being of its citizens, such as what we call social security in the United States. To some extent, governments have always engaged in some social welfare activities, such as poor relief. The past century has seen an enormous extension and diversification of such activities. Today most advanced countries practice the welfare state theory to the extent of providing a wide variety of welfare services for their citizens. The theory may be stated as the belief that, within the framework of a free enterprise economy, it is the proper function of government to take whatever action may seem appropriate to provide for the economic and cultural well-being of its citizens.

EXPANDING ROLE OF GOVERNMENT

An Age of Big Government. We live in an age of big government. Whatever theory or combination of theories may be followed, and whatever structure governments may have, governments everywhere engage in functions that were undreamed of when the United States became independent. This is an inevitable consequence of other changes that have taken place. The enormous growth of population, the clustering of people into cities, and the tremendous growth and diversification of industry, largely as a consequence of a spiraling output of inventions, have created myriad problems with which government must cope. These new functions have fallen mainly to national governments because the tasks are beyond the capacity of local units.

Regulatory Functions. Many of these functions are regulatory in character. Regulation of the economic processes has grown enormously in recent decades in industrialized free-enterprise countries. One aspect of it which has loomed large in most Free World countries, and especially in the United States, is the effort to preserve competition by preventing competing concerns from combining into monopolies. Most governments now set minimum wages and restrict the hours and regulate the working conditions of labor. Many practices of business in general have been brought under legal control. Two types of business are under especially stringent controls, usually through special administrative agencies created for the purpose. First are businesses that deal in other people's money, such as banks, stock exchanges, and insurance companies. Second are industries that are in the nature of public utilities or, in the language of the common law, "are vested with a public interest." These include railroads, air lines, telecommunications, and other industries on which the public depends for essential services.

Government Enterprise. Today almost all governments engage in some business enterprises, either on a basis of socialist theory or just as a matter of expediency. The oldest government enterprise is the post office. In addition to this, often in conjunction with it, most European governments also operate their railroads and their telephone and telegraph lines. Some of them operate their radio and television broadcasting facilities. A number of governments also engage in other lines of business, such as electric power and steel production, often in competition with private enterprise. Most governments operate their central bank, which is usually the only agency in the country which can issue currency. Local governments frequently operate such public utility enterprises as water supply, electric power, and public transportation. Continental European cities commonly maintain a municipal theater or municipal opera, and some of them run a wide variety of local businesses. As previously noted, in the Soviet Union and other Communist countries all economic enterprises are owned and operated by the government.

In continental European countries, these government enterprises are directly under the management of a cabinet department or its equivalent at the local level. The English-speaking countries usually put the management of each industry in the hands of a non-partisan or bi-partisan board or commission, with members appointed for long, rotating terms to avoid political pressure. Another device used in Britain and the United States is the government corporation. Thus the British Broadcasting Company and the American Home Owners Loan Coporation are entirely government owned, but as corporations they can do business without administrative interference by government officials. Some Latin American countries use a mixed device in which the government holds stock, often a controlling interest, in private corporations. This cuts the government in on management and profits, but still leaves the way open to attract private investment.

Service Functions. In almost all countries, including our own, governments at different levels provide a number of services to their citizens, either free to the user or supplied at merely nominal charges. National governments forecast the weather, and engage in research activities in agriculture, science, and economic matters, making their findings available to persons concerned. They usually have programs for the conservation of natural resources. They also usually provide some public health services and often recreational facilities. Still other service functions are highway building and maintenance, and public education.

Grants-in-Aid. Grants-in-aid are financial grants from a higher level of government to a lower level to aid in meeting the cost of some project or activity. Government grants for one purpose or another have been made throughout recorded history, but grants-in-aid, as the term is now understood, probably began with federal land grants in the United States. Even before the Constitution was adopted, the old Congress of the Confederation, in the Ordinance of 1785, set aside one section (square mile) of land in each township (six miles square) to be granted to each state that might be formed out of the Northwest Territory for the purpose of providing public schools. During the Civil War, the Morrill Land Grant Act granted public land to every state for the purpose of establishing an agricultural college. There being no more good public land in 1917, when Congress decided to make grants to the states for road building, money was granted instead of land. Today the federal government makes grants to the states for a wide variety of public welfare projects. We usually speak of this as federal aid. The states, in turn, grant money to cities, school districts, and other subdivisions for various purposes.

The term *grants-in-aid* originated with the British. Around the beginning of the present century, the British national government began making grants to counties and boroughs to aid in financing schools, local roads, poor relief, and other local projects. Today the device is used in almost all countries.

MAJOR TYPES OF GOVERNMENT

Two Main Classes. Most present-day governments fall into one of two main classes. These are totalitarian or authoritarian on the one hand, and free or responsible on the other. There are major varieties in each class which may be presented simply in the form of an outline.

Totalitarian or authoritarian.
  Absolute monarchy.
  Personal dictatorship.
  Ideological:
    Fascistic.
    Communistic.
Free or responsible.
  Presidential.
  Cabinet.
  Variations.

Totalitarian or Authoritarian. These terms do not mean quite the same thing. Totalitarian government is total government. There is no aspect of the life of the people over which it may not exercise power. The citizen exists for the state and, even though some civil rights may be promised on paper, he actually has no rights which the government can be compelled to respect. Authoritarian government rests, or claims to rest, on some absolute authority, and so can not be held responsible by the people whom it rules, or by any other earthly power. Governments in this class have both groups of characteristics so, as applied to them, the terms may be used interchangeably.

Absolute Monarchy. Absolute monarchy, which survives today only in a few relatively unimportant countries, is the oldest form of totalitarian or authoritarian government. The monarch has total power over his people. He may claim that his authority is derived from the Deity (divine right), but he acknowledges responsibility for his acts to no one on earth.

Personal Dictatorship. Personal dictatorship is much like absolute monarchy. The dictator, who usually has seized power by military force or *coup d'état,* is not apt to take a monarchical title (though a few have done so) and can not claim his authority by divine right or from inheritance. He may make some meaningless gestures of following constitutional forms or acknowledging responsibility to the people by holding controlled elections, but in reality his authority rests on force and he exercises total power. A variant of the personal dictatorship might be called the group dictatorship. Instead of a single dictator, there is a group of several persons, usually military men, which the Latin Americans call a *junta.*

Ideological Totalitarianism. Many present or recent totalitarian governments are or were expressions of an ideology. In these, the final authority is the party which embodies the ideology, though the leader of the party may scarcely be distinguishable from a personal dictator. These governments may have a paper constitution, which is honored only in the observance of certain formalities. There is usually a pretense of a parliament, but it consists of hand-picked "yes men." Only *the* party is permitted to operate, and there is no political freedom of choice. The constitution may contain something like a bill of rights, but the people have no means of holding the government responsible or of compelling respect for their rights.

There is no limit to the possible number of ideologies, but in the present century there have been two main varieties: Fascistic and Communistic. In the period before and during World War II, the Fascistic variety was dominant. Beginning with Fascism in Italy, it became Nazism in Germany, Falangism in Spain, and had other names in still other countries. Today, Communism is the prevailing type of totalitarianism.

Free or Responsible Government. In contrast with totalitarian regimes, all free or responsible governments have certain characteristics in common. They are based on the doctrine that the state is the body of citizens acting collectively and hence, that the state exists for the citizen, not the citizen for the state. The voters always have the means to hold the government responsible through free elections, in which two or more political parties or two or more candidates for each office may compete for votes. The civil rights of citizens are not only guaranteed by law, but are enforceable in the courts. There are two main varieties, presidential and cabinet or parliamentary.

Presidential. The presidential type of government, of which the United States is the oldest and best example, is based on the principle of separation of powers. This means that each of the three main branches, executive, legislative, and judicial, is sufficiently independent in the exercise of its discretionary powers that no one can be controlled by either or both of the other two. There are "checks and balances" by which each branch may exercise restraints on the other two but, particularly between the executive and the legislature, these do not go as far as in cabinet government. A deadlock between these can not be broken either by the executive dissolving the legislature or the legislature forcing the resignation of the executive by a no-confidence vote. Elections are held on a regular schedule. Normally there is a single executive, usually called a president, though Switzerland and Uruguay have executive councils.

Cabinet. The cabinet system, also called the parliamentary system, developed in Great Britain and has spread, with variations, to most of the countries of Western Europe and to many of the new nations of Asia and Africa. In this arrangement, there is a plural executive, the cabinet, nominally appointed by a titular chief-of-state, but actually selected by the leader of the majority party in parliament or the leaders of parties which enter into a coalition. The prime minister, who is always the leader of the majority party or one of the parties in a coalition, is head of the cabinet and effective head of government, but he can make decisions only with the consent of his cabinet colleagues. In most countries, the prime minister and members of the cabinet are also members of parliament; in countries where they are not, they may still introduce legislation and participate in parliamentary debates. The cabinet prepares all important legislation and acts as a steering committee of parliament. If parliament rejects any important "government" bill, the prime minister and cabinet must either resign or have the chief-of-state dissolve parliament and call an election. Thus, as between executive and legislature, there is no separation of powers. In cabinet-governed countries, there is a separate ceremonial chief-of-state, in whose name executive action is taken and to whom the cabinet resigns. He may be either a hereditary monarch or an elected president. He acts only on the "advice" of the ministers and has very little discretionary power. Members of parliament are elected for maximum terms of five to seven years, but their tenure may be ended sooner by a dissolution. Immediately following a dissolution, an election is called and new terms begin. In two-party countries, the effect is to give the voters an indirect referendum on the issue that caused the dissolution. In multiple-party countries, it does not necessarily work out that way.

Variations. There are variations of cabinet government in different countries. In multiple-party countries, such as Italy, where it is almost impossible for one party to hold a majority of seats in the lower house of parliament, a cabinet must be made up of a coalition of parties. In this case, the chief-of-state may have some discretion in deciding which party leader to ask first to "form a government." However, no cabinet can take office until it receives a vote of confidence from parliament. Moroever, parliament may force the resignation of the prime minister and cabinet at almost any time (there are a few restrictions), which makes for instability of the executive with frequent cabinet crises.

In West Germany, the Chancellor has far more independence

of action than the typical prime minister and it is difficult, almost to the point of impossibility, for parliament to force his resignation. In France, the Fifth Republic combines what is essentially a presidential type of government with many of the forms of a cabinet system. Most observers believe that this is made to work only by the personality of President De Gaulle. There are still other variations in other countries. Usually, the prime minister and cabinet are "responsible" (in the sense of being required to resign in response to a no-confidence vote) only to the lower house of parliament, but in a few countries they are equally responsible to both houses.

METHODS OF CHANGING GOVERNMENT

Routine. In all free countries, there are constitutional provisions for orderly change in the personnel of government. Basically this means that, either at set times or when there is a dissolution of parliament, the voters may select new members of the legislative body (at least of the lower house), and sometimes other public officials, in freely contested elections. In cabinet-governed countries, changes of prime minister and cabinet may take place between elections. In countries with the presidential plan, there is provision for someone to take over the executive functions in case of the death, resignation, or disability of the president. These changes are not regarded as breaking the continuity of government and have no direct effect on the country's diplomatic relations.

Constitutional. In most countries it is also possible to change the government by changing the constitution, either by amending the old one or by adopting a new one. If this is done in accordance with the provisions of the old constitution, it likewise does not legally break the continuity of government and does not require new diplomatic recognition.

Irregular. Governments are also changed from time to time, sometimes very drastically, by such irregular methods as *coup d'état* and revolution. The distinction between these is somewhat hazy but, in general, *coup d'état* (literally "stroke of state") means the seizure of power by a dictator by intrigue and threat of force, but with a minimum of violence. As a legal term, revolution means any change of government by illegal means, but we use that term commonly to mean the overthrow of a government and the creation of a new one by armed revolt. These changes by irregular means do break the continuity of government. Many of the acts, and often the debts, of the previous regime are repudiated. Diplomatic recognition by other countries is terminated automatically, and the new regime must go about seeking diplomatic recognition. To avoid this necessity, the *coup d'état* will sometimes go through the motions of following constitutional forms, such as forcing the old head of government to resign after designating the leader of the *coup* as his successor, or having the change ratified by a plebiscite. Other governments, however, are apt to regard such a device as a mere subterfuge and withdraw diplomatic recognition anyway.

Totalitarian governments sometimes have constitutional provisions for orderly change, but changes are always controlled by the dictator or ruling party. Real change of regime in a totalitarian state can come about only by these irregular means: revolt of the armed forces (popular revolt is impossible); death of the dictator; collapse of the regime due to defeat in war. To these we might add the slow process of evolution, which appears to be taking place in the Soviet Union.

TEST-YOURSELF QUIZ

Without referring back to the text, check the answer or completion in each question that you think is right. Then turn to answers on page 236 and see how well you have done.

1. Sovereign powers are:
( ) a. Those exercised arbitrarily by a monarch or a dictator.

( ) b. Those exercised by a government independently of any other government.

( ) c. Powers granted to a government by another government.

( ) d. "General welfare" or "police" powers.

2. Most Free World countries apply which of these theories of the functions of government?

( ) a. Mercantilism.

( ) b. *Laissez faire.*

( ) c. Socialism.

( ) d. Welfare state.

3. In most Free World countries, the government exercises, to some extent, all but one of these groups of functions. Which one?

( ) a. Control of the private life of individuals.

( ) b. Regulation of some types of private business.

( ) c. Carrying on of some business enterprises.

( ) d. Providing certain services to the people.

4. The term "grants-in-aid" refers primarily to:

( ) a. Foreign aid programs.

( ) b. Dividing a set proportion of the revenues of the central government among local governments.

( ) c. Grants of money by a higher level of government to lower levels for specific purposes.

( ) d. Government loans to private individuals or business firms.

5. The most significant classification of modern governments is into:

( ) a. Monarchies and republics.

( ) b. Personal dictatorships and regimes based on an ideology.

( ) c. Totalitarian and free.

( ) d. Presidential and cabinet.

6. The usual way of changing policy-making officers in a free country is:

( ) a. Legislation.

( ) b. Elections.

( ) c. *Coup d'état.*

( ) d. Revolution.

7. By which of these means is it not possible to change a totalitarian government?

( )   a. Elections.
( )   b. Intrigue.
( )   c. Military revolt.
( )   d. Death of the dictator.

8. A totalitarian government may make a hollow pretense of:
( )   a. Having the general approval of the people.
( )   b. Following a liberal constitution.
( )   c. Being based on an authority claimed to be infallible.
( )   d. Being responsible to representatives of the people.

SUGGESTIONS FOR DISCUSSION

1. Distinguish sovereign powers and delegated powers of government.
2. What is the police power? How is it apt to create problems in a federal union?
3. What are the traditional functions which most governments possess?
4. Compare and contrast these theories or doctrines of proper government functions: mercantilism, *laissez faire,* socialism, welfare state.
5. Discuss and evaluate the major types of functions which most governments have taken on during the last century.
6. What are grants-in-aid? Why have they become so important in recent years?
7. Contrast the two main classes of modern governments and distinguish the main varieties of each.
8. Summarize and evaluate the principal ways in which governments may be changed.

BIBLIOGRAPHY

Arendt, H., *On Revolution* (New York, 1963).

Barbu, Z., *Democracy and Dictatorship* (London, 1956).

Beers, S. H., and Ulam, A. B., Eds., *Patterns of Government* (New York, 1962).

Bowie, R. R., and Friedrich, C. J., *Studies in Federalism* (Boston, 1954).

Brewster, R. S., *Government in Modern Society* (Boston, 1963).

Brogan, D. W., and Verney, D. V., *Political Patterns in Today's World* (New York, 1963).

Brown, D. F., *Growth of Democratic Government* (Washington, D. C., 1959).

Cole, T., *European Political Systems* (New York, 1959).

Harris, R., *Independence and After* (Fair Lawn, N. J., 1962).

Jouvenel, B. de, *Sovereignty* (Chicago, 1963).

Nova, F., *Contemporary European Governments* (Baltimore, 1963).

Postgate, R. W., Ed., *Revolution from 1789 to 1906* (New York, 1962).

Schermerhorn, R. A., *Society and Power* (New York, 1961).

Verney, D. W., *Analysis of Political Systems* (New York, 1960).

7

The Legislature

All modern states, except outright dictatorships
and the few remaining absolute monarchies, have
some kind of legislative body which, in theory
if not in fact, represents the people of the country.

In totalitarian governments this is little more than a shallow pretense. The official party picks the candidates, there is only one candidate for each position, and the voter can vote only for the official candidate or, in some countries (at his own peril) cast a negative vote. Since the voter has no freedom of choice, the legislators are not really representative of the people as that term is understood in the Free World. Moreover, these legislative bodies meet only for a few days in each session. Other than listening to speeches by party officials, all they do is ratify by acclamation the decisions of the party leader or ruling council of the party. In Free World countries, however, a genuine effort is made to make at least one house or chamber of the legislature truly representative by letting the voters choose its members in freely contested elections. Moreover, in these countries the legislature is a real deliberative body, debating legislative issues freely and voting on them either according to political party doctrines or according to the member's individual judgment.

Names. The British Parliament is the oldest legislative body, having developed step-by-step over a period of a thousand years, and it has served as a model for most others. Many countries have taken over the name *Parliament* for their national legislature. Beyond this, though, the word *parliament* (without capitalization) is used as a general name for any legislative body. The American term *Congress* is used in all the Latin American countries and in some others scattered over the world. The Russians call theirs the *Supreme Soviet,* and some countries use the name *National Assembly*. Where there are two houses or chambers, each has its own name.

Size. The size of legislative bodies varies greatly. In small countries, units of federal unions, and local governments, they are usually relatively small, varying from less than a dozen to around a hundred and fifty members. In larger countries, the most directly elected house or chamber is apt to have from four hundred to six hundred members. The Supreme Soviet of the Soviet Union has about two thousand. It is considered a sound principle of political science that a legislative body should be large enough to represent all interests and groups, and large enough to have real deliberation, but not large enough to become unwieldy.

Bicameral. Details of structure vary greatly from country to country, but overall structure falls into one of two classes, bicameral and unicameral. A bicameral legislature consists of two distinct groups of members, selected on different bases and usually for different terms. These are called *houses* in English-speaking countries; elsewhere, they are usually called *chambers*. They meet, deliberate, and vote separately and, with occasional exceptions, a measure must pass both houses or chambers to be enacted. The more directly elected is called the lower house or first chamber; the other, the upper house or second chamber. Each, of course, has its individual name in a particular country. Originally, the two houses were supposed to have equal, if not identical powers, but in the present century there has been a tendency to reduce the powers of the upper house or second chamber. A notable exception is the United States where the

Senate not only retains its special powers of confirming appointments and approving treaties, but has more influence on legislation than the House of Representatives.

Formerly in all constitutional monarchies, and still in some of them, membership in the upper house is hereditary, or partly hereditary and partly appointive. Some other countries also have appointive second chambers. In these situations, the upper house has very little power in legislation. In federal unions, the upper house or second chamber is usually intended to represent the component units rather than the population in general. The United States Senate was originally set up on this basis, with state legislatures choosing the Senators. With the coming of direct election of Senators, this aspect largely disappeared.

Probably the basic reason for bicameral parliaments is that the British Parliament evolved this way and other countries copied it. It is argued, however, that a bicameral structure serves the purpose of "checks and balances" and helps to prevent the enactment of hasty or ill-considered legislation.

Unicameral. A unicameral legislature consists of a single house or chamber. A few national governments have unicameral parliaments, and frequently the component units of federal unions have unicameral legislatures. Very commonly, except in Britain, governments of subdivisions have unicameral councils. In the United States and Canada, most city councils are unicameral. In the national parliament of Norway, and in county and municipal councils in Britain, the voters elect the members without distinction as to the chamber in which they are to serve. After election, the legislative body itself designates about one third of its members to serve as an upper chamber. The main arguments for the unicameral plan are that it eliminates duplication of work, prevents two chambers shifting responsibility to each other, and gets legislative work done more quickly and efficiently.

FUNCTIONS OF LEGISLATURES

Legislative. The most obvious function of legislatures is legislation or the making of laws. Their legislative power is almost always restricted by the constitution and is usually shared with the executive. In passing laws, the legislature is supposed to represent the best interests and, as far as practicable, the considered wishes of its constituents. There is always a question as to how far, in voting on a controversial measure, a legislator should follow the known wishes of the people who elected him, and how far he should rely on his own best judgment as to the merits of the bill. There is no categorical answer to this question. In countries where party discipline is much stronger and party doctrine much better defined than in the United States, legislators usually feel that they must vote according to the dictates of their party.

Financial. The financial function is equally important with the legislative. Under nearly all modern constitutions, all government funds must be raised by the legislature, either through taxation or by authorizing borrowing. In some cases, as in many of the "states" of the United States, the legislature can only propose loans and must refer them to the voters in a referendum. Financial management is usually delegated to the executive, but all funds must be appropriated by the legislative body before the executive can spend them. In some countries, such as Great Britain, the legislative body can only accept or reject the executive budget entire, and rejection calls for either a resignation of the cabinet or a dissolution of parliament. In other countries, though, such as the United States, the executive can only recommend and the legislature may reduce, increase, or modify the budget figures as it sees fit.

Constituent. Most parliaments and legislatures of the units in a federal union also have constituent functions. Usually they can submit constitutional amendments which must be ratified by popular referendum or other prescribed means. In some cases, they may call constitutional conventions. Also they usually may enact what we may call constituent legislation. This means passing acts which, in form, are ordinary legislation, but which have the effect of adding to or modifying the constitution. In the Fifth French Republic, the constitution refers to such acts as organic laws. Such legislation may cover such things as the creation of administrative machinery, prescribing the manner of holding elections and determining the outcome, and prescribing the manner in which the executive and the courts shall operate. In the United States, all federal courts, except the Supreme Court, have been created by acts of Congress.

Other. Through their financial control and political pressure, legislatures can exercise influence, sometimes very strong influence, in the shaping of executive policies, both domestic and foreign. They sometimes exercise administrative supervision by holding administrative agencies responsible to them rather than to the executive. In common law countries, they have judicial power in cases of impeachment. They may authorize the government to go into various kinds of business. Finally, transcending all their other functions, they have the function of representing the people of the state or lesser unit as a body politic, on the principle of government by the consent of the governed.

BASES OF REPRESENTATION

Territorial Districts. The most common basis of representation in legislative bodies is territorial districts, which may or may not coincide with or be composed of units of local government. In unitary states, the entire country is divided into representative districts, which may be known by different names in different countries. In federal unions, representatives, at least for the lower chamber, are apportioned among the component units and each unit is then divided, usually by its own legislature, into representative districts. Representatives in lower chambers are almost always apportioned according to population. Some upper houses, especially in unitary states, are apportioned similarly, but with different (and usually larger) districts. If the upper house is hereditary, there is no formal apportionment at all; if it is appointive, there may or may not be a territorial basis of apportionment. Some federal unions give their component units equal representation in the upper house, as in the case of the United States Senate and Swiss Council of States; others assign arbitrary numbers of upper chamber members to their units.

Single-Member Districts. Most commonly, but not always, members of the lower house are chosen in single-member districts that are required to be as nearly equal in population as possible. In two-party countries, this means that the house will reflect quite accurately the political alignment of the voters. It does not work that way, though, in multiple-party countries, and this fact has given rise to various schemes of proportional representation.

Plural-Member Districts. Plural-member districts, sending two or more members from each district, are usually but not always found in connection with proportional representation which we shall discuss presently. In federal unions the component unit usually constitutes a plural-member district for the upper chamber. Thus in the United States each "state" is a two-member district for the election of Senators.

Proportional Representation. There are several schemes of proportional representation, all aimed at giving each political party representation in a legislative body in proportion to the number of votes cast for its candidates. All of the plans are based on plural-member districts, and most of them involve the use of party lists of candidates. Some of them also involve preferential voting, in which the voter indicates his first and second choice of candidates. In the most common arrangement, an electoral quota (number of votes required to elect a candidate) is set; sometimes this is a mathematically determined electoral quotient and sometimes it is set arbitrarily. The voter votes only for the party list of his choice. As many candidates are elected from each list as the party receives votes in multiples of the quota. Sometimes, as in pre-Hitler Germany and present-day Italy, remainders above this number are applied to the election of candidates from a higher (regional or national) list. Usually candidates on the list are declared elected in the order previously determined by the party agency which made the nominations. In Italy, the voter may indicate his order of preference, and these preferences are averaged to determine the order in which candidates are declared elected.

Reapportionment. Wherever representation is distributed according to population, reapportionment or redistricting is necessary from time to time to adjust to population shifts. Most constitutions make provision for this. In some countries it is done on a set schedule, as every ten years in the United States. In others, it is done when the parliament or some other agency of government decides that population changes require it. Most commonly it is done by the legislative body itself, but in some countries or parts of countries it is the responsibility of an administrative agency.

Occupational Groups. A few countries, the Republic of Ireland for example, base representation in their second chamber on occupational groups. Mussolini first introduced the idea during his rule in Italy. Those who favor the plan argue that it provides more adequate representation of all economic interests than is possible with territorial districts. Several countries have taken up the idea to the extent of providing for economic councils, whose members are selected on an occupational basis. However, these councils are not really a part of the parliament, but have only advisory powers.

Mass Representation. Mass representation means that all members of a legislative body are elected at large from the entire government unit. City councils and the legislative bodies of other small subdivisions are often chosen on this basis. The arrangement works well enough in government units with small populations, but appears impractical where large populations are involved. At present, no national parliament is elected on a mass basis. The *Reichstag* in Hitler's Germany and, for a time, the Chamber of Deputies in Mussolini's Italy, were "elected" on a mass basis, but the voter could vote only to approve an official list of candidates.

RELATIONS OF LEGISLATURES WITH OTHER BRANCHES

Executive. There are always close relationships between the legislative and executive branches. In totalitarian governments, the legislature is completely subservient, and even in Free World countries, the people look to the executive for legislative leadership. Under the cabinet system, the ties are particularly close. The prime minister and cabinet members, if not members of parliament as they are in many countries, take part in the work of parliament. The cabinet drafts all important legislation, and parliament gives priority to "government" bills over private members' bills. At the same time, the executive is "responsible" to parliament and must resign if parliament votes "no confidence."

In the presidential system, the executive can only recommend legislation and exert various indirect pressures to secure its enactment. Neither he nor his cabinet members, though, can take a direct part in the work of the legislature. The legislature can not force the resignation of the executive, but it can restrict his actions through its financial control, by legislating many of the rules under which the executive branch operates and, in some cases (as in the government of the United States), actually creating and changing the machinery of the executive branch. Usually the legislature has power to impeach the executive, but this power is seldom used. Under most presidential constitutions, the executive may veto acts of the legislative body. Some of these constitutions permit the legislature to override a veto by some special majority or some special procedure.

Judicial. Relations of the legislature with the judiciary are less close than with the executive, but there are some checks and balances between them. The legislature enacts, with some participation by the executive, the laws which the courts apply, and can usually legislate some of the rules and procedures under which the courts operate. In some cases, such as the federal government of the United States, the legislature creates (and can abolish) the lower courts. Where the impeachment power exists, it applies to judges as well as to executive officers. The courts, in turn, interpret and apply the laws the legislature enacts, and sometimes change their meaning by interpretation. In the United States and some other countries that have copied our arrangement, the courts have a near-veto on legislative acts through judicial review of legislation. Several countries have established special constitutional courts which have some power, but less than American courts, to nullify legislative acts which they hold to be in violation of the constitution. Everywhere, though, except in totalitarian governments, every effort is made to give the courts enough independence of both the executive and the legislative branches so that their decisions will not be controlled by political considerations.

TEST-YOURSELF QUIZ

Without referring back to the text, check the answer or completion in each question that you think is right. Then turn to answers on page 236 and see how well you have done.

1. A legislative body may be considered truly representative only if:
( ) a. The voters vote for the members.
( ) b. The voters may choose between or among rival candidates of parties.
( ) c. Members are elected from single-member districts.
( ) d. Members are chosen under "proportional representation."

2. The second chamber or "upper house" of a bicameral legislative
    body best serves the purpose of "checks and balances" when:
( ) a. Its membership is hereditary or appointive.
( ) b. Its members are elected on a different basis than members of
        the other chamber.
( ) c. Its members are elected on the same basis as those of the
        other chamber.
( ) d. Its members are chosen from their own number by legislators
        elected without reference to the chamber in which they are
        to serve.

3. Next to law making, the most important business of legislative
    bodies under the presidential type of government is:
( ) a. "Constituent" functions.
( ) b. Holding the executive responsible.
( ) c. Control of finances.
( ) d. Conducting investigations.

4. The one of these bases of representation that is used most rarely is:
( ) a. Single-member districts.
( ) b. Plural-member districts.
( ) c. Mass or "at large" representation.
( ) d. Representation based on vocational groups.

5. The purpose of proportional representation is:
( ) a. To secure representation of political parties in proportion to
        their voter strength.
( ) b. To distribute representation among areas in proportion to
        population.
( ) c. To make sure that even the tiniest political parties are repre-
        sented.
( ) d. To provide for non-partisan representation.

6. The relationship of the legislative body to the executive is closest
    under:
( ) a. Totalitarian government.
( ) b. The cabinet system.
( ) c. The presidential system.
( ) d. A system of "checks and balances."

7. A major argument in favor of a unicameral legislative body:
( ) a. It is more truly representative than a bicameral body.

( ) b. It emphasizes the common interest rather than special interests of groups.

( ) c. It eliminates partisan politics.

( ) d. It is more efficient than a bicameral body.

8. The constituent functions of many legislative bodies usually include all but one of these powers. Which one?

( ) a. Power to submit amendments to the constitution.

( ) b. Power to suspend the constitution.

( ) c. Power to pass legislation which has the effect of adding to the constitution.

( ) d. Power, in some circumstances, to call a constitutional convention.

SUGGESTIONS FOR DISCUSSION

1. To what extent and in what sense is it true that nearly all modern states have representative legislative bodies?

2. Why do political scientists often refer to all legislative bodies as parliaments?

3. Distinguish, and compare the advantages and disadvantages of, bicameral and unicameral legislatures.

4. Besides law making, what are the common functions of legislative bodies?

5. What is "proportional representation" and why is it used in some countries?

6. What do you think of the scheme of basing representation on occupational groups?

7. What is to be said for and against each of these bases of representation: single-member districts, plural-member districts, mass?

8. Discuss the relations of the legislative branch with the judiciary.

BIBLIOGRAPHY

Hanson, A. H., *Parliament at Work* (Toronto, 1961).

Haskins, G. E., *Growth of English Representative Government* (New York, 1963).

Hoogestraat, W. E., and Sekkink, D. E., *Modern Parliamentary Practices* (Minneapolis, 1963).

Hughes, C., *The Parliament of Switzerland* (Fair Lawn, N. J., 1963).

Interparliamentary Union, *Parliaments* (London, 1962).

King-Hall, S., and Ullmann, R. K., *German Parliaments* (New York, 1954).

Patterson, S. C., *Toward a Theory of Legislative Behavior* (Stillwater, Okla., 1963).

Raalte, E. van, *Parliament of the Kingdom of the Netherlands* (London, 1959).

Wheare, K. C., *Legislatures* (Fair Lawn, N. J., 1963).

Wohlke, J. C., *The Legislative System* (New York, 1962).

Young, R. A., *The British Parliament* (London, 1959).

8

The Executive

In literal meaning, the executive branch of government is the branch which executes the laws. It is that, but it is also much more. It has some part in the making of the laws. Except insofar as policies are dictated by the constitution or by legislation, the executive branch makes the policies of a government, both domestic and foreign.

Through the appointing power, the executive has great influence on the conduct of administration. In the government of a sovereign state, the executive conducts the foreign relations of the country. "Executive branch" is a broad term and includes, besides the executive proper, a host of executive officers of various grades and various degrees of authority.

Chief of State and Head of Government. The chief of state is the formal or ceremonial head of state. He (or she) may be a hereditary monarch or an elected president. All executive acts are done in his name and he must, himself, perform many of the formal acts of government. The head of government is the working chief of the government. He is either *the* executive or the chief member of a plural executive, such as a prime minister. As head of government, his main business is to formulate policy and make decisions.

Under the presidential plan of government, these roles are combined in the same person. The President of the United States, for example, is both chief of state and head of government. Under the cabinet system, though, the two are separate persons, though both are considered parts of the executive branch. In this situation, the chief of state acts only on the "advice" of the ministers, and has little or no discretionary power. It is the prime minister and cabinet who are the real executive.

TYPES OF EXECUTIVES

Single and Plural. The single executive arrangement, which usually goes with the presidential plan, combines all supreme executive power in a single individual. Thus, the Constitution of the United States declares, "The executive power shall be vested in a President of the United States of America." There are, of course, other executive officers, but they are subordinate to and responsible to the supreme executive. With a plural executive, executive powers are shared among several persons.

The Cabinet as Plural Executive. The most common type of plural executive is the cabinet under the cabinet system of government. Executive power belongs to the cabinet as a whole and most major decisions must be voted in a cabinet meeting. The prime minister is chief of the cabinet and is considered the head of government. He may even have some individual discretionary power of his own. In principle, though, he is only "first among equals" and can act, by "advising" the chief of state, only with the approval of his cabinet colleagues. Here and there we find deviations. The Chancellor of West Germany is more like a single executive than a typical prime minister, even though there is a separate chief of state and he is theoretically responsible to the *Bundestag.* There is a similar arrangement in some of the newer and less developed countries.

The Executive Council. Switzerland and Uruguay give the executive power to a council of several members. In its relation to other branches of government, this executive council is more like a president under the presidential plan than a cabinet under the cabinet system. The presidency of the council is rotated among the members annually and the president for the year performs the ceremonial functions of a chief of state. The council as a whole is the executive, and policy decisions are made by a vote of the members. A similar arrangement is sometimes used in local governments in some countries.

The American "States." Most of the "states" of the United States have a type of plural executive that we may call the divided executive. The governor is the *chief* executive and head of government, and has the most extensive executive powers. However, there are several other executive officers, elected independently of the governor, over whom he has no control. This sometimes prevents the forming and carrying out of consistent policies. Several of the "states" have taken steps to remedy the situation.

METHODS OF SELECTION

Heredity. Only in the few remaining absolute monarchies, and in those constitutional monarchies (chiefly in underdeveloped countries) where the monarch retains the major executive power, can it be said that the executive is selected by heredity. Hereditary succession had some advantages, such as the opportunity to have the heir trained for the job, but it had the great disadvantage that the character and ability of the executive were left to chance.

Direct Election. Many modern executives, where the presidential system prevails, are elected for fixed terms by popular vote. Some national presidents are chosen this way, especially in smaller countries. The governors of component units of federal unions are usually directly elected, as are the chief executive officers of subdivisions. This is considered the most democratic method of selection, but it may not be practical in situations where most of the voters lack the education or the means of information to make wise choices. Some of the states that have separate chiefs of state select this official by direct election.

Indirect election. There are several forms of indirect election. One is election by the legislative body. In a few countries that have cabinet government, the legislative body actually elects the prime minister and cabinet. In most of them, the prime minister and other ministers are formally appointed by the chief of state, but he must appoint those who can get votes of confidence in parliament. Another indirect method is choice by the legislatures or other official bodies of the divisions of the country. Still, a third method is election by an electoral college which, in turn, is usually popularly elected. In the United States, election of the President and Vice President by an electoral college has become a modified form of direct election. The voter considers that he is voting for the presidential candidate, but the distribution of electoral votes may modify the outcome.

Appointment. The executive of a sovereign state may be appointive in form, like the prime minister and cabinet in many cabinet-governed countries, but can not be in fact. However, the chief executive officer of territorial divisions of a country are sometimes appointed by the executive of the central government.

Irregular. In revolutionary situations and in totalitarian governments, the executive may be selected in irregular ways. He may simply seize power. He may be "proclaimed" by the ruling clique of a party, or he may "proclaim" himself president or head of government under some other title. Sometimes he is merely taken for granted as the chief of the revolution. Sometimes he may go through the formality of election, but with the voters having no freedom of choice.

POWERS AND FUNCTIONS OF THE EXECUTIVE

Scope of Powers, Duties, and Functions. It is not necessary to distinguish powers, duties, and functions of the executive. Strictly speaking, a power is something he may do; a duty is something he is obliged to do; a function is something he is expected to do. Actually, the three are so intertwined that a single executive act may involve two or all three. Here we list the principal things that executives do.

Executive Functions. As distinguished from other categories of powers and functions of executives, those that are executive in the strict sense include several things. First, he is obligated to uphold the constitution and to see that the laws are faithfully executed. He does this mainly through his power to appoint and remove subordinate executive officers. He may also issue directives to these officers, indicating how their duties are to be performed. Then he is the chief policy maker. In formulating policy and making policy decisions, he may have the advice of subordinates or of anyone else he cares to consult, but the responsibility is his. Usually, decisions of subordinates may be appealed to him through appropriate channels, and his decision is final.

Administrative. The elaborate administrative machinery of a government comes to a focus in the executive. With some limitations, such as the requirement of Senate confirmation in the United States, the single executive, or the department head in a plural executive, appoints and can remove the chief administrative officers and assumes political responsibility for their work.

Legislative. The ways in which the executive is related to the regular process of legislation have already been indicated. He may also have what is called delegated legislative power. Sometimes the constitution, but more often the legislative body, delegates to the executive the authority, within specified limitations, to issue orders that have the effect of making law. Such legislative executive acts are called orders in council in Britain, executive orders in the United States, and decrees in most other countries. The usual condition is that, within a certain number of days, the legislative body may annul such acts by merely adopting a resolution. After that, the legislature can overrule them only by enacting a law through the regular legislative process.

Judicial. Executives have one judicial power, the power to grant pardons or other forms of clemency to persons convicted of crimes. Formally, the pardon power belongs to the chief of state, but if this is a separate position, he acts only on the advice of an executive official, usually the minister of justice. Where the positions of chief of state and executive are combined, as in the American presidency, the executive both makes the decision and issues the pardon. In most cases, the person who can make the decision is guided by the advice of experts, either officials of the Department of Justice (or its equivalent) or by an official board of criminologists.

Military. The chief of state, if there is one, is always the formal commander in chief of the armed forces, but the effective military power rests with an executive official. In countries like Switzerland and the Soviet Union which have no real chief of state, but only an official who performs the ceremonial functions, the supreme military power belongs to the executive. In presidential governments like the United States, the president is the formal commander in chief as chief of state, but also has the effective military authority as executive.

The military power includes the power to appoint uniformed military officers and to issue directives to them. It also includes authority to make final decisions on military policy and to enter into military agreements with heads of other governments. Usually, too, it includes the power to establish martial law in emergencies, and to make the final decision on appeal in convictions by military courts. In time of war, the commander in chief has emergency powers which include the issuing of military orders to the civilian population which have the force of law. It was under such authority that Lincoln issued the Emancipation Proclamation.

It is a rule of common law, which many other countries have taken over, that military power must be kept subordinate to civilian authority. This means that the effective commander in chief and the heads of all military departments in the executive branch must be civilians. In the United States, this requires that when a general is elected President, as has happened several times, he must resign his military rank and any pay that goes with it, and become plain "Mister."

Diplomatic. In unitary states and the central government of federal unions, the executive is charged with the conduct of the diplomatic relations of his country and the making of final decisions in matters of foreign policy. There is always a department in the executive branch which handles routine diplomacy and makes minor decisions, but the responsibility for final decisions rests with the single supreme executive or with the plural executive as a group. Besides, present-day world conditions have necessitated an increasing amount of what is called summit diplomacy. Heads of government communicate directly and sometimes meet in person in what are called summit conferences. The handling of foreign relations is the most difficult and exacting responsibility of the executive of any important country.

Political. Finally, the head of government is *ex officio* the head of his political party. What this amounts to in practice varies greatly from country to country. Under cabinet government in a two-party country, it is a great advantage because it enables him to command the parliamentary majority he needs. Under cabinet government in a multiple-party country, the prime minister can usually command the votes of members of his own party in parliament, but he must bargain with the leaders of other parties in forming and maintaining a coalition cabinet. In one-party countries (totalitarian), the executive is a virtual dictator if he is the real party chief. If, as sometimes happens, the real party boss (and hence dictator of the country) is another person, the chief executive is only a puppet for such a person.

In a situation like that in the United States, where party doctrines are hazy and party discipline low, the executive's position as head of his party is apt to be more of a headache than a help. He can not command the votes of members of his party in the legislative body and often must seek the support of members of the opposition party for his legislative proposals. At the same time, he must try to conciliate all factions of his party and hold the party together for election campaigns.

EXPANDING ROLE OF THE EXECUTIVE

Former Legislative Preëminence. At the time of the American and French Revolutions, preëminence in all countries that had ceased to be absolute monarchies was given to the legislative branch. This was unquestionably the reason why, in the Constitution of the United States, the article on the legislative branch was placed ahead of the article on the executive and elaborated in much more detail. In Britain, where the monarch had deteriorated into a mere figurehead, even though George III was trying unsuccessfully to revive royal leadership, Parliament was considered supreme. In the British colonies in America and in France, as a reaction against monarchism, the feeling spread that only elected representative bodies could speak with the sovereign voice of the people, and that executive power should be reduced to a minimum. Most of the "state" constitutions adopted during the American Revolution, reduced the power of the governor almost to the vanishing point, leaving him little more than a ceremonial chief of state. In several of them, he was elected by the legislature for a one-year term, so that he was only an agent of the legislature. Although a reaction had set in in the "states" before the adoption of the federal Constitution, with the powers of the governors being restored bit-by-bit, with longer terms and popular election, it was several decades before preëminence began to shift markedly to the executive branch.

Swing to Executive Predominance.

During the nineteenth century, preëminence in government in most countries was shifting from the legislature to the executive. The actual change over came in different ways in different countries, and nowhere was it a steady progression. Each country had its periods of strong and weak executives. The process was accelerated after the beginning of the present century and even more after World War II. Not only did people turn more and more to the executive for legislative leadership, but growing population, the development of new industries and other activities, the increasing complexity of social and economic structure, and changing world conditions, all created new functions for the executive branch and new responsibilities for executive decisions. At the same time, legislative bodies proved less able to deal with new problems without executive guidance and the quality of legislative leadership within the parliaments tended to decline. Everywhere today the vital center of government is the executive.

RELATION OF THE EXECUTIVE TO OTHER BRANCHES

Legislative.

We have already covered adequately the relation of the executive branch to the legislative branch of government. The formal relationship differs drastically under the principal types of government. However, certain features of the relationship are quite general. The executive always proposes, and in some cases can virtually dictate, a legislative program and a financial budget. In varying degrees, the executive guides the actual work of the legislative body. Under the cabinet system, members of the cabinet participate directly in the work of the legislature. Parliament can force the executive to resign, and the executive can, under some limitations, have the parliament dissolved and an election called. Under the presidential system, none of these things can happen, but the executive can exert various pressures to secure the enactment of measures. In most presidential governments, the executive may veto acts of the legislature, but there is usually a provision under which the legislature may override the veto. In some governments, such as the Fifth French Republic, West Germany, and some of the American "states," the executive has an item veto on appropriation bills. That is, he may veto individual items without vetoing the entire bill. In a few situations, the executive may reduce the amount of an appropriation without vetoing the bill.

On the other side, the discretion of the executive in policy making may often be restricted by legislative enactment; he can not make a policy that is contrary to law. He must depend on the legislature to provide the money for everything he does. Usually, the departmental organization of the executive branch and the administrative machinery through which most executive policy is carried out are provided for by legislation.

Judicial. Despite the deliberate effort in most governments to keep the judiciary independent of political control, the executive has several points of contact with it. In most national governments, the executive appoints the judges (in the United States, with the consent of the Senate), either for life terms or for terms running until compulsory retirement at a specified age. In a few national governments, and in many of the American "states," judges are appointed for a fixed term of years. In cabinet-governed countries, the appointing officer is apt to be a cabinet member other than the prime minister. In Britain, it is the Lord Chancellor; in most countries, the minister of justice. A few countries have judicial commissions which make the selections, with formal appointment by the chief of state. Once a judge is appointed, the executive has no further control over him. However, if sufficient vacancies occur, the executive may sometimes be able, by appointing judges with his own political philosophy, to influence the general pattern of court decisions interpreting the laws or the constitution.

The influence of the courts on the executive and executive policy is very limited. The courts may, to some extent, restrict the executive's latitude in policy making by the interpretations they place on laws or constitutional provisions. In the United States, the Supreme Court can declare an act of the President unconstitutional, but rarely does. If an executive officer is accused of crime, he must first face impeachment proceedings in the legislature. Only if he resigns or is removed, may he be held for trial in court.

TEST-YOURSELF QUIZ

Without referring back to the text, check the answer or completion in each question that you think is right. Then turn to answers on page 236 and see how well you have done.

1. The type of plural executive found only in "states" of the United States is:
( ) a. Cabinet.
( ) b. Executive council.
( ) c. Divided executive.
( ) d. Chief executive with advisory council.

2. The only method of selecting top executives not used in Free World countries is:
( ) a. Direct election.
( ) b. Indirect election.
( ) c. Nominal appointment by chief of state on basis of parliamentary majority.
( ) d. Appointment by a higher authority.

3. In ideological totalitarian governments, the top executive is usually selected by:
( ) a. Heredity.
( ) b. Popular election.
( ) c. Ruling clique of "the party."
( ) d. Revolution.

4. Three of these statements characterize the chief of state in a cabinet-governed country. Which does not?
( ) a. He acts only on the advice of his ministers.
( ) b. He is also head of government.
( ) c. He performs many ceremonial functions of government.
( ) d. All executive acts are done in his name.

5. Three of these are normally functions of the executive. Which one is not?
( ) a. To decide law suits on appeal from the courts.
( ) b. To supervise administration.
( ) c. To exercise leadership in legislation.
( ) d. To supervise and direct the armed forces.

6. The positions of chief of state and head of government are combined in:
( ) a. The cabinet system.
( ) b. The presidential system.
( ) c. The soviet system.
( ) d. The "chancellor" system.

7. A head of government is usually, along with his other functions:
( ) a. Also chief of state.
( ) b. Head of a cabinet.
( ) c. President of an executive council.
( ) d. Official head of his political party.

8. Usually, the most important relationship of the executive and judicial branches is:
( ) a. The pardoning power of the executive.
( ) b. Appointment of judges by the executive.
( ) c. Power of the courts to limit executive authority.
( ) d. Power of the executive to remove judges.

SUGGESTIONS FOR DISCUSSION

1. Distinguish clearly "chief of state" and "head of government." In what situations are the positions combined? Do all countries have a chief of state?
2. Compare and evaluate the various types of plural executives.

3. What would you consider the good and bad features of each of the various methods of selecting executives?
4. Discuss in some detail the various powers and functions of executives.
5. How and why has predominance in government shifted from the legislative branch to the executive?
6. What is the significance of the statement that a separate chief of state "acts only on the advice of his ministers"?
7. What are the various relations between the executive and the legislative body under the cabinet system? How are these different in two-party and multiple-party countries?
8. How are the relations between the executive and the legislative branch under a presidential system different from what they are under a cabinet system?

BIBLIOGRAPHY

Binkley, W. E., *President and Congress* (New York, 1962).
Carter, B. E., *The Office of Prime Minister* (Princeton, N. J., 1956).
Daalder, H., *Cabinet Reform in Britain, 1914-1963* (Stanford, Cal., 1963).
Horn, S., *The Cabinet and Congress* (New York, 1960).
Jennings, W. I., *Cabinet Government* (New York, 1959).
Vanderbilt, A. T., *The Doctrine of the Separation of Powers and Its Present-day Significance* (Lincoln, Neb., 1963).

9

The Judiciary

The judiciary, or judicial branch of government, consists of the courts. A court, which is a single judge or panel of judges acting jointly, is an official agency of government to settle disputes in accordance with law. Some courts also do some other things, but their main business is to settle disputes that are brought before them by contending parties, called litigants.

The party bringing the suit is called the plaintiff; the party being sued is the defendant. In criminal trials, the state or the sovereign is the plaintiff and the accused person is the defendant. Besides the judge or judges, there are other officers of the court. There is an officer, usually called either sheriff or marshal in English-speaking countries, who executes the orders of the court and has custody of prisoners. All but the lowest courts have clerks with whom cases are filed and who keep records of all court proceedings. In courts that try criminal cases, there is a prosecutor and sometimes a public defender. In common law countries, any lawyer licensed to practice in a court is considered an officer of that court.

Types of Courts. The prevailing type of court in any country depends on the legal system that country follows, but there are some distinctions that apply everywhere. One is between petty courts and major courts. A petty court, usually with a non-professional judge such as a justice of the peace or police judge, settles minor disputes and/or tries persons accused of minor offenses. A major court is any one above the petty rank. The lowest major court, called a trial court or court of first instance, is the one in which most of the important cases are tried. It also takes cases on appeal from the petty courts. This brings up another distinction, that between courts of first instance and appellate courts. An appellate court, with a few exceptions, gets cases only on appeal from lower courts. In common law countries, and with some specified exceptions in Roman law countries, the appellate court does not retry the case but only reviews it. This means that it goes over the records of the trial to determine whether errors have been made either in procedure or in the decisions of the judge or judges in interpreting and applying the law. When the appellate court finds legal grounds for doing so, it may usually reverse or modify the judgment of the trial court, or may order the case retried. It is a rule of common law that an appellate court will not reverse the verdict of a jury in a criminal case but, if it finds grounds for believing that the verdict is wrong, must send the case back to the trial court for retrial.

Procedure. Court procedure depends on the system of law that is applied. In trials in common law countries, almost always before a single judge, the judge is required to maintain absolute impartiality. Each party to the suit has a lawyer (called counsel) who calls in witnesses, questions his own witnesses and those of his opponent, and argues his client's case. In all criminal trials, except in petty courts, and in civil cases where the money or value of property involved exceeds a certain amount, there is a jury. The jury decides questions of fact (guilty or not guilty in a criminal case) and sets the amount of damages in damage suits. The judge decides all questions of law and procedure.

In Roman law countries, trials are before a panel of three or more judges assisted, in some countries, by two or more lay assessors. These lay assessors are neither lawyers nor professional judges. In some countries, but not all, they are required to be experts in the subject matter under litigation. They sit with the judges, question witnesses, and advise the judges on decisions, but have no vote in reaching decisions. Some appellate courts in the American "states" use similar assistants, but they are required to be lawyers. Roman law judges take a more active part in trials than do common law judges. They question the witnesses, have more discretion in procedure, and are not required to maintain such strict impartiality. The lawyers only argue the case. Some Roman law countries have introduced jury trial, borrowed from the common law, for limited classes of cases. Procedures under Communist and Islamic law are similar to Roman law procedure, but with even fewer safeguards for litigants and especially for defendants in criminal cases.

SYSTEMS OF COURTS

Regular Courts.   In every country, the regular courts, those which handle the ordinary civil and criminal cases, are grouped into several levels in what is called a court system. The arrangement is always pyramidal. At the base of the pyramid are the petty courts. Above them is the lowest regular trial court, then an appellate court of intermediate grade, and at the top a supreme court or, as it is called in several countries, a court of cassation. Some countries have parallel pyramids for civil cases and criminal cases. Some have a judicial council or commission at the top which does not actually hear cases, even on appeal, but directs the administration of the court system.

In federal and quasi-federal unions, we may find any one of several situations. Each component unit may have its own pyramid of courts with a parallel federal pyramid, as in the United States. Another plan, as found in West Germany, makes all the courts federal, with the units serving only as areas of jurisdiction. Still another arrangement, as found in the Soviet Union, is to have no regular federal courts except the supreme court, leaving federal cases to be carried through the lower levels in the courts of the component units. In unitary states, of course, all courts are "national," though the governmental divisions of the country may be used as areas of jurisdiction.

Special Courts. Outside the regular court structure, all larger countries have special courts for certain classes of cases that require different handling than ordinary litigation. Thus, the United States has its Court of Claims and its Court of Customs Appeals. Some of the American "states" have their own special courts of one kind or another. One that is found in every "state" is a probate court, usually one to each county, which is really more of an administrative agency than a court. It deals mainly with administering the estates of deceased persons and the carrying out of wills. If there is litigation in these matters, the case goes to a regular court for trial.

Administrative Courts. Several countries have created administrative courts to deal with such administrative matters as labor relations, business regulation and, sometimes, public administration. A few countries have a full pyramid of administrative courts reaching from the local level up to the central government level. More commonly, there is only an administrative court in the national capital which hears appeals from the decisions of administrative agencies and sometimes from local governments. These administrative courts follow a different procedure from that of litigation in the regular courts.

SELECTION AND TENURE OF JUDGES

Appointment. The historic method of selecting judges, and still the most common and most generally satisfactory, is by appointment. Formal appointment is by the chief of state, but the selection is made by an executive officer. Thus British judges are appointed by the monarch, but are selected by the Lord Chancellor. In the United States, federal judges are appointed by the

President, but the appointment must be confirmed by the Senate. The requirement of Senate confirmation rarely causes trouble in the selection of Supreme Court justices and judges of the courts of appeal, but in choosing district judges the President usually finds it expedient to follow the recommendations of the Senator or Senators of his political party for the state in which the district is located.

In national governments, appointment is usually for a life term, though some countries have modified this by compulsory retirement at a certain age. In those American states in which judges are appointed by the Governor, appointment is for a usually fixed term of years. Some of the "states" also have compulsory retirement at a certain age.

Bureaucratic Selection. In France, West Germany, and a few other countries, being a judge is a profession. Young men who wish to enter it must first meet high educational requirements. They then receive special training in an institute conducted by the government. They gain admission to the judicial ranks, at the lowest level, by competitive examinations. After that, it is a matter of winning promotions, which often involve being shifted from one part of the country to another. Selection for the top judicial positions, for which there are always more eligible candidates than vacancies, is made by a council of top-ranking judges, with formal appointment by the chief of state.

Election. In most of the American "states," in the Soviet Union, and in a few other countries, judges are elected by popular vote for a fixed term of years, but are usually eligible for reëlection. There are several objections to this method of choice, the most important being that the voters are not in a position to evaluate the technical qualifications needed, and the popular election puts the judge under obligations to a political party. At least two of the "states" have sought to meet these objections by a device that combines features of bureaucratic selection, appointment, and election. When a vacancy occurs, a commission, consisting at least in part of lawyers, submits to the Governor the names of three persons selected on the basis of qualifications. The Governor appoints one of the three. After the new judge has served a short probationary term, his name is submitted to the voters in an election, without political party designation, with the question, "Shall Judge So-and-so of such-and-such a court be retained?" The voters vote yes or no.

Tenure. It is generally agreed by political scientists that life tenure for judges, especially in the regular courts above petty grade, is much preferable to fixed terms, though much is to be said for compulsory retirement at a specified advanced age. This frees the judge from the temptation to be influenced in his decisions by considerations of what may be expedient for reelection or reappointment. True, life tenure makes it difficult to get rid of a bad judge, but this problem rarely presents itself.

Removal of Judges. A dictator or absolute monarch may remove judges at will, but this destroys the impartiality of the courts and makes them mere tools of autocracy. In common law countries, judges may be removed by impeachment if they are guilty of misconduct in office. In some countries, they may be removed "for cause" by the constitutional court or by a judicial commission of top-ranking judges. Early in this century, several of the American "states" adopted provisions for the recall of judges by popular vote. In most of them, the device has either fallen into abeyance or has been abolished. It is a sound principle of political science that a judge should not be subject to removal just because some of his decisions are unpopular. Judges who deserve removal for misconduct are rare.

LAW AND LEGAL SYSTEMS

Meaning of Law. Law is any rule or set of rules governing conduct or human relations which is enforced by the courts.

The word is used with various shades of meaning, but we need not concern ourselves with these. Likewise law or laws may be classified in several different ways, but the only classification we need to consider is according to source.

Customary Law. Originally all law derived from customs, though some ancient peoples attributed their customary law to divine command, as did the Old Testament Hebrews. At first the monarch or his agent simply enforced accepted customs as law. As civilization developed and life became more complicated, it became necessary to standardize and systematize these customs into specific rules of law. The judge or magistrate, in deciding a case, would formulate the custom he was applying into a specific rule, and keep a record of it. Then judges or magistrates would compare notes, and if similar cases had been decided in different ways, they would decide among themselves which rule was the best and henceforth all would apply that rule. If they could not agree, they might refer the matter to the monarch for final decision. It was in this way that the Roman law developed in the Roman Empire and the common law in medieval England. A similar process took place in other parts of the world. We may think of customary law, then, as law that originated in customs and was given form by court decisions. Today most rules of customary law have been superseded by statutes, but when no statute quite fits the case, the judge still applies the rule of customary law.

Statutes. A statute is a law that has been enacted by some properly constituted law-making authority. Originally statutes were the decrees of monarchs, but in modern times they are usually enacted by a parliament or other legislative body. A statute will nullify any rule of customary law that conflicts with it. However, a study of the statutes of almost any country, especially in the Free World, will show that most of the basic statutes are restatements, perhaps with some modification, of old rules of customary law.

Judge-Made Law. Customary law was judge-made in a sense, but when it was taking shape judges were only standardizing and reconciling rules of custom. In modern times, judges are applying rules of law that already exist, usually as statutes or constitutional provisions. However, these rules are not always sufficiently clear that they may be applied literally to the case in hand. This means that, to apply the law, the judge must first interpret it to fit the particular situation and this interpretation may, in effect, amount to making a new law. If a judge's interpretation is challenged, it may be appealed up to the highest court of the state, but the interpretation of that court is final and can be changed only by a new legislative enactment. All courts of the state will then follow it. Moreover, judges follow precedent. If the application of a particular rule of law is not clear in a case, the judge will look up the records of similar cases, and will follow the rule as interpreted in these earlier cases. Thus, judicial interpretation has the effect of making new laws.

Doctrine of Natural Law. Throughout the later middle ages and early modern times, there was general acceptance of the doctrine of natural law, which theologians equated to Divine Law. This doctrine held that nature itself (or the Creator) has set up the basic rules of human conduct and human relations and that all man-made enactments should conform to this natural law. Today this doctrine, as such, is not generally believed, but there is a widespread conviction that ethical principles, derived from age-long human experience, should govern the making and application of laws.

Legal Systems. As customary law developed in a particular area, such as the Roman Empire or medieval England, the numerous rules fell into a pattern which was distinctive from the patterns of other areas. This, in turn, came to be formalized into what we may call a legal system. Each system developed legal principles which control the application and interpretation of the specific rules. Moreover, as statutory law came to play an ever larger role, these same legal principles largely controlled the making of statutes. Consequently, both the customary law and the statutory law of a country fit into the same pattern and are a part of its legal system.

A number of legal systems have developed at different times in different parts of the world, but only four are of major importance in modern times: Roman law; common law, Communist law, and Islamic law.

Roman Law.   The system of Roman law developed through several centuries. Starting with customary law, it was supplemented by statutes under the republic and by judicial interpretation and decrees of the emperors under the empire. It was codified under direction of the Emperor Justinian in the sixth century. It had great influence on the canon law of the middle ages, and became the basis of law in all countries of Western Europe in early modern times. Napoleon Bonaparte had a new and modernized code prepared, and, in the form of the Code Napoleon, it is today the basic legal system in the countries of western continental Europe and Latin America. It has also exerted great influence on the legal systems of several other countries.

Common Law.   As already noted, the common law, or as it was orginally called the common law of England, developed in the royal courts of later medieval England. It had crystallized completely by the beginning of the modern era. A similar, but slightly different, system of common law developed in Scotland. Today the common law is the basic legal system of Great Britain, the United States, and the nations of the British Commonwealth.

More than any other legal system, the common law seeks to safeguard the rights of litigants, particularly of persons accused of crime. Among its characteristics are trial by jury, the axiom that an accused person is legally innocent until proved guilty, and the concept of due process of law. Due process of law, often shortened to "due process," means different specific things in different situations, but in general it means the right of a person, especially an accused person, to defend himself and his rights. He is always entitled to a fair trial or hearing before an impartial tribunal, with the right to present testimony and have his case judged on its merits. Court procedures in common law countries are adapted to this end.

Communist Law. Communist law is based on the doctrines expounded by Nicolai Lenin, who claimed to be interpreting the doctrines of Karl Marx. It holds that Communist Party doctrine is the only truth, that any deviation from it is error, and that willful defiance of it is criminal. In cases in which Communist Party doctrine is not involved, the rules and practices of Roman law are followed in Communist countries. In cases of "crimes against the state," however, the defendant has little opportunity for self-defense, and the court procedure is directed at extorting confessions, rather than securing a fair trial.

Islamic Law. Islamic law, based on the Koran, is the basis of the legal system in most Moslem countries. In earlier times, the judge applied the words of the Koran as a law. As these countries became modernized, the Koran was supplemented by decrees of rulers and still later by modern legislation, and the need of judicial interpretation to meet changing conditions produced a large volume of judge-made law. Today most Moslem countries have made heavy borrowings of rules and procedures from other legal systems, chiefly Roman law.

Codes of Law. A code of law is a written compilation of all the rules and procedures, based on both customary law and statutes, in a legal system. The oldest code on record is that compiled under the direction of the Babylonian King Hammuarabi about 1700 B.C. The early books of the Old Testament, written several centuries later, contain a less formal codification of Hebraic law. The ancient Athenians had codifications attributed to Draco and Solon, and the early Roman republic had a compilation called the Twelve Tables. We have already mentioned the codes of Justinian and Napoleon. The common law has never been formally codified, although Sir William Blackstone's *Commentaries on the Laws of England,* written in the 1760's, amounts almost to a codification. In the United States, the individual states issue periodic compilations of their revised statutes which serve the purpose of codes of law.

JURISDICTION AND FUNCTIONS OF COURTS

Jurisdiction. Jurisdiction is defined by the dictionary as the right or power to exercise judicial authority. However, the word has two shades of meaning that are pertinent here. One is the scope of cases that may come before a court. In this connection, we speak of original and appellate jurisdiction. If a court has original jurisdiction, it gets the case initially for trial; if it has appellate jurisdiction, it gets the case only on appeal from a lower court. In some countries, certain courts have jurisdiction only in civil cases or those in which one party sues another, while other courts have jurisdiction only in criminal cases. The Constitution of the United States lists the classes of cases that may be brought in federal courts, leaving the jurisdiction in all other cases to the courts of the "states."

The other special shade of meaning has to do with the geographic area over which a court has jurisdiction. Lower courts are very numerous and each has jurisdiction only in a small area, usually a governmental subdivision. As we move up the pyramid, we find that each level of courts above the petty level has a larger geographical area, each consisting of several of the jurisdictional areas of courts next below it. At the top of the pyramid, the supreme court has jurisdiction over the entire territory of the state.

Functions of Courts. The primary function of courts is to settle disputes between litigants by applying the law in suits brought before them. As already noted, this involves the incidental function of interpreting the law. But courts also do other things. In some situations (though never in the federal courts of the United States) they will give advisory opinions as to what is legal to organs of government. They also give declaratory judgments, declaring the legal rights of parties to a dispute, without requiring that a suit be filed and the case brought to trial. In most countries, they may issue decrees of bankruptcy, and they sometimes administer property that is in litigation. They issue equity orders (some countries and some of the American "states" have separate courts of equity), and orders, such as summonses and subpoenas, to compel the attendance of persons in court. In the United States, they administer naturalization.

RELATION TO OTHER BRANCHES OF GOVERNMENT

Executive. In most countries, the executive appoints the judges, but does not have power to remove them and has little or no control over them once they are appointed. Usually acts of executive officers are subject to scrutiny by the courts to determine their legality or, in the United States, their constitutionality. The responsibility of the executive to see that the laws are faithfully executed includes, along with much else, what is usually called law enforcement. This means the prevention or punishment of violations of criminal law. Law enforcement may sometimes involve the use of military force, a discretionary power of the executive, but in most cases it means the prosecution of alleged offenders in court. Prosecution is a function of a law officer in the executive branch. He brings the charges, though in common law countries indictment by a grand jury may be required, and he, perhaps through a subordinate, acts as attorney for the prosecution in court. It is a principle of both common law and Roman law that a private party can not sue the sovereign without his consent. However, a number of countries, including the United

States for certain cases in federal courts, have enacted statutes authorizing such suits. When the government is sued, a law officer of the executive branch is the defense attorney.

Legislature. In many countries, including the federal government in the United States, the legislature may create and abolish courts at some levels, define the scope and area of their jurisdiction, and prescribe by law some of the rules under which they operate. Unless a question of constitutionality is involved, and even then in Great Britain and a few other countries, the legislature can overrule the judicial interpretation of a law by changing the law. Only in the United States must the appointment of judges be approved by one house of the legislative body, the Senate.

Judicial Review of Legislation. Judicial review means that the judge or judges of a court may review the actions of an organ or agency of government for the purpose of discovering and correcting errors. The actions of lower courts are reviewed by higher courts. The actions of administrative agencies are almost always subject to judicial review. In the common law countries and some others, this is by the regular courts; in some countries, it is by special administrative courts. In some situations, actions of the executive are subject to judicial review to test their constitutionality. In some countries this is by special constitutional courts, but in the United States and countries that have copied our plan, it is by the regular courts. In common usage, though, when we use the term *judicial review* without a qualifying phrase, we mean judicial review of legislation.

As already noted, a few countries provide for a sort of judicial review of legislation by special constitutional courts. Judicial review of legislation to determine its constitutionality as a function of the regular courts is typically American, though it has been copied by some other countries, chiefly in Latin America. It grew out of the "royal disallowance" of colonial times, in which a high court in England, miscalled the Judicial Committee of the Privy Council, could "disallow" an act of a colonial legislature which it found to be in conflict with the charter of the colony or with the constitutional laws of England. It was first applied by an American court in the famous "Know Ye" case in Rhode Island in 1786, before the Constitution of the United States was written. The Constitution failed either to grant or to prohibit the power to the federal courts, not because the delegates to the Constitutional Convention ignored it, but because they could not agree. Chief Justice John Marshall asserted the power for the federal courts in the case of Marbury *vs.* Madison in 1803, and it has been taken for granted ever since.

The principle involved is simple. Different kinds of law are of different grades of authority. When a court, in deciding a case, finds two laws of different grades in conflict with each other, it will apply the law of higher grade and declare the law of lower grade to be null and void. Thus, any statute will overrule common law; a "state" statute will overrule a city ordinance; the "state" constitution will overrule a "state" statute; the Constitution of the United States, which declares itself to be the supreme law of the land, will overrule any law of lower grade, including federal statutes. In a few countries, the constitutional court will rule a question of constitutionality without having a case before it, but in the United States the courts will pass on the constitutionality of a law only in deciding a regular suit that has been brought before them for trial or review.

We are apt to think of judicial review of legislation as a prerogative of the Supreme Court alone. Actually, any court from the lowest up, may hold a law to be unconstitutional if, in a case it is trying or reviewing, it finds that the law invoked is in violation of any higher law, including the Constitution of the United States. Nearly always, however, if a law of any importance is held unconstitutional by a lower court, the case will be carried up on appeal and the Supreme Court will have the final word. The Supreme Court may reverse its decision later, after changes in personnel, but the only way a Supreme Court decision on the constitutionality of a law may be reversed otherwise is by amending the Constitution.

TEST-YOURSELF QUIZ

Without referring back to the text, check the answer or completion in each question that you think is right. Then turn to answers on page 236 and see how well you have done.

1. Trial by jury is most characteristic of countries using:
( ) a. Common law.
( ) b. Roman law.
( ) c. Islamic law.
( ) d. Communist law.

2. Generally speaking, the least satisfactory method of selecting judges is:
( ) a. Executive appointment for a specified term of years.
( ) b. Executive appointment for life or until a set retirement age.
( ) c. Bureaucratic selection.
( ) d. Popular election.

3. In most common law countries, judges may be removed only by:
( ) a. Dismissal by the executive.
( ) b. Action of a judicial commission.
( ) c. A recall election.
( ) d. Impeachment.

4. An appellate court is characterized by:
( ) a. Being any court above the "petty" level.
( ) b. Never trying a case.
( ) c. Being usually a panel court.
( ) d. Having the power of judicial review of legislation.

5. A code of law is:
( ) a. A statute book.
( ) b. The particular legal system used in a country.
( ) c. A compilation of all the rules of law and procedure used in a particular legal system.
( ) d. Criminal law as distinct from civil law.

6. The basic principle underlying judicial review of legislation is:
( ) a. The courts determine what the law is.
( ) b. When laws of different grades apply in a case, the higher law is enforced.
( ) c. The courts must adapt the law to fit conditions of the time.
( ) d. The courts must make the law fit the policies of the executive.

7. A court may have any or all of these functions except one. Which one?
( ) a. Settle disputes.
( ) b. Administer property.
( ) c. Interpret the law.
( ) d. Confiscate property.

8. The jurisdiction of a court refers to:
( ) a. The kinds of cases or geographic area over which it has authority.
( ) b. The kind of law it applies.
( ) c. The functions of special courts.
( ) d. The composition (judges and other officers) of the court.

SUGGESTIONS FOR DISCUSSION

1. What are courts? What are their various functions?
2. What is meant by saying that, in most situations, an appellate court does not retry a case, but only reviews it?
3. How definite is the distinction between courts of first instance and appellate courts?
4. What are some of the major differences in court procedure under common law and Roman law?
5. What are administrative courts and how do they differ from "regular" courts?
6. Distinguish customary law, statutory law and judge-made law.
7. What are legal systems? What are the principal ones now in operation?
8. What is involved in judicial review of legislation? Compare the American plan with the constitutional court plan used in some countries of Europe.

BIBLIOGRAPHY

Abraham, H. J., *The Judicial Process* (Fair Lawn, N. J., 1962).

Berman, H. J., *Justice in the U. S. S. R.* (Cambridge, Mass., 1963).

Ensor, R., *Courts and Judges in France, Germany and England* (New York, 1933).

Hazard, J. N., *Settling Disputes in Soviet Society* (New York, 1960).

Jackson, R. M., *The Machinery of Justice in England* (London, 1964).

McWhinney, E., *Judicial Review in the English-Speaking World* (Toronto, 1961).

Mayers, L., *The American Legal System* (New York, 1964).

Paton, G. W., *A Text-Book of Jurisprudence* (Fair Lawn, N. J., 1964).

Redmond, P. W. D., *General Principles of English Law* (London, 1964).

Roche, J. P., and Levy, L. W., Eds., *The Judiciary* (New York, 1964).

Schwartz, B., Ed., *The Code Napoleon and the Common Law World* (New York, 1956).

Wagner, W. J., *Federal States and Their Judiciary* (New York, 1959).

10

Public Administration

We speak of the administration of a president or a prime minister, meaning his tenure of office, the people directly associated with him, and just about everything pertaining to his office and its functions. However, when we use the word administration *without a qualifying article, it takes on a different meaning. Administration means the carrying out of policy—getting things done.*

Public administration means the administration of public or governmental affairs as distinct from private or corporate matters. It means putting into operation the policies or programs of government. An administrator may sometimes have to make minor policy decisions in carrying on his work, but he does so only subject to a higher authority.

Scope of Public Administration. All the myriad activities which governments carry on, outside law making, executive policy making, and the work of the courts, have to be administered, and so come within the scope of public administration. We can mention only a few of the main categories.

First, there are the so-called housekeeping functions of government: collecting the taxes, paying the bills, selecting personnel, and all the other chores involved in operating the government itself. Then, there are regulatory functions. Most modern governments regulate many types of private enterprise, and administrative machinery is needed to carry out the regulation: making rules, issuing licenses, deciding disputes, making inspections, and conducting investigations. Nearly all governments carry on a wide variety of service activities, and each of these activities is a job for administration. Many governments operate some government enterprises, and managing each of these is a job of administration.

ADMINISTRATIVE AGENCIES

What They Are. Any individual or group of individuals that is charged with carrying on a particular government function, in accordance with policies prescribed by law, is an administrative agency. Putting it the other way around, an administrative agency is an organ of government charged with carrying on a particular activity or executing a particular policy. There are several types, as we shall see presently, each best adapted to a certain kind of administrative work.

Types of Agencies. A single-headed agency, one headed by a single administrator, is best adapted when the functions of the agency are largely routine, with little occasion to make policy decisions or settle disputes. A single administrator can best supervise and direct such work as forecasting the weather, collecting the taxes, or operating public parks. A single administrator with an advisory board is in order if, although the major work of the agency is routine, there are frequent occasions to lay down rules or make policy decisions. A plural-headed agency—a board or commission—is to be preferred when the chief work is regulatory, involving the making of rules and decisions. When much of the work is of this nature, but there is also a great deal of routine administration to be done, a board or commission with a single administrator subject to its authority is often the best arrangement. A device used in the United States and Great Britain for carrying on some government enterprises is the government corporation. This is a corporation entirely owned by the government, but having much of the freedom of action of a private corporation in carrying on business. In the United States, we also find a few examples of what is called an authority, such as the Tennessee Valley Authority, which combines the advantages of the government corporation with some regulatory powers.

In Great Britain, local administration is entrusted to committees of the county and borough councils. However, these committees limit themselves to making such policy decisions as are required and leave the routine administration to professional administrators. A similar arrangement is found in the Soviet Union and some other Communist countries. In some countries, local administration is left to local executive officers.

Powers. The powers of an administrative agency depend largely on what is to be administered. Where the work is largely routine in character, the powers of the head of the agency or the agency proper hardly extend beyond supervising the work and deciding differences of opinion among subordinates. A regulatory agency must have extensive powers to lay down rules for the type of business it is regulating, to investigate violations of these rules and to impose penalties, to settle disputes, and to settle such questions as which applicants shall receive licenses. The rule-making power is called quasi-legislative. Such rules by an administrative agency actually are law of a minor grade, and are enforceable in the courts unless they are overruled by regular legislation or by a court decision that they exceed the powers of the agency. The power to make decisions, after a proper hearing of the parties involved, is called quasi-judicial. These stand in law as though they were court decisions unless they are overruled by a regular court on appeal.

Agencies operating government enterprises have most of the usual powers of business management. Those operating public services have such powers as are considered necessary in the particular service they are rendering. In any case, an administrative agency has only the powers that are given to it by law, and in most countries all acts of administrative agencies are subject to judicial review. That is, a person who considers himself injured by the action of an agency may appeal to a court. The court will not pass on the merits of the administrative act as such, but will rule on such questions as whether it exceeded the legal powers of the agency, followed proper procedure, or deprived the party of his legal rights.

Sources of Authority. Administrative agencies are creations of the state, and their authority is conferred on them by the state in its sovereign capacity. In some countries, and in some of the American "states," some administrative agencies are provided for in the constitution. More commonly, they are created by statute, as are all federal agencies in the United States and all administrative agencies in Great Britain. The statute (or constitutional provision) creates the agency, provides for its organizational structure and the selection of its personnel, and confers its powers.

Degrees of Independence. The heads of administrative agencies (or members of the boards or commissions if they are plural-headed) are normally appointed by the chief of state. If that official is not also head of government, he makes the appointment on the recommendation of an executive officer, usually the head of the cabinet department to which the work of the agency is most directly related. Once appointed, the agency's independence of executive control varies, not only from country to country, but in the same country.

In the United States federal government we distinguish presidential agencies, departmental agencies, and independent agencies. The distinction does not hold elsewhere, but it illustrates degrees of independence and responsibility. The presidential agencies, such as the Bureau of the Budget and the Central Intelligence Agency, are grouped into the Executive Office of the President and are subject to his direct supervision and control. Departmental agencies are grouped into the cabinet departments.

Sometimes the whole department is the agency (as the Post Office Department) and sometimes each of its bureaus is a separate agency (as the bureaus in the Department of the Interior). These agencies are responsible to the President through the bureau chief and/or the head of the department. About all that the independent agencies have in common is that they are not in either of these groupings, and they differ greatly in their degree of independence. Regulatory agencies, with rule-making and decision-making power, are almost completely independent of executive control. The President can remove members of the commissions only for misconduct and after a hearing. This is done deliberately to free these agencies from political control and to render them impartial. Agencies conducting business are subject to executive policy making, but their heads or members can not be removed for political reasons. Agencies whose functions are largely routine are subject to about as much control as the President cares to exercise, but he rarely interferes with their operations. Usually their heads are not changed with changes of political parties in the White House. All are subject to control by Congress through legislation, and to judicial review of their actions in the courts.

CENTRALIZATION AND DECENTRALIZATION

Centralized Administration. In some countries, notably authoritarian ones such as Spain and Portugal, all public administration is centralized in the national government. All agencies are "departmental" agencies in that they head up in one of the cabinet departments. Local administrators merely carry out orders from the national capital.

Formerly, in France and Italy local administration was centralized almost to this extent. However, both countries have moved in the direction of decentralization. In both, the principal local administrators are still appointed by the central government and are responsible to it. Even so, they are advised by local councils and have considerable autonomy in carrying on their work.

Decentralized Administration.   Nowhere is public administration completely decentralized. Agencies administering national matters or matters that are nationwide in scope are always centralized, either in a cabinet department or in a central agency, and local administrators in these areas are subject to central direction and control. In some places, however, administration of strictly local matters is almost completely decentralized. In the "states" of the United States, for example, there are "state" agencies for statewide matters, but local administration is carried on either by popularly elected town or county officials or by appointees of the mayors or city managers of cities. Great Britain gives responsibility for most local administration to committees of the county and borough councils. These committees, however, limit their administrative work to general supervision, and leave the actual administration to professional administrators. In the Soviet Union, formal responsibility for administration at the various government levels is assigned to committees of the soviet (council) at each level. The actual work of administration, though, is done by appointed administrators whose real direction comes from the Communist Party. Other countries have varying degrees of centralization and decentralization.

Federal Unions.   In most true federal unions and many quasi-federal states, the component units have their own administrative machinery distinct from, and largely independent of, the administrative agencies of the central government. In cases of conflict of jurisdiction, that of the central government agency usually prevails. In some countries, notably West Germany, appeals may be taken from agencies of the component units (*Länder* in West Germany) to corresponding agencies of the central government. In the United States and Canada, the only appeal from "state" or provincial agencies is to the courts in judicial review.

SELECTION OF PERSONNEL

Levels of Personnel. The heads of agencies and members of plural-headed agencies are usually appointed, often for fixed terms and sometimes on the basis of special qualifications. Below these is an important group of administrators whom we may call agents of the agencies. They are such officials as trial examiners, attorneys, division chiefs, and regional directors. Subject to the higher authority of the agency proper, they represent the agency and exercise some of its powers, and usually have considerable leeway in doing so. In some countries they are appointed by the central government; in others, they are considered part of the civil service and are selected under a merit system; most commonly, the agency has a free hand in selecting them. Finally, there is the vast army of employees who do the routine work. These are the people with whom we are chiefly concerned in this section.

The Civil Service. These administrative employees comprise what most countries call the civil service. Strictly speaking, the term civil service means any government employment and/or the persons engaged in such employment. In practice, the term *civil service* is used to designate administrative employees outside the military services. In some countries the civil service includes the foreign service; in others, the United States among them, the foreign service is a separate category. Commonly, policy-determining officials at or near the top, and casual and temporary employees, are not considered a part of the civil service.

Bureaucracy. Another term that is much bantered about is bureaucracy, but its meaning depends on who is using it. Literally it means government by bureaus. Some people use the term as synonymous with civil service. Others mean by it the higher ranking officials in the civil service who are suspected of exercising more influence than they should on policy making. It would seem best to limit the term bureaucracy to the closely knit and self-perpetuating groups in the civil service of some countries, such as West Germany, which exercise administrative power, including policy making, almost independently of effective control by responsible political officials.

Selection of Civil Service Personnel. The oldest method of selecting civil service employees was by appointment, with the appointing officer having full freedom of choice. This arrangement still exists in a few countries and in some of the "states" of the United States; there are even some vestiges of it in the United States federal government. A careful and conscientious official can and sometimes does make excellent appointments, unless the number to be made is staggering, but there is always the temptation to appoint one's friends or political supporters, or to use the "patronage" to build up a personal or partisan political organization. The arrangement can easily deteriorate into a corrupt "spoils system." Nominally in the Soviet Union, and actually in some of the "states" of the United States, many local administrative employees are popularly elected. There is little to commend popular election of nonpolicy-making government personnel except the tradition that it is democratic. Most countries have adopted some kind of merit system for most of their civil service employees.

Merit Selection. A merit system is an arrangement for selecting and promoting civil service employees on the basis of merit. The employee gets into the service initially through a competitive examination, sometimes with educational prerequisites. He is promoted partly on the basis of his service record and partly on the basis of further examinations. Since one of the goals is to free the administrative employees from partisan politics, a merit system carries with it security of tenure to the extent that the employee can be dismissed only for good cause or in reduction of the service; never because of a political party change in the executive or through personal favoritism. Use of the merit system tends to make the public service a career or even a profession, rather than just a job, but this works out to different degrees in different countries. Details of the system vary greatly from one country to another.

PRINCIPLES OF PUBLIC ADMINISTRATION

Expanding Scope of Public Administration. In all important countries, growth of population and the rapidly growing complexity of economic life are continually creating new tasks which governments must undertake. Each of these new activities, as well as each of the older ones, must be administered by a suitable administrative agency with a large staff of employees. Hence, public administration, both in the importance of the work it does and in the number of people engaged, has become the biggest part of big government. Its study has become a field in itself (as a division of political science) and it is developing its own scheme of law, called administrative law. Because of the great importance of public administration in the lives of ordinary citizens, most political scientists agree that certain principles should be followed in managing the civil service.

Primary Purposes. There are two primary purposes of civil service management, and all arrangements should be contrived, as far as humanly possible, to serve these purposes. The first of these purposes is efficiency. The job, whatever it is, needs to be done well, in accordance with the laws that provide for it, and without waste or duplication of effort. The second purpose, which applies particularly to agencies with quasi-legislative, quasi-judicial, or policy-making powers, is strict impartiality. As far as human ingenuity can achieve it, these agencies should be so constituted that personal or political considerations will never enter into their decisions. Many areas have "conflict of interest" laws which forbid any person to hold a position as administrator who has any financial or personal interest in any business or other activity with which the agency concerned may have dealings.

Effective Selection. One thing that is necessary to attain these purposes is the effective selection of personnel. No merit system has yet been devised which is free from defects, and perhaps none ever can be. Even so, it is the concensus of opinion among political scientists that, whatever its faults, it is the best arrangement now available for recruiting all civil servants except policy-making officials at the top (though some countries include many of these) and casual and temporary employees. The competitive examination leaves much to be desired as a basis for initial selection. It is usually supplemented by personal interviews of the applicant by a higher official and, in selecting especially trained experts, it is sometimes dispensed with entirely. Nevertheless, with the huge numbers to be recruited, it appears to be the most feasible device.

There are two types of entrance examinations called "comprehensive" and "practical." Except for minor clerkships and positions requiring special skills, the British use "comprehensive" examinations. These examine the applicant on his general education, without reference to his qualifications for a particular job. They are based on the assumption that the new civil servant is entering a life career which carries social prestige, along with possibility of promotion all the way up to the position of permanent secretary of a cabinet department. In the United States, we use the "practical" examination, which examines the applicant on his qualifications for a particular job or particular type of work, without reference to the career possibilities of the civil service. It is noteworthy that, over the years, the two countries have been moving more and more toward a common basis, combining features of both plans.

It is entirely legitimate to set up educational prerequisites for taking the examination. This is done in some cases in all countries, and in all cases in some countries. In countries such as France and West Germany, where public administration is considered a profession, special training is required before taking the entrance examinations. Most countries have a prerequisite of citizenship, which may or may not enhance the efficiency of the service. In the United States, we add a loyalty check as a prerequisite.

The usual practice is placement in the order of examination grades from the top down to a minimum grade which is required for placement at all. In some situations, this rating on the placement scale is weighted by other factors, such as previous experience in a similar type of work or personality factors. This is probably justifiable. In the United States, we also weight the rating with veteran preference. A war veteran is given a bonus of several points added to his examination grade; a disabled veteran or widow of a veteran is given even more bonus points. There are arguments for this on ethical grounds, but political scientists agree that it works against the efficiency and morale of the service.

Morale. Another situation which can contribute greatly to the impartiality and efficiency of public administration is high morale and a strong loyalty to the service among the administrative employees. There is no pat formula for achieving this, but there are several things which can contribute to it. In such countries as Great Britain and West Germany, where the civil service carries high social prestige, this is a major factor in maintaining morale and loyalty to the service. Almost everywhere, security of tenure is an important factor. All merit systems provide some measure of security of tenure. The problem is to give enough security to promote morale and still not make it impossible to get rid of misfits. Another necessity is to have a sufficiently high pay scale and enough "fringe benefits" (including retirement with a pension after a long period of service) to make public employment competitive with private employment. Most countries do reasonably well on this score. Finally, the management of the service must give employees a feeling that they are being fairly dealt with. Arrangements for promotion must be such as to eliminate any hint of personal favoritism. The rules of work, dealing with such matters as tardiness, absenteeism, and insubordination, must be stringent enough to be effective, but not so stringent that they breed discontent. The employees must be able to complain and be heard about their grievances without impairing their standing, and their suggestions for improvement should be welcomed. There may be other factors that will enter into the picture, but whatever *can* be done *should* be done to promote high morale and loyalty to the service among the employees.

RELATION TO OTHER BRANCHES OF GOVERNMENT

The Executive. Administration is always considered a part of the executive branch of government so that, in a sense, the head of government is, among other things, the chief administrator. However, as we have noted previously, the degree of executive control varies, not only from country to country, but among different agencies within the same country. Usually the top administrators are executive appointees and are expected to work in harmony with executive policy. The head of government, directly, through the head of a cabinet department, or through a special agency like the United States Civil Service Commission, which is responsible to him, can make and modify rules for the recruitment and management of the civil service.

The Legislative Branch. Administration is always subject to a large measure of legislative control. Unless provided for in the constitution, administrative agencies are created by statutes enacted by the legislative body. Again, unless the powers, duties, and functions of an agency are spelled out in the constitution (something that is rarely done), it is the legislative body which confers the power, assigns the functions, and stipulates the procedure of administrative agencies. In practically every case, it is laws enacted by the legislative body which are to be administered. In some countries, notably Great Britain and the United States, the national legislature (Parliament or Congress) maintains a measure of supervision over administration by making some agencies responsible to it rather than to the executive.

The Judiciary. Practically everywhere, acts of administrative agencies are subject to judicial review on complaint of an aggrieved party, either in the regular courts or in special administrative courts. In countries that have special administrative courts, these courts will sometimes pass on the merits of administrative rulings or decisions. The more common rule, universal in common law countries, is that a court will only review an action of an administrative agency to determine first, whether the agency has acted within the powers conferred on it by law, or second, whether it has deviated from proper procedure in a manner that deprives the aggrieved party of any of his legal rights. In a few situations, such as administering naturalization in the United States, or handling the estates of deceased or bankrupt persons, the courts themselves act as administrative agencies.

TEST-YOURSELF QUIZ

Without referring back to the text, check the answer or completion in each question that you think is right. Then turn to answers on page 236 and see how well you have done.

1. The type of administrative agency best suited for carrying on technical but routine functions is:
( ) a. Single administrator.
( ) b. Single administrator with advisory board.
( ) c. Board or commission.
( ) d. Government corporation.

2. An administrative agency has the powers that:
( ) a. It decides it needs to perform its functions.
( ) b. Are directed by executive order.
( ) c. Are conferred on it by law.
( ) d. Are given to it by order of a court.

3. Regulatory agencies are often given a large degree of independence in order to:
( ) a. Protect the tenure of top administrators.
( ) b. Prevent personal or political pressure from influencing their decisions.
( ) c. Prevent the courts from overruling their decisions.
( ) d. Keep the executive from becoming too powerful.

4. Administrative agencies are normally subject, in some degree, to all but one of these controls. Which one?
( ) a. Directives from the executive.
( ) b. Legislation.
( ) c. Popular elections.
( ) d. Judicial review by the courts.

5. The method of selecting civil service employees which political scientists regard as least satisfactory is:
( ) a. Executive appointment.
( ) b. Merit system.
( ) c. Selection by committees of a legislative body.
( ) d. Popular election.

6. All but one of these are objectives to be sought in administering civil service. Which one is not?
( ) a. To provide as many jobs as possible.
( ) b. To get work done efficiently.
( ) c. To make sure that agencies maintain strict impartiality.
( ) d. To maintain high morale among employees.

7. The term "bureaucracy" is used most appropriately in the meaning of:
( ) a. Government by bureaus.
( ) b. The civil service in general.
( ) c. A self-perpetuating civil service which operates with little or no control by the political authorities.
( ) d. Top-ranking officers in the civil service.

8. Normally, the primary responsibility of administrative agencies is to:
( ) a. The executive.
( ) b. The legislative body.

( ) c. The courts.
( ) d. The voters.

SUGGESTIONS FOR DISCUSSION

1. Compare the meaning of "administration" and "the administration."
2. See how many functions of public administration you can think of and try to rate them in the order of their importance.
3. What are quasi-legislative and quasi-judicial powers? Why do some administrative agencies have them?
4. Why is a board or commission preferable to a single administrator when the functions of the agency are mainly regulatory?
5. Compare the degree of independence of agencies with various types of functions, and try to explain the reason in each case.
6. Why is the classification of administrative systems into centralized and decentralized necessarily inexact?
7. What is a merit system and how does it work? What advantages does it have over other methods of selecting administrative employees?
8. Explain, and see if you can justify, the principles laid down for good public administration.

BIBLIOGRAPHY

Baum, B. H., *Decentralization of Authority in a Bureaucracy* (Englewood Cliffs, N. J., 1961).

Dawson, R. G., *The Civil Service in Canada* (New York, 1939).

Dimock, M. E., and G. G. O., *Public Administration* (New York, 1964).

Gladden, E. N., *An Introduction to Public Administration* (London, 1961).

Gladden, E. N., *The Essentials of Public Administration* (New York, 1955).

Kilpatrick, F. P., and others, *The Image of the Federal Service* (Washington, D. C., 1964).

Morstein-Marx, F., *Elements of Public Administration* (Englewood Cliffs, N. J., 1959).

Nelson, D. H., *Administrative Agencies of the U. S. A.* (Detroit, Mich., 1964).

Rowat, D. C., *Basic Issues in Public Administration* (New York, 1961).

Sharp, W. R., *The French Civil Service: Bureaucracy in Transition* (New York, 1931).

Sisson, C. H., *Spirit of British Administration* (New York, 1959).

Von Mises, L., *Bureaucracy* (New Haven, Conn., 1962).

11

The Electorate and Elections

*Everywhere today, except in the few remaining
absolute monarchies, government is presumed
to rest on the consent of the governed, given through
direct or indirect elections. But who may participate in these elections? Obviously not all
inhabitants of the country, not even all the citizens,
but only those persons who possess the suffrage
or the "right" to vote.*

Strictly speaking, as noted previously, voting is not a right but
a privilege and a duty, given by the state to such persons as, it
is assumed, will exercise it in the best interests of the community.
This may be done in the constitution or by legislative action, or
by a combination of the two.

   Restrictions on Voting.   Everywhere there are restrictions
on suffrage. These usually take the form of requirements which
the would-be voter must meet in order to qualify. In earlier times,
the qualifications commonly included the ownership of a minimum value of real estate, or the payment of a minimum amount
of taxes on real estate, and often the holding of specified religious
beliefs. Today, these requirements exist in only a few places.
Until fairly recently, women were not allowed to vote, and there
are still a few countries where they can not qualify. Occasionally,
racial restrictions are imposed, as in the Republic of South Africa

where, in most elections, voters must be "white," and in Liberia where only members of the Negro race can vote.

Present day restrictions have to do mainly with citizenship, age, and residence. Normally, citizenship is, though it need not be, a requirement for voting. Prior to World War I, about a third of the "states" in the United States permitted aliens to vote if they had taken the first step toward naturalization and could meet other requirements. In the British Commonwealth of Nations, those countries which acknowledge the Queen as their titular sovereign permit any British subject to vote if he can meet age and residence requirements, even though he be a citizen of another Commonwealth country. There is always a minimum age requirement. Most commonly this is the traditional twenty-one years, though in some countries it is lower and in some, higher. A few countries have different age requirements for voting for different offices. Finally, there is almost always a residence requirement. The voter must have lived in a designated area a specified length of time in order to qualify. This is sometimes a double or even triple requirement: in most of the "states" of the United States, the voter must have lived in the "state" for six months or a year, and in the subdivision where he seeks to vote (county, township or precinct) for thirty, sixty, or ninety days; in a few of the "states," he must have lived in the "state" a certain length of time (usually a year), in his county, so many days, and in his precinct, a fewer number of days. A few whole countries (mostly in underdeveloped areas) and some of the American "states" also have educational or literacy requirements. Also, in a few countries, voting age depends on marital status; a person may vote at a younger age if married than if unmarried.

Negative Restrictions. Besides these positive requirements, suffrage laws commonly impose some negative restrictions: things that will deprive an otherwise qualified person of the "right" to vote. These usually include mental incapacity (if officially adjudged), conviction of major crimes, dishonorable discharge from the armed services, and (in the United States and Communist countries) legally proved disloyalty. There is a widespread mis-conception in the United States that these things deprive a person of his citizenship. They do not. They only deprive him of the "right" to vote.

Is Voting a Duty? It is commonly accepted that those who have the "right" to vote have a moral duty to do so. In a few countries, Belgium for example, it is a legal duty, with fines or other penalties imposed on those who fail to vote. This is called compulsory voting. Elsewhere, it is argued that if a person can vote and fails to do so, he has no grounds to complain if the gov-ernment is not run to suit him. There is much to be said for this. Most political scientists would agree that voting is a moral obliga-tion, but they would go further and insist that the moral obligation is not just to-vote, but to vote intelligently. Voting consistently for a party label, regardless of candidates or issues, voting for a candidate because he has an attractive personality, or voting a certain way because a friend has asked one to do so, is at best an inadequate way of meeting one's moral obligation. If voting is to be fully meaningful as giving the "consent of the governed" and expressing the considered "will of the people," the voter needs to inform himself as fully as he can about candidates, issues, and party positions, and then vote according to his best judgment as to what is best for the community or the country. The voter will, of course, be influenced by the effect certain policies may be expected to have on his own interests. This is a part of getting the "will of the people," since responsible officials must seek to harmonize or compromise conflicting interests. Even so, the voter will do well to be sure he is voting from enlightened self-interest, and not from mere whim or prejudice.

VOTERS' LISTS

The Need for Voters' Lists. Except in rural areas where everyone knows everyone else, it is necessary that, when a voter appears at the polling place, persons conducting the election have a ready means of knowing whether or not he is a qualified voter. To provide this means, it is the almost universal practice to prepare lists of qualified voters and to revise these lists prior to each important election. The responsibility for compiling and revising the list is given to some public official or group of officials. Methods of going about it vary. In some countries, the responsible official or agency compiles and revises his lists on the basis of reports from minor local officials who are presumed to know who are qualified voters in their respective areas. In other countries, the lists are based on official records of local communities, which include records of persons who have come of age or moved into the community as well as those who have died, moved away, or otherwise become disqualified. Only in the United States is the initiative placed on the voter himself by requiring that he register. But even with registration, unless the voter is required to register anew for each election (a practice that is no longer common), the responsible officials still have the responsibility of keeping the lists "purged" of names of persons who have died, moved, or otherwise become disqualified. This is difficult.

Checking the Lists. With or without voter registration, the lists must be checked continually. Mistakes can be made and sometimes are. Every effort must be made to ensure that each name on the list is that of a qualified voter, and to remove all other names. In countries that do not keep public records of changes in residence, it is extremely difficult to know who has moved out of the election area or moved into it the required length of time before an election. In case of question, the burden of proof is placed on the voter. The voter should have, and usually does have, an opportunity, if his name is omitted or dropped from the list, to appear before the proper official and offer proof that it should be included.

Identifying the Voter. Especially in large urban communities, these lists may not be enough. If a would-be voter appears at the polling place and gives a name on the list, the election officials may not know whether or not he is the person he says he is. So far, no over-all plan of voter identification has appeared, but several expedients are used here and there. An old device, now generally discarded, was to permit the voter to "swear in" his vote; he swore, under the penalties for perjury, that he was a qualified voter, and this was accepted as proof. In some countries, the voter whose identity is questioned may be required to bring in a sponsor, who is known to the election officials, who will testify to his identity. In some situations, he may present identifying documents, such as his social security card or driver's license. A device used in many places in the United States is the signature card. Where this is used, every voter, before he is given a ballot (no matter how well known he may be to the election officials) is required to sign an identification card or slip, and this signature is compared with the signature on his registration card.

ELECTIONS

Meaningfulness of Elections. Elections are held, or at least provided for, almost everywhere, but their meaningfulness depends on the character of the government. In most totalitarian states, elections are held in which the voter has no freedom of choice. If they have any meaning at all, it is only in giving the voters a feeling of participation by registering their approval of the regime. Even in Communist China, which has never had an election, the constitution promises the election of a national assembly at some indefinite time in the future. In personal dictatorships, elections are either "postponed" indefinitely (though always promised) or, if held, are so "rigged" that they offer no challenge to the power of the dictator.

In the Free World, however, elections really determine who shall run the government and, to a great extent, what policies shall be followed. Members of the legislative body (at least one chamber of it) are elected in free competition. Under the cabinet system, this amounts to indirect election of the head of government (the prime minister), since he is selected on the basis of party strength in parliament. Under the presidential system, the head of government is popularly elected, either directly or indirectly, in free competition. Moreover, in the Free World, many issues are referred directly to the voters for decision.

Types of Elections.   Elections may be classified on several different bases. One classification is into elections of officers and referenda on issues. Since an election of officers usually takes the form of competition between or among political parties, we may defer the discussion of these elections to the next chapter. There are several varieties of referenda. In many countries around the world, and in the "states" of the United States, constitutional amendments or new constitutions are submitted to the voters for approval in what the Europeans call a plebiscite. This word literally means "decree of the people," but practically it means the same as our word referendum. In most of the "states" of the United States, the constitutions require that bond issues and tax increases above certain levels be submitted to the voters in referenda. In Switzerland, Italy, some of the "states" of the United States, and a few other places, there is provision for what is called "initiative and referendum." In the "initiative," a proposal for a law (or in some cases, a constitutional amendment) is placed on the ballot by a petition signed by a specified number of voters. If a majority of voters approve it in an election, it becomes law. In the "referendum," a similar petition places on the ballot a measure passed by the legislative body, and the vote in an election determines whether or not it shall become law. In cabinet-governed countries, particularly if there is a two-party system, an election following a dissolution of parliament over a particular issue amounts to a referendum on that issue, since the voters will decide it by electing legislators who favor or oppose it.

Another classification of elections is into general and special. A general election is one held throughout a country (or component unit of a federal union), either on a set schedule or following a dissolution of parliament, primarily for election of members of the legislative body. In some countries, other officials may be elected or referenda voted on at the same time. A special election is one of limited scope, held at a different time than the general election, for a special purpose such as filling a vacancy or voting on a referendum question. We may also contrast with general elections, local elections. We can not class these as special elections because they are usually held on a set schedule, usually at a different time than the general election. They are mainly for the election of local officials, including members of local legislative bodies, but some local referendum questions may be voted on also.

Conduct of Elections. Responsibility for conducting elections is vested in a permanent official, usually in addition to other duties. An exception in some localities in the United States is a board of election commissioners which devotes full time to election matters. This official designates the persons who conduct the election in each polling place, and may or may not count the votes. In France, the prefect of the *department* is in charge of elections. He designates four "assessors," usually local officials, in each polling place, to conduct the election and count the votes. In Britain, the job is divided. The sheriff for the county and the mayor for the borough is the "returning officer" who designates "assistants" in each polling place to conduct the actual election, but all ballots are sent to the "returning officer" to be counted. The clerks of the borough and county councils are the "registration officers," who prepare and revise the voters' lists. In most countries the executive or chief administrator of the main local government unit is in charge of elections. In the United States outside New England, except where there is a board of election commissioners, the county clerk makes all arrangements for the election. However, most of our "states" have a requirement, not found elsewhere, that each polling place be manned by six persons, three from each major political party, who conduct the election and count the votes.

Ballots.   Almost everywhere in the world, except in some larger American cities that use voting machines, voting is by paper ballot provided by the election authorities. In most countries, voting booths are provided in which the voter may mark his ballot in secret. The ballot is marked with an "X" in a square or similar space provided to indicate each candidate or party list voted for. On referendum proposals, there is a space to mark "X" for "yes" or "no." On an older form of ballot, that still survives here and there, the voter crossed out the names of candidates for whom he did not wish to vote and on referendum proposals, crossed out "no" to vote "yes," and *vice versa.* There may be two or more ballots to be marked in the same election.

There is sometimes a problem of arranging names on the ballot. In Great Britain, where the general election ballot contains the names of only two or three candidates for Parliament, and the local ballot (in county and borough elections held at a different time than the general), only the names of two or three candidates for councilman, there is no problem. Much the same is true in many of the countries of western continental Europe. Where there is proportional representation, there is a question of the order of the names on the party lists since, except in Italy where the voter may express a preference, candidates are declared elected in the order in which their names appear on the list. The order is determined by the party organ, usually a committee, which makes the nominations. The real problem is in the United States. Not only do we elect federal, state, and county officers in the same election, but we include many state and county administrative positions as elective. As a consequence, the ballot may contain as many as a hundred names, with the voter asked to make two dozen or more choices.

We have developed two plans for arranging the names. The oldest, still used in about a third of the "states," is the party column ballot. All the candidates of a political party are listed in a column under the party name and party emblem, with the highest office to be filled at the top of the column, the lowest, at the end of the column, and the others, in between in the order of their importance. There is a square beside each name in which the voter may mark an "X" to vote for an individual candidate, but there is also a circle at the head of the column in which the voter may mark an "X" to vote a "straight" party ticket. The other plan is the office block ballot. This ballot has a "block" or box for each office, arranged from the highest to the lowest, with the names of all candidates for each office, with party designation, in the box for that office. In some "states," the names in each box are arranged alphabetically; in others, the parties are rotated. There is no place on the ballot to mark an "X" for a "straight" party ticket; each candidate must be voted for separately. This is intended to encourage independent voting.

Short Ballot Reform. The requirement of making so many choices at once is baffling to many voters. The average voter finds it virtually impossible to know the merits or the views of so many candidates. All too often, he makes his choice for President or Governor, and then votes a "straight" ticket of the party of his chosen candidate for the top office. Candidates for minor positions are said to "ride into office on the President's coat tails." Some propose to remedy this situation by holding federal, state, and county elections at different times, just as municipal elections are now generally held at a different time from the general election. Most American political scientists favor the so-called "short ballot" reform. This proposal would shorten the ballot by having only policy-determining officers elected, with all the others appointed by the executive or selected under a merit system. This would bring our "states" and counties into line with the practice of the federal government and most American cities, as well as most other countries of the world. Most politicians oppose the "short ballot," ostensibly because it would be undemocratic, but actually because it would tend to weaken their political organizations.

SOME CONSIDERATIONS REGARDING ELECTIONS

Frequency. In countries having presidential-type governments, along with some others, general elections occur on a set schedule because legislators and all other elective officers have fixed terms. With cabinet-type government, a general election is held either at the expiration of the maximum term of members of the legislative body or following a dissolution of parliament. Everywhere, local elections come on a set schedule, with municipal elections held at a different time from other elections. After a revolutionary change, an election may be called at any time. When we add to these, special elections to fill vacancies or to vote on referendum proposals, and—in the United States—"primary" elections to make nominations, elections may come at very frequent intervals. It is a principle of political science that elections should be frequent enough to keep the voters interested and challenged, but not frequent enough to become burdensome. How frequent is *too* frequent may vary with circumstances. Frequency may be reduced by combining several elections into one as, in the United States, federal, "state," and county elections are usually combined. This reduces expense and saves voters' time, but it may confront the voter with too many simultaneous choices.

What the Voters are Asked to Decide. We have already suggested some of the things the voter is asked to decide. Usually he indicates his choice of a political party by voting for candidates of that party. Either through his choice of a party or by voting for individual candidates with whose ideas he agrees, he indicates the general policies he wishes. If there is a sharp division between parties or candidates on particular issues, the voters decide the issue by electing the party or the candidate whose stand on the issue most of them approve. Besides, the voters decide many issues directly by voting on referendum proposals.

It is axiomatic that the fewer decisions a voter is asked to make at one time, the more likely he is to make intelligent decisions.

In countries where the voter chooses only between two or among three or four candidates for legislator or local councilman, and where "plebiscites" are held at a different time, this consideration does not present a serious problem. However, with a situation such as exists in most of the "states" of the United States, the voter is confronted with a number of simultaneous choices that is utterly baffling. There is no easy solution of the problem. The "short ballot" reform would probably help, but would not eliminate the difficulty entirely. The decisions to be made could be distributed among more elections, but this, besides increasing expense, would weary the voter with too frequent elections. Another partial answer would be to allow elected representatives more discretion in settling issues that now have to be submitted to the voters, such as tax increases and bond issues. This is done in our federal government and in most governments of the world. In our "states" and counties, though, this runs up against the insistence of the taxpayers on keeping their hands on the purse strings.

The Education of Voters. It is also axiomatic that the better educated the voters are, the more adequately they function as an electorate. This applies not only to general education, but to education in public affairs and the workings of government. This is an especially baffling problem in the newly emerging nations where a majority of the people are illiterate and where no one has had experience with self-government. Even in the most advanced countries, where there is almost no illiteracy and where free mass media of communication, newspapers, radio and television, reach almost everyone, all too many voters do not understand the problems and issues of government and are not sufficiently interested to inform themselves.

Governments usually do something to educate the voters. In totalitarian countries, the government seeks to mold the thinking of voters completely through one-sided propaganda and by denying access to other sources of information. In Free World countries, the government tries to keep the people as fully informed as considerations of national security will permit, with news releases, press conferences, and public addresses, over radio or television, by responsible officials. Civic organizations do all they can to generate voter interest and to spread information on public questions. Pressure groups seek to convert voters to their particular points of view. Adult education facilities offer instruction in public affairs. In the last analysis, the problem is to develop enough feeling of responsibility in the individual voter so that he will keep himself informed.

Preferential Voting. Preferential voting means that the voter, instead of marking an "X" to vote for an individual candidate or party list, indicates his first, second, and perhaps third, choice by marking numerals in the squares beside the names. The device is used in some plans of proportional representation. In Italy, as we have seen, a literate voter may indicate the order in which he prefers candidates for parliament be declared elected on the party list. Where it is used by itself in a direct election, preferential voting works this way. If any candidate receives a clear majority of first choices, he is elected. If no one has such a majority, the second choices are counted and added to the first. If any candidate has a majority of the combined first and second choices, he is elected. If necessary, third choices are counted and added in the same way.

Preferential voting is used in some American cities in municipal elections if there are more than two parties or other organized groups competing. It also has untapped possibilities. In many smaller American cities, municipal elections are non-partisan. The present practice is to hold a primary election in which the names of all candidates who have filed for any elective office appear on the ballot, and the voter votes for his choice. The two candidates for each office who receive the highest and second highest votes in the primary are then the candidates between whom the voter chooses in the regular municipal election. By preferential voting, it could all be done in one election. Many of the Southern "states" require a majority vote to nominate in the primary. If there are more than two candidates for an office and no one receives a majority, a "run off" primary is held later in which the voters choose between the two highest. Here also, preferential voting would make it possible to do it all in one election.

TEST-YOURSELF QUIZ

Without referring back to the text, check the answer or completion in each question that you think is right. Then turn to answers on page 236 and see how well you have done.

1. Present day qualifications for voting in most countries do not include:
( ) a. Citizenship.
( ) b. A residence requirement.
( ) c. Minimum voting age.
( ) d. Payment of certain taxes.

2. The most intelligent voting is based on:
( ) a. Party loyalty.
( ) b. Serious evaluation of candidates and issues.
( ) c. The feeling that it does not matter how one votes since his vote will not count much anyway.
( ) d. Disregarding all factors but self-interest.

3. The chief purpose of voters' lists is:
( ) a. To get more people to vote.
( ) b. To favor one political party.
( ) c. To make sure that only qualified persons vote.
( ) d. To keep members of minority ethnic and religious groups from voting.

4. A general election is:
( ) a. One held throughout a country to elect officers.
( ) b. One called to vote on a referendum proposal.
( ) c. One for the election of the chief of state or head of government.
( ) d. One for the nomination of candidates.

5. A bi-partisan board in each polling place to conduct the election and count the votes is characteristic of:
( ) a. Great Britain.
( ) b. Western continental Europe.
( ) c. The United States.
( ) d. The Soviet Union.

6. Elections should be held:
( ) a. Very frequently to keep the voters interested.
( ) b. As rarely as possible to save expense.
( ) c. Frequently enough to keep the voters interested, but not so frequently as to become a burden.
( ) d. For all levels of government at the same time.

7. In most countries, an otherwise qualified voter may lose his right to vote by any three of these conditions. Which one will not disqualify him?
( ) a. He is convicted of a serious crime.
( ) b. He fails to register his party affiliation.
( ) c. He is legally adjudged mentally incompetent.
( ) d. He is dishonorably discharged from the armed services.

8. An election is fully meaningful only if:
( ) a. The government is controlled by the free choice of the voters.
( ) b. Nearly all adults have the right to vote.
( ) c. Most of the people vote in the election.
( ) d. The election is not "rigged."

SUGGESTIONS FOR DISCUSSION

1. Is voting a right, a privilege or a duty? How would you qualify your answer?
2. Enumerate past and present restrictions on suffrage. Which would you approve and which would you disapprove?
3. In most situations, why is it considered necessary to prepare voters' lists ahead of elections? Which of the ways in which this is done would you consider the best?
4. On what does the "meaningfulness" of elections depend?
5. What are the purposes for which referenda or plebiscites are used?

What is meant by the "initiative and referendum"? Is it used any-where outside the United States?

6. Compare the conduct of elections in several countries.

7. What problems may arise in arranging names on the ballot? What are some of the ways in which the problem is solved? Why do we hear of "short ballot reform" only in the United States?

8. In what senses is the education of voters important in various parts of the world?

BIBLIOGRAPHY

Alford, R. R., *Social Class and Voting in Four Anglo-American De-mocracies* (Berkeley, Cal., 1961).

Birke, W., *European Elections by Direct Suffrage* (Leyden, Nether-lands, 1961).

Bone, H. A., and Ranney, A., *Politics and Voters* (New York, 1963).

Butler, D. E., Ed., *Elections Abroad* (London, 1959).

Butler, D. E., *The Electoral System in Britain since 1918* (Fair Lawn, N. J., 1963).

Institute of Electoral Research, *Parliaments and Electoral Systems* (London, 1961).

Lee, E. C., *The Politics of Nonpartisanship* (Berkeley, Cal., 1960).

O'Leary, C., *The Irish Republic and Its Experiment with Proportional Representation* (Notre Dame, Ind., 1961).

Tingsten, H. L. G., *Political Behavior* (Englewood Cliffs, N. J., 1963).

Williamson, C., *American Suffrage* (Princeton. N. J., 1960).

12

Political Parties

Political parties are of several kinds. Some stand for fixed principles of government. Others are only rival organizations to contest elections. Others have still other characteristics. But in one form or another, political parties are found almost everywhere. Except in a few situations where nonpartisan elections are held, political parties are the medium through which the electorate functions to participate in government.

Because of the wide variation in the characteristics of parties, a political party can be defined only as an organized group of politicians and voters which presents candidates in elections and seeks to control government by winning elections.

Legal Status of Parties. Normally, political parties are recognized by law and, in some cases, are strictly regulated by law. However, in most countries, their organization and methods of operations are governed by custom and tradition. In absolute monarchies and some dictatorships, political parties are forbidden. Even in these places, however, there are divisions of opinion and attitude among the people which amount to rudimentary political parties. They may even have "underground" organization, though they can not function normally by participating in elections. In totalitarian countries, there is an "official" party or coalition of parties, which alone can present candidates in elections. In these countries, too, there are apt to be "underground" parties which either plot revolutionary activity, or offer passive resistance to the regime.

PARTY SYSTEMS

Meaning. Some countries operate with only one party, others with two principal parties, and still others with such a multiplicity of parties that it is virtually impossible for any one ever to win a clear cut victory in a national election. We refer to the particular situation in a country as the party system of that country. Except where the party system is prescribed by law, the arrangement we find in a country depends on the history, the traditions, and the poltical experience of the country.

One-Party System. In a one-party system there is only one political party. This party automatically wins all elections because its candidates have no opposition. In totalitarian governments, this arrangement is prescribed by law. There is an official party, dominated by the dictator or elite oligarchy, and no opposition parties are permitted to exist. In ideological totalitarianism, this party (Communist, Fascist, or what have you) stands for the accepted ideology. A pretense of other parties is sometimes permitted, but only so long as these "parties" accept the dominant ideology and work in permanent coalition with the official party; they can never offer real opposition. In Free World countries, there may be local areas where one party is so predominant that it amounts to a one-party system in strictly local politics (as formerly in the "Solid South" in the United States), but this is a result of a special set of circumstances. There may be brief periods in free countries when there will be only one party (as in the United States in 1820), but this is only a stage in a realignment of parties, and never lasts long. The normal thing is for the voters to divide into parties, if they are permitted to do so.

Two-Party System. In a two-party system, such as we have in the United States, there are only two parties that are important enough to be real contenders in elections, although other lesser parties may exist also. This arrangement may exist as a transitional stage in a country that is emerging from a revolutionary period (as Turkey) or one that has recently been under foreign occupation (as Austria). However, as normal politics on a relatively permanent basis, it is found only in the English-speaking countries. Probably the main reason it exists in these countries is that it is based on a tradition that goes back to the formation of the original political parties (Whigs and Tories) in England in the late 1600's. It does have some important advantages, though. It is much easier for a voter to choose between two parties than to pick among several. If the "ins" are voted out, the "outs" come in, so that coalition governments are rarely necessary. This makes for stability and continuity of national policy. There is also the disadvantage that the voter can not always find a party that expresses his political philosophy or his views on issues, and so must evaluate individual candidates rather than just the stands of parties.

Multiple-Party System. The normal tendency in free politics is for voters to divide into several parties, each voter adhering to a party which stands for his political philosophy or the special interests of a group to which he belongs. This gives rise to the multiple-party system. There may be anywhere from three or four to two dozen or more parties. In Germany, just before Hitler took over, there were twenty-five parties represented in the *Reichstag.* The arrangement has the advantage that a voter may express his wishes by voting for a party, and need not bother about individual candidates. Its great disadvantage is that it makes for instability in government. Almost never will a single party win a complete victory in a national election, so that government must be carried on by a coalition of parties. Under a presidential plan of government, the coalition is formed before the election to support a candidate for president, but a president so elected has great difficulty trying to please the various party groups that have helped elect him. In many countries of Latin America, attempts are often made (and sometimes succeed) to throw such a president out of office by armed uprising. Under the cabinet plan of government, the cabinet must be made up of leaders of several parties in a coalition. Such coalitions are notably unstable, with the result that cabinet crises are frequent. In pre-Hitler Germany, it was the inability to continue to form coalitions that opened the way for Hitler to come to power, and it was a similar situation that brought about the downfall of the Fourth French Republic.

TYPES OF PARTIES

Bases of Classification. Political parties may be classified on several different bases: according to membership; according to strength; according to basic character; and whether popular or parliamentary.

According to Membership. Parties are classified according to membership into open, enrolled, and closed. The important parties in most free countries have an open membership. Anyone may adhere to any party. In the United States, for example, a person becomes a Republican or a Democrat merely by deciding that he is one. He may, if he wishes, contribute to the funds of his party or work for its success in elections, but he is not required to do so. He need not vote consistently for the candidates of his party. Except, in some cases for voting in primary elections, he need not even divulge his party preference. A person may, if he chooses, be an "independent" voter and not consider himself a member of any party. Much the same situation prevails with regard to the larger parties in most countries of the Free World.

In some countries, some parties, usually the smaller ones, have what we may call an enrolled membership. To become a member of the party, a voter must join it formally, pay dues, and carry a membership card. Any voter may, of course, vote for the party's candidates, but only party members have a part in nominating candidates and deciding party policies. Formerly some minor parties in the United States had such enrolled membership.

In totalitarian countries, the official party always has a closed membership. Party membership carries an elite status and special privileges, so that it is greatly to be desired. The applicant for party membership must be admitted to the party, sometimes must go through a probationary period for indoctrination and to test his loyalty to the party ideology, and may be expelled from the party for any transgression of party discipline. Obviously, a party of this type can exist in a free country only as an underground conspiracy.

According to Strength.   A classification that is very significant under a two-party system, but is meaningless elsewhere, is into major, minor, and third. It is based on two criteria, strength and permanence. A major party is one which has relative permanence and enough voter strength to be a real contender in national elections. In the United States, the Democrats and Republicans; in Britain, the Conservatives and the Labor Party; in Canada, the Conservatives and Liberals, are the major parties. A minor party is one with relative permanence, but not enough voter strength to be a real contender in national elections. In the United States, the Socialist and Prohibitionists parties are examples. Since these parties have no chance of success, one may wonder why they exist. In theory, they always hope to grow into major parties, though most of their adherents probably do not hold the hope very seriously. Sometimes, as in the case of the Prohibitionists, they feel that they are upholding a cause. Sometimes, like the American Socialists, they feel that they are making a real contribution by advancing ideas which will be taken up by the major parties. Occasionally, some of them draw enough "protest" votes to hold the balance of power in an election.

A third party is one which springs up quickly and presents a considerable show of strength in one national election, but does not attain permanence. If it survives the one election, it shrinks into a minor party. In some cases, a third party splinters off from a major party, as did Theodore Roosevelt's Progressives in 1912, or the so-called "Dixiecrats" in 1948. Sometimes it represents a widespread protest movement, as did the People's Party (the "Populists") in 1892. Third parties sometimes play a significant role in shaping the course of political events. Once in the United States (the Republicans) and once in Britain (the Labor Party), a third party has achieved permanence and become a major party.

According to Basic Character. Classified according to their basic character, there are several varieties of parties and, in some cases, varieties of varieties. We can mention only the principal types. It must be noted, though, that these types are not mutually exclusive. A particular party may have some or all of the characteristics of two or more types. Moreover, a party may originate as one type and change over into another.

Doctrinal Parties. The doctrinal party conforms to the traditional definition of a political party as a group that stands for definite principles or doctrines and seeks to put these into effect in government. The American Prohibition Party is a good example. The ideological parties of totalitarian countries are essentially doctrinal parties, though they may have some of the characteristics of other types. In multiple-party countries, most of the parties are usually doctrinal in character. Even in two-party countries, the major parties may preserve some doctrinal traits, as to the Conservative and Labor Parties in Great Britain. Our own Democratic and Republican Parties were originally partly doctrinal in character, though they have now lost most of this character. The changeover takes place because the issues that call the party into existence are settled or cease to be considered important, but the party as an institution goes on and, as new issues arise, differences of viewpoint on the new issues cut across party lines.

Leadership Parties. A leadership party is one which is formed around an individual leader. It consists largely of his personal following and is, in a sense, a lengthened shadow of the leader. Hitler's National Socialist Party in Germany was of this type. So was the party of General De Gaulle in France from the end of World War II until the establishment of the Fifth Republic. When it first came into power, the Democratic Party in the United States was largely the personal party of Andrew Jackson. Such a party may also be doctrinal, insofar as the leader stands for particular doctrines. A leadership party can not continue as such indefinitely. Leaders are not immortal, either physically or politically. When the leader drops out of the picture, his party either disintegrates or turns into another type.

Coalition Parties. A coalition party must be distinguished carefully from a coalition *of* parties. In a coalition *of* parties, two or more party organizations agree to cooperate to conduct a campaign or to form a cabinet, but the parties in the group retain their identity. The coalition may break up and each party go its own way. In a coalition party, two or more party organizations combine into a new organization and adopt a new party name. The component groups usually have little in common beyond opposition to the party or coalition in office. Consequently, a coalition party may be effective in opposition, but when it wins an election and comes into office it is apt to break down. In the United States, the Democratic Republican Party (1828-1832) and the Whig Party (1836-1854) were of this type.

Special Interest Parties. A special interest party is one which exists to uphold or advance the particular interests of a particular group of people. There are almost as many varieties of this type as there are varieties of interests: economic, social, ethnic, regional, and even religious. The American People's Party of 1892 spoke for the farmers. Originally the Labor Party in Britain was the political mouthpiece of organized labor. Some countries have peasant parties, and West Germany, for a while, had a refugee party. In multiple-party countries, parties whose purpose is to serve the interests of business or industry usually exist, though they are apt to take misleading names. Formerly, parties to uphold the interests of particular social classes were found in many countries. Regional parties exist or have existed in many places. The old German Empire had a Bavarian party, and in pre-Communist Yugoslavia all parties were regional, representing the various areas which, after World War I, were combined into the Yugoslav state. In its early years, the Republican Party in the United States was a regional party, standing for the sectional interests of the North as against those of the South. In the old German Empire and the pre-Hitler German republic, the Center Party was the political voice of the Catholic Church.

Institutional Parties. An institutional party is one which has become an institution. Usually with few if any distinctive principles or doctrines, other than those held by the whole country, it maintains an active organization to contest elections and to enjoy the fruits of victory. As an institution, it holds the loyalty of great numbers of voters. It may adopt a "platform," which nominally takes stands on issues to appeal to voters, but more often than not the "stands" on real issues are evasive, while unreal issues are dreamed up for the campaign and very trivial ones magnified far beyond their real importance. Such a party tries to appeal to as many special interest groups as possible and to antagonize as few as possible. The real purpose is to win the election. In two-party countries, the major parties always tend to develop in this direction, but in the United States the development has gone further than anywhere else. Except for subversive doctrines, which both Democrats and Republicans rule out, we find almost every shade of opinion on every major question among adherents of both of our major parties, and in legislative bodies, Congress and the "state" legislatures, voting on controversial questions almost always cuts across party lines.

Parliamentary and Popular Parties. A parliamentary party is the organization of partisans in the legislative body. A popular party is an organization of voters and politicians to make nominations and conduct election campaigns. The two original parties in England (the first anywhere in the modern world) were of the parliamentary sort. Members of Parliament banded together into rival groups (which soon acquired the names of Whig and Tory) to contest issues before Parliament, chiefly the question of whether James, the brother of Charles II, should be permitted to accede to the throne. When an election came, members and rival candidates appealed to the voters as Whigs and Tories, but had no voter organization to conduct the campaign. Much the same happened in the United States after the Constitution went into effect. Members of Congress who favored Alexander Hamilton's financial proposals organized to support his legislative program and took the name of Federalists. Opponents of the Hamiltonian program organized similarly, and took the name of Republicans. When elections came, each group appealed for votes in support of its viewpoint, but at first neither had an organization among the voters. The Republicans, under the leadership of Thomas Jefferson, were the first to develop a popular organization, following the model of the Committees of Correspondence of the Revolution.

In most countries today, members of each party in the legislative body have their "parliamentary" organization. In cabinet-governed countries, it is apt to be this "parliamentary" party, rather than the convention or "congress" of the popular organization of the same party, which picks the official party leader who is automatically the party's candidate for prime minister. In most countries the ties between the parliamentary and popular parties are so close that the distinction has become almost meaningless. In Great Britain, however, it is still of considerable significance.

STRUCTURE OF PARTIES

Party Organization. The structural organization of parties varies, not only from country to country, but sometimes among the parties of the same country. There is, however, a somewhat standardized pattern that is followed with variations. Usually the working organization of the popular party consists of a pyramid of committees of party leaders, or at least of active party workers. Members of the committees at the lowest level, functioning for the smallest government unit, are commonly selected, at least in theory, by party voters at the local level. In most countries, the selection is made in a "mass meeting" of party voters, often attended only by active party workers, with the real choices being made by party leadership at a higher level. In some countries, committees at lower levels are simply appointed by higher leadership. In some of the "states" of the United States, members of the local party committees are elected in primary elections conducted by the regular election authorities.

There are usually party conventions, called congresses in some countries, at various levels of government. In some unitary countries, such as Britain, there is only one such party conclave held at the national level. These conventions or congresses select the party committees at their level, decide questions or party policy (including stands on issues), and select the party's campaign leader. In the United States, this leader is called the chairman of the central ("state") or national committee, but in most countries he is called the secretary of the party. In federal unions, and in unitary states that have regional congresses or conventions, those below the top level sometimes select the delegates or representatives to the national convention or congress.

Party Discipline and Loyalty. A political party always makes an effort to exercise discipline over its members and to hold their unswerving loyalty. In the ideological parties of totalitarian countries, strict party discipline is maintained with at least an appearance of loyalty. Elsewhere, the discipline which the party can exercise over its adherents depends largely on the extent of party loyalty, and this varies greatly. The proportion of adherents who are loyal to the party under all circumstances is apt to be high in doctrinal and special interest parties; low in institutional parties. The effectiveness of a party in campaigning and in government depends largely on its ability to hold its voters in line in elections and to hold its legislators in line in legislative bodies.

FUNCTIONS OF PARTIES

Common Functions. Certain functions are, supposedly, common to all political parties, but effectiveness in performing these functions varies with circumstances. Parties nominate candidates for office, present issues to the voters, conduct election campaigns, assume responsibility for government when in office, and constitute a "loyal opposition" when out of office. They may also operate as propaganda agencies and sometimes function as charitable organizations.

Nominating Candidates. Everywhere elections are held (except in some local situations where elections are non-partisan), political parties nominate candidates. Formerly, in the United States, nominations were made at every level of government by party conventions, and candidates for President and Vice President are still made in national conventions of the parties. Some of the "states" still have nomination by conventions, but a large proportion have substituted nomination by primary election. The voters, who for purposes of the primary declare themselves to be adherents of a particular party, choose the nominees from persons who have "filed" for the nomination. In a few other countries, nominations are made by the party conventions or congresses, but more commonly they are made by the party committees at the various government levels. In Britain, no party nominations are made, but the party committees "adopt" a candidate who has filed for member of Parliament or borough or county councillor.

Presenting Issues. In totalitarian countries, there are no issues for the voters to decide. In other countries, the parties, in their campaigns or party declarations, undertake to present issues which the voters can help to decide by voting for the candidates of one party or another. Doctrinal and special interest parties are usually quite forthright in this. Their stands on issues, at least those which concern their doctrines or special interests, are consistent and well known. In cabinet-governed countries, an election called upon a dissolution of parliament may amount to a referendum on the issue that caused the dissolution. This is especially true in two-party countries. Institutional parties, even those which retain some doctrinal coloration like the major parties of Great Britain and Canada, often find it difficult to face up to real issues because they are trying to appeal to a wide variety of special interest groups. When they can not avoid making statements on highly controversial issues, their statements are usually so vague as to be almost meaningless. Still, they must have issues to campaign about, so they do one or both of two things. In their party statements and campaign oratory, they magnify trivial differences of viewpoint into earth-shaking issues, or they invent issues out of whole cloth. Each party proclaims that it, in contrast to its rival or rivals, stands for such things as peace, prosperity, and honesty in government. In this situation, the voter, if his vote is to carry weight in settling major issues, must look into the views and past record of individual candidates.

Conducting Campaigns. Some political campaigns are very heated, others very calm. Much depends on the amount of voter interest that can be aroused. In some countries, especially those that are politically immature, campaigns are often accompanied by violence. Generally speaking, party campaign managers will use every device that is not illegal which they think may win votes—if they can raise the necessary funds. Party rallies, and speechmaking by candidates and party dignitaries, once the main features of campaigns, are still much used. Putting up posters, advertising in the press, editorials in friendly newspapers and magazines, and buying time on radio and television, are all standard devices. Personal campaigning—handshaking, ringing doorbells, and sending appeals by mail—usually play a part. Bales of campaign "literature" are distributed, especially in the United States.

To some extent, parties are campaigning all the time. It is sometimes said in the United States that the next campaign begins the morning after election, and much the same is true in most countries. Also in the United States, the campaigns of individuals for nominations begin several weeks, or even months, before the primary or convention, but the party organization is usually neutral in these contests. The active campaigns of the parties are short in most countries. In Britain, they can not last longer than three weeks, and they are not much longer in other European countries. In the United States, they last from the primary or convention to the election, and that is usually several months. The national conventions which nominate candidates for President and Vice President are held in midsummer of election years (the exact time is set by the national committee of each party), and the campaign lasts from then until the general election in November.

Party Responsibility. In theory, the party or coalition in office is responsible for the conduct of government, and can be held answerable to the voters in elections. In two-party countries with the cabinet system, this party responsibility works out fairly well. The party with a majority in parliament automatically controls the executive, and will run the government according to its party policies. In an election, the voters may reject these policies by voting the party out of office and the rival party in. In multiple-party cabinet governed countries, responsibility has to be to parliament. It is hardly feasible to hold a coalition directly responsible to the voters, because policy making is shared by several parties, and each party operates independently in elections. Moreover, in these countries, dissolutions of parliament are difficult and very rare, so an election seldom hinges on a single issue.

Under presidential government, the party to which the president belongs is considered the party in office, and the voters tend to regard that party as responsible for the conduct of government. However, it is not uncommon for one or both chambers of the legislative body to have majorities of the opposite party and if the country is also multiple party, all parties in the legislative body, except that of the president, are usually in opposition to him. When, as in the United States, the parties are of the institutional type without clear-cut positions, the confusion is worse confounded. The President's party will claim credit for everything that has been done that appears to please the people, and blame the opposition party for all that has gone wrong. A check of voting records in Congress usually shows, however, that all important bills have been passed or defeated by combinations of Republican and Democratic votes. Under these circumstances, real party responsibility scarcely exists.

The Role of Opposition.   Opposition can be a very important and useful function of parties that are not in office. They keep the party or parties in office on the alert, restrain any tendency to excessive partisanship, and force compromises and adjustments. Under cabinet government, especially in multiple-party countries, they hold the threat of throwing the governing group out of office by a vote of censure or a vote of lack of confidence. Even under presidential government, they are an effective counter balance to the party or parties in power. At least one opposition party is necessary to responsible government.

THE ROLE OF PARTIES IN DIFFERENT TYPES OF GOVERNMENT

Always Important.   Except in absolute monarchies, political parties are always important, and they have potential importance even in absolute monarchies. Outside small local areas, where non-partisan government sometimes operates successfully, it seems impossible to carry on modern government without them. Even so, their role varies with the type of government.

Totalitarian Government. In ideological totalitarianisms, the official party is the government to all intents and purposes. Government officials, even the members of the hand-picked legislative body, take orders from the head or ruling oligarchy of the party. While there is no real government responsibility, the voters are given a feeling of participation by being permitted to vote for the candidates of the party.

In personal dictatorships, all parties except that of the dictator are usually suppressed by law, but they are apt to continue to exist as "underground" conspiracies plotting the overthrow of the regime. While the dictator may resort to tyranny and brutality to stamp them out, he is still compelled to moderate some of his actions and to make concessions to what these suppressed parties stand for, sometimes even going so far as to follow constitutional forms. His own party provides him a pretext for power and creates some appearance of popular support.

Two-Party Cabinet Government. In two-party cabinet government, the role of parties is vital. The majority party of the moment runs the government according to its policies and is responsible to the voters for its conduct. Even so, it is subject to many restraints by the opposition party, which offers the voters an alternative program when an election comes. The British government, for example, could not function without two major parties.

Multiple-Party Cabinet Government. In multiple-party cabinet government, the role of parties is somewhat different, but just as important. First, there is usually a party to express each political viewpoint and to speak for each special interest. Consequently, the voter may express his will by voting for a party, without concerning himself with individual candidates. In fact, where proportional representation is used, he may not have a chance to vote for individual candidates, but can only vote for the party list of his favorite party. Party discipline is usually strong, so that a party's members of the legislative body can be depended to vote consistently according to the party line. Since government must usually be by a coalition, no single party can be held responsible for the conduct of the government, but each party in the coalition—or in opposition—is responsible to its adherents to uphold the party point of view.

Presidential Government in Multiple-Party Countries. As in other multiple-party countries, there is apt to be a party to represent each point of view or special interest. There may also be some leadership parties. The president is usually elected by a coalition of parties, so that his responsibility to the voters is personal, rather than partisan. Normally, he will try to act along the lines of his own party views, but he must make concessions to the other parties that helped elect him, and try to work out compromises that will satisfy them all. He can not dissolve the legislative body legally (though he sometimes does so anyway if violence is threatened) and he can not be thrown out of office by a vote of censure (though, especially in Latin America, ways are sometimes found to force his resignation). He must get along with the legislative body as best he can. The parties give expression to viewpoints, and provide the voter with an assortment of choices. Usually party regularity in voting is the rule rather than the exception.

Presidential Government in Two-Party Countries. The United States is the only major country with this situation, and it is complicated in our country by the fact that the parties are of the institutional type. The parties nominate candidates, conduct campaigns, and have an important role in organizing the government. But we do not have "party government" in the sense that it operates in Great Britain. Party responsibility scarcely exists. It is the President, the Senator, or the Representative whom the

voter holds responsible, rather than the party. Each of the major parties has a large following of loyal adherents who always vote a straight party ticket, but it is the independent voters and voters with only mild party leanings who decide elections. These vote for their choice of individual candidates, regardless of party label. The parties are necessary, but their role is different than in most other countries.

TEST-YOURSELF QUIZ

Without referring back to the text, check the answer or completion in each question that you think is right. Then turn to answers on page 236 and see how well you have done.

1. Under conditions of free politics, the usual tendency is for people to:
( ) a. Unite into one political party.
( ) b. Group themselves into two parties.
( ) c. Form a number of parties.
( ) d. Have no political parties at all.

2. By definition, a political party must:
( ) a. Stand for distinctive principles or policies.
( ) b. Be an organized group to nominate candidates and participate in elections.
( ) c. Have an enrolled or "card carrying" membership.
( ) d. Be large enough to be a real contender in elections.

3. The major parties in the United States are:
( ) a. Doctrinal parties.
( ) b. Leadership parties.
( ) c. Special interest parties.
( ) d. Institutional parties.

4. A political party is most apt to assume real responsibility to the voters for government action (or opposition) under:
( ) a. A two-party system in a cabinet-governed country.
( ) b. A two-party system in a country with presidential type government.

( ) c. A multiple-party system in a cabinet-governed country.
( ) d. A one-party system in a totalitarian country.

5. A political party is most apt to carry out the function of presenting real issues to the voters under:
( ) a. A two-party system in a cabinet-governed country.
( ) b. A two-party system in a country with presidential type government.
( ) c. A multiple-party system in a cabinet-governed country.
( ) d. A one-party system in a totalitarian country.

6. Party loyalty and discipline are apt to be greatest and continue longest among members of:
( ) a. An institutional party.
( ) b. A coalition party.
( ) c. A leadership party.
( ) d. A doctrinal or special interest party.

7. The classification of parties that is significant only in two-party countries is:
( ) a. According to membership.
( ) b. According to strength.
( ) c. According to basic character.
( ) d. Into parliamentary and popular.

8. The strictly institutional party (with few or none of the characteristics of other types) is apt to be found only in a country with:
( ) a. Two-party cabinet government.
( ) b. Multiple-party cabinet government.
( ) c. Presidential government and a multiple party system.
( ) d. Presidential government and a two-party system.

SUGGESTIONS FOR DISCUSSION

1. Try to work out a definition of a political party that will fit all types of parties, including those in totalitarian countries.
2. What are the three types of party systems found in different countries. Compare and evaluate their characteristics.
3. Compare the meaning of party membership under totalitarian and

"free" government. In what situation is party membership least significant?

4. Why does the classification of parties into major, minor and third apply only in countries with a two-party system? Distinguish between minor and third parties.

5. Compare the characteristics of the different types of parties as classified according to basic character. May the same party have some of the characteristics of more than one type?

6. Distinguish parliamentary and popular parties. Why is the distinction more important in some countries than in others?

7. What is the typical plan of party organization? What are some of the variations?

8. What are the functions that parties are generally assumed to have? How does the performance of each of these functions vary in different situations?

BIBLIOGRAPHY

Alford, R. R., *Party and Society: the Anglo-American Democracies* (Chicago, 1963).

Armstrong, J. A., *The Politics of Totalitarianism* (New York, 1961).

Bailey, S., Ed., *Political Parties and Party Systems in Britain* (New York, 1952).

Barron, R. W., *Parties and Politics in Modern France* (Washington, D. C., 1959).

Council on Foreign Relations, *Political Handbook of the World* (New York, 2 vol., 1961 and 1962).

David, P. T., and others, *The Politics of National Party Conventions* (New York, 1964).

Duverger, M., *Political Parties* (New York, 1959).

Emerson, R., *Political Modernization: the Single-Party System* (Denver, Col., 1964).

Goldwin, R. A., Ed., *Political Parties, U. S. A.* (Chicago, 1964).

Goodman, W., *The Two-Party System in the United States* (Princeton, N. J., 1964).

Key, V. O., *Politics, Parties and Pressure Groups* (New York, 1964).

Meyer, E. W., *Political Parties in Western Germany* (Washington, D. C., 1951).

Michels, R., *Political Parties* (New York, 1962).
Neumann, S., Ed., *Modern Political Parties* (Chicago, 1956).
Riker, W. H., *The Theory of Political Coalitions* (New Haven, Conn., 1962).

13

Public Opinion

If the average person were asked the meaning of public opinion he would probably say that it is the opinion of the public. Actually, the public as a whole rarely has an opinion. Only a great crisis can produce anything even remotely approaching unanimity of opinion on any question.

Not only do different groups and even individuals hold differing opinions on almost every public question, but these opinions run the whole gamut of intensity from mere passive leanings to militant demands for action. Moreover, on almost any issue we might pick at random, we would find that a large proportion of people have no opinion at all. The reactions to a major governmental proposal would run something like this. At one end of the spectrum there would be a group of staunch supporters of the proposal ready to take various kinds of action to bring it about. On the favorable side, opinion would shade out through decreasing degrees of intensity to a middle ground of complete indifference. At the other extreme would be a similar group of bitter opponents of the proposal, ready to campaign actively against it. Unfavorable opinion would likewise shade out through declining degrees of intensity to the middle ground of complete indifference. The size of the indifferent middle group will vary with the success or failure of the efforts of proponents and opponents to win converts to their respective points of view.

Weight of Opinion. What counts, in this absence of any really concerted opinion, is what we may call the weight of opinion. This means the comparative influence that can be exerted in one direction or the other by proponents and opponents of the proposal in question. There are three main factors, and perhaps some lesser ones, that determine the weight of opinion: the number of people who hold an opinion, the intensity with which they hold it, and the number and importance of influential individuals who hold it.

Numbers. Numbers do count, especially when a public opinion is expressed at the ballot box. Numbers also carry weight in applying pressures on government. That is why such efforts are made by groups on both sides of a question to win converts. But numbers alone are not enough. The opinion of the majority is not necessarily the effective public opinion.

Intensity. If a viewpoint is to become effective in shaping events, it must be held not only by large numbers of persons who agree with it passively, but by some who feel strongly enough to do something about it. At the core, there must be leadership, possibly a single leader but more often a relatively small group of dedicated leaders, who will form pressure groups, engage in lobbying, and conduct propaganda campaigns. There must be even larger numbers who will attend rallies, write to their congressman or members of parliament, and do other things to show more than a passing interest.

Important Persons. Furthermore, a viewpoint can be aided mightily if it is held publicly by persons of influence or importance. The more of them the better. Big names carry weight, both in making converts to the cause, and in influencing legislators and other government officials.

Segments of Opinion. Public opinion is not even as simple as this. On a very specific question it may be possible to classify opinions into "for" and "against," but on broader issues there are usually a number of segments of opinion. Different groups and individuals will have opinions that bear on the issue, being clearly for or against it only with qualifications or reservations. Each special interest group is apt to form such a segment and view an issue in the light of what effect it may have on its special interest. Judgments on issues may be conditioned by prejudices or traditions, or people may be carried away by some spectacular event, only to change their ideas when the excitement dies down.

ROLE OF PUBLIC OPINION IN GOVERNMENT

Important Everywhere. Practically all governments try to have a favorable public opinion and seek its support for their acts. Responsible governments usually try to follow it. In those situations where it appears impractical to responsible officials to follow the weight of public opinion, a responsible government tries to explain its actions to the public. Even an irresponsible government, whether revolutionary or totalitarian, finds the support of public opinion a tremendous asset.

Irresponsible Governments. The importance which irresponsible governments attach to the support of public opinion is indicated by the lengths to which they go to cultivate it. Not only do they deluge their people with propaganda, but they try, through censorship and other means, to suppress the expression of any hostile opinion or the spread of information which would cause dissatisfaction. This applies generally to all types of irresponsible government, even personal dictatorships and absolute monarchies. Even the use of terror is aimed in part at creating a favorable public opinion. A revolutionary regime always seeks to justify itself to its own people, and to opinion abroad. The ideological totalitarianisms devote great efforts to propagating their ideology as a means of building public opinion in their support.

Responsible Governments. In responsible governments of every type, the weight of public opinion is often a determining factor in the shaping of government policy. These governments, too, seek to cultivate a favorable public opinion, but they are sensitive to adverse trends and will usually modify their policies or actions to conciliate hostile public attitudes. After all, the weight of public opinion is the "will of the people," on which all free government is based.

FORMATION AND CULTIVATION OF PUBLIC OPINION

Spontaneous Opinion. To some extent, public opinion forms spontaneously. Many people will react to the news that is available to them by forming opinions on problems and questions in the news. Where the news is controlled, as in totalitarian states, most people will accept it as true and fall into line with the viewpoint which the distorted news suggests, but there may also be a negative reaction. People who want to think for themselves may feel that something is being kept from them and form a hostile attitude toward the regime, even though they may not dare to express it openly. In a free country where the news is uncensored, reactions will normally run the usual gamut, with amount of "pro" and "anti" sentiment, and of indifference, varying with the interest appeal of the particular situation.

Cultivated Opinion. Ordinarily, this spontaneous opinion will be strong enough to produce action only among individuals and groups who feel that their special interests, beliefs, or prejudices are affected. These persons and groups, some "pro" and some "anti," then set about to cultivate a weight of opinion favorable to their own views. Governments too, even in free countries, seek to cultivate favorable opinion by such means as news releases, press conferences, and speeches by public officials. Political parties never cease their efforts to generate public opinion that will bring them votes. Thus, much of public opinion (most of it that is effective) is deliberately cultivated.

Propaganda. Most of the devices used to generate or influence public opinion fall under the head of propaganda. Propaganda may be defined simply as any effort by anyone to influence the views or actions of others. The word has acquired a bad implication because of its use in war and diplomacy, but actually whether it is good or bad depends on whether or not one agrees with it. In a very real sense, commercial advertising is propaganda; so is a clergyman's sermon. Whenever an individual or group— or government—tries to influence the views of people, the effort is, by definition, propaganda.

Forms of Propaganda. The forms that propaganda takes in the cultivation of public opinion are almost unlimited. It runs all the way from simple conversation to heavily financed intensive campaigns. Some of the devices are writing letters, holding rallies, paying for advertising, issuing propaganda "literature," picketing, and parading. If there is a segment of the press committed to a certain viewpoint, these newspapers will print editorials favorable to their position and may even color their reporting of the news. The enlisting of important or influential people in the cause is an effective means of winning converts. So is enlisting the support of civic, religious, and fraternal organizations that have a reputation for disinterested action for the public welfare. Any trick may be used that will win friends and influence people.

MEASURING PUBLIC OPINION

Importance of Evaluation. Government policy makers, the news media, and even the general public are concerned with trying to measure or evaluate the weight of public opinion. To news men and the public, it is mainly a matter of news interest. To the politician, it is an important aid in planning campaign strategy.

To the government policy maker, it is vital information. Government policy must be harmonized with the weight of public opinion to command the popular acceptance which is imperative in free government, and is highly valuable even in totalitarian regimes.

Public Opinion Polls. Chiefly in the United States, but to some extent in other countries, public opinion polls are used to measure the weight of public opinion in exact percentages. A large number of individuals, supposedly a good cross section of the segment of the public that is being polled, are asked to indicate, in regard to a particular matter, whether they are for, against, or undecided, and their answers are translated into terms of percentages. Those who conduct the polls claim a high degree of accuracy (within two or three per cent) for their results. That these polls are highly useful is not open to question. However, their failure in several notable instances to predict correctly the outcome of elections is a strong indication that the reliability is considerably less than is claimed for them. There are some inherent weaknesses. Someone must decide what individuals will be queried, and that judgment is not always good. Again, the individual questioned may give one answer to the poll taker and register a different one at an election. Another weakness is that the polls do not provide for recording varying shades of opinion. Finally, the person being polled may not take the procedure seriously and may give facetious answers.

Press Reaction. An older device, still in use everywhere in the Free World, is gauging the reaction of the press on controversial issues. Percentage accuracy is not claimed for this method, but persons who become skilled in gauging press reaction can usually come up with a reasonably accurate evaluation of the weight of public opinion. Newspapers either attract readers who agree with their editorial viewpoint or adapt their editorial comment to coincide with the views of their readers. In using press reaction as an index to the weight of public opinion, certain factors must be taken into account. Newspapers and magazines are not all equal in significance. The most obvious difference is in the size of their circulation, but almost equally important are the reputation and known bias (if any) of the publication. Again the significance of a publication for this purpose must be down graded if the publication is the organ of a group or organization with a fixed viewpoint, or the mouthpiece of a highly opinionated individual. Finally, if the circulation of the publication is local or regional, it may reflect local or regional views accurately enough, but this may be only a small segment of national public opinion.

Organized Groups. Organized groups not only take stands on controversial issues, but sometimes engage in extensive propaganda campaigns to win converts to their viewpoints. In some situations it is possible, by balancing off the organizations that favor and those that oppose a course of action, to make a fairly good evaluation of the weight of public opinion. The size of the membership of each organization must be taken into account, as well as the extent to which the rank and file membership can be depended upon to follow the stand taken by their governing body. The general importance of an organization, and the extent to which it can influence the attitude of non-members, must also be taken into account along with the fact that each organization will seek to create the impression that it represents a larger segment of public opinion than it does.

Informal Methods. For the most part, however, persons who consider it necessary to their calling to evaluate public opinion depend on informal methods. It is sometimes said that news men and politicians (and most policy making government officials are also politicians) develop a sixth sense for the perception of public opinion. They take into account the results of the methods we have been discussing, but they also watch for many small "straws in the wind." They observe reactions to public speeches, check bits of conversation, and note overtones of public discussions. They look behind the open statements of proponents and opponents to analyze the motivation. In other small ways, they are able to sense the drift of public opinion.

PUBLIC OPINION IN ACTION

Modes of Expression. Bearing in mind that there is rarely a unified public opinion on anything, but that, on any important question, there are segments and gradations of opinion, we must look to these parts of public opinion for modes of expression. Some of these modes of expression are very simple. People who hold views only mildly, will express them only in such ways as private conversation, taking part in group discussions, and the choice of what they read or listen to on radio and television. Those who hold views more enthusiastically will try to do something about their opinions and use various kinds of action to propagate their viewpoints and make them effective.

Voting. The simplest form of action, in which the most people will engage, is voting in elections, and trying to persuade others to vote, to uphold one's particular viewpoint. This voting may be direct on referendum proposals. It operates indirectly in voting for a political party which stands for the viewpoint in question or for candidates who agree with the voter's ideas. It also operates in persuading government officials that a majority of the voters want certain action or policies in government. In political campaigns, parties or candidates will seek to win votes by appealing to the views or interests of as many voters as possible.

Petition. All free countries guarantee the right of petition, and this provides a relatively simple action for registering segments of public opinion. Besides the traditional form of signatures to a written request for government action (or protest against it), there are several other forms of petition. One is the writing of letters to legislators or other officials. Another is the adoption of resolutions, either by existing organizations or by "rallies" called for the purpose, and the publication of these resolutions or the sending of them to public officials. Lobbying, which we shall discuss presently, is also considered a form of petition.

Pressure Groups. A pressure group may be defined as any group which seeks to exert pressure to achieve or prevent some governmental action. They are of many varieties. The simplest we may call an *ad hoc* pressure group. This is a group put together to work for a single short-range objective. Its organization is apt to be simple, and it usually dissolves when its objective is attained or hope of attaining it is abandoned. Somewhat similar is the long-range single-purpose group. It, too, is formed to work for a single objective, but one which will require a long period of time to attain. Its organization is apt to be more complete and of a more or less permanent nature. An example in the United States was the old Woman Suffrage Association which, when the Nineteenth Amendment was adopted, reorganized itself into the League of Women Voters.

Another type of pressure group is the civic organization which takes "stands" on issues and works actively for or against proposals for governmental action. These organizations exist primarily to promote some civic objective, but they also act as pressure groups. Another type, with myriad variations, is the special interest organization. There are farmers' organizations, labor organizations, business organizations, professional organizations, religious organizations, and many other varieties. These usually exist to advance the interests of the group in other ways, but they operate as pressure groups when governmental action, which would affect their interests, is contemplated.

Lobbying. Pressure groups use all the forms of propaganda to win support for their objective and the forms of petition that have been mentioned to influence government action. Their major weapon, however, is lobbying. This word has acquired an unfavorable connotation because of abuses that crop up from time to time, but lobbying is an entirely legitimate device. It means, simply, presenting one's views on a question, with supporting arguments or evidence, to legislators or other policy-making officials in an effort to secure the action one desires. It is carried on in various ways including personal conferences, sometimes during meals paid for by the lobbyist or his backers. Probably the most effective lobbying is done in open hearings before legislative committees.

Picketing and Demonstration. Lobbying sometimes takes the forms of picketing or demonstrations, but these are also used as propaganda devices to win support for a viewpoint. Picketing consists of standing or walking back and forth, singly or in small groups, carrying placards which proclaim the grievance or wishes of the picketing group. Demonstrations involve larger groups—often very large. The "demonstrators" usually parade, singing or chanting, and carrying placards. Sometimes they will cluster at a strategic spot and listen to fiery speeches. Demonstrations sometimes get out of hand and turn into riots. The effectiveness of these devices is open to question, but they continue to be used. At times they appear to arouse more hostility than support for the viewpoint they are upholding.

The Press. We should not drop this discussion without mentioning the press (a term we may use to include radio and television along with newspapers and magazines) as an instrument of public opinion in action. Special interest organizations often have their own publications which always uphold the viewpoint of the organization. These publications help to hold organization members in line, but have little influence on non-members or on government action. All of the mass news media are available for paid advertising by pressure groups or other propagandists. Individual newspapers and magazines often take sides editorially on controversial issues, sometimes even going so far as to color their presentation of the news. In this way, they operate as propaganda instruments. Occasionally a periodical publication will conduct a long campaign of months or years duration in behalf of some reform or other government action. Finally, through their "letters to the editor" column, newspapers provide a forum for the views of individuals and groups. Thus, the press not only expresses public opinion, but helps to shape it.

TEST-YOURSELF QUIZ

Without referring back to the text, check the answer or completion in each question that you think is right. Then turn to answers on page 236 and see how well you have done.

1. The weight of public opinion includes all but one of these factors. Which one?
( ) a. The number of people who hold the opinion.
( ) b. The intensity with which the opinion is held.
( ) c. The "big name" people who support the opinion publicly.
( ) d. The endorsement of political parties.

2. In a "free" country, active public opinion is stimulated most effectively by:
( ) a. Spontaneous reaction to the news.
( ) b. Efforts of the government.
( ) c. Efforts of interested groups to cultivate it.
( ) d. Activity of political parties.

3. In evaluating public opinion for policy-making purposes, government officials are apt to rely mainly on:
( ) a. Public opinion polls.
( ) b. Press reaction.
( ) c. Informal methods.
( ) d. Propaganda of organized interest groups.

4. The expression of public opinion aimed at influencing government in which most people engage is:
( ) a. Voting in elections.
( ) b. Petitioning the government.
( ) c. Pressure group activity.
( ) d. "Demonstrations."

5. Usually, the most effective lobbying is done:
( ) a. In personal conferences with legislators or other officials.
( ) b. In open hearings before legislative committees.
( ) c. By bribing public officials.
( ) d. By presenting petitions of pressure groups.

6. The press is most effective as an instrument of public opinion:
( ) a. Through the publications of special interest organizations.
( ) b. By reflecting the views of its readers.
( ) c. Through the "letters to the editor" column.
( ) d. Through editorial propaganda.

7. Which one of these could not operate as a pressure group?
( ) a. A reform organization.
( ) b. A civic organization.
( ) c. An occupational organization.
( ) d. A political party organization.

8. Besides the sending of signed written petitions, the "right of petition" covers all but one of these. Which one?
( ) a. The writing of letters to legislators or other officials.
( ) b. Propaganda directed to the general public.
( ) c. Adoption of resolutions by organizations or special "rallies."
( ) d. Non-violent picketing and demonstrations.

SUGGESTIONS FOR DISCUSSION

1. Try to formulate a good, workable definition of public opinion.
2. Since public opinion is so intangible, why is it so important that even totalitarian governments make a great effort to cultivate it?
3. What is meant by "weight of opinion"? How and why is it important?
4. How do government officials evaluate public opinion?
5. What is propaganda? What are some of the forms it may take?
6. What are the principal ways in which segments of public opinion operate to influence government?
7. What are pressure groups? What are some of the kinds? Do you consider them good or bad?
8. What is lobbying? What are some of the forms it may take? Do you think it should be prohibited?

BIBLIOGRAPHY

Banfield, E. C., *Political Influence* (Don Mills, Canada, 1961).

Berdes, G. R., *Up from Ashes* (Milwaukee, 1964).

Christenson, R. M., and McWilliams, R. O., *Voice of the People* (New York, 1962).

Ehrmann, H. W., Ed., *Interest Groups on Four Continents* (Pittsburgh, 1961).

Key, V. O., *Public Opinion and American Democracy* (New York, 1964).

Lane, R. E., and Sears, D. O., *Public Opinion* (Englewood Cliffs, N. J., 1964).

La Palombara, J. G., *Interest Groups in Italian Politics* (Princeton, N. J., 1964).

Roche, J. P., and Levy, L. E., Eds., *Parties and Pressure Groups* (New York, 1964).

Schettler, C. H., *Public Opinion in American Society* (New York, 1960).

Wilson, F. G., *A Theory of Public Opinion* (Chicago, 1962).

Zeigler, H., *Interest Groups in American Society* (Englewood Cliffs, N. J., 1964).

14

Intergovernmental Relations

*Every sovereign state is divided into intermediate
and local units for some functions of government.
There are, almost always, at least two levels,
and some countries have three or four. These are
always administrative districts of the central
government, but in most Free World countries,
some or all of the local units have some measure
of self-government.*

In true federal unions, the component units ("states," provinces, or whatever they may be called) possess some governmental powers in full sovereignty, though they may also serve as administrative districts for the federal government. In quasi-federal states, the component units have some distinctive powers of their own, but, at least in some situations, these may be overruled by the central government.

Intermediate and Local Units. A unitary state is usually divided into primary intermediate units such as the British counties, the French *departments,* and the Italian provinces, which are both administrative areas for the central government and units of local self-government. In Britain, administration is sufficiently decentralized that county administration is largely in the hands of the county councils with some supervision and direction by the administrative organs of the central government. In France and Italy, the prefect, an agent of the central government, dominates the administration of his *department* or province, but he is advised by an elected council. In some countries, there is a secondary intermediate unit between the primary unit and the central government, such as the "regions" in Italy. The primary unit is usually divided into local areas, such as the British boroughs or the French and Italian communes. In Britain, the boroughs are self-governing municipalities, not necessarily contiguous. Areas in between boroughs are subject only to the administrative authority of the county. French and Italian communes are territorial subdivisions; there is no area that is not in a commune. Neither are there distinct municipalities; a city is just a large commune. Arrangements in other countries vary in detail, but are usually similar to the French and Italian plan. In some of them, cities do have a municipal status apart from the local area in which they are located.

Relations.   All of these divisions and subdivisions are subject to the authority of the central government, and are under some measure of legislative, administrative, and judicial control. Strictly local units may or may not be subject to administrative control by the primary unit of which they are part. Usually these internal units have no direct relations with each other, though their mayors or other chief administrators may sometimes have unofficial meetings to discuss common problems. Sometimes they may be allowed to enter into contractual relations with each other with regard to exchange of facilities.

Federal Unions.   In federal unions (including most quasi-federal states) the intermediate and local areas are divisions and subdivisions of the component unit of the union, the "state," province, *Land*, or whatever it may be called. They stand in the same relation to it that, in a unitary state, they would have to the central government. In quasi-federal unions, like West Germany, the central government may have some direct control over them, but in a true federal union they have no relations whatever with the federal government. In the United States, in recent decades, we have overstepped this rule by the federal government making grants-in-aid to cities. The grants, however, are not made directly to the city; they are made to a local "authority" which the act of Congress requires to be set up to receive and administer the grant.

Relations of the component units to the federal government are spelled out in the federal constitution which provides for apportioning powers of sovereignty between the central government and the units. There is also an agency, the Supreme Court in the United States, which can settle disputes over powers in borderline cases. The people of the units are, of course, subject to national law, but the federal government can not legislate for the unit itself. Usually the component units function as such in the election of members of the federal legislative body and, in the United States, in the election of the President. They may also play a part, as in the United States, in the process of amending the federal constitution.

The component units of a federal union have no formal relations with each other, such as exchange of diplomats, but they may enter into agreements with each other on matters not covered by federal laws or regulations. In the United States, the consent of Congress is required for formal interstate agreements, but informal agreements are often made on minor matters. Normally, units of a federal union are not permitted to have relations of any kind with a foreign state. In the United States, the "states" may, with the consent of Congress, enter into agreements with neighboring countries on non-political subjects, such as building bridges across boundary rivers or regulating traffic across the border. The constitution of the Soviet Union permits the member "union republics" to have foreign relations, and two of them, Byelo-Russia and the Ukraine, are charter members of the United Nations. For all practical purposes, though, the monolithic control of the entire Soviet Union by the Communist Party makes this privilege meaningless.

INTERNATIONAL RELATIONS

Meaning and Scope of Term.   Sovereign states always have relations of one sort or another with other sovereign states, and these relations are known, not quite accurately, as international relations. The relations may be friendly or unfriendly, close or distant, formal or informal. They include diplomacy, various kinds of commitments, and sometimes war.

Diplomacy.   Diplomacy means simply the conduct of international relations through governmental agencies. In normal or routine diplomacy, the state accredits to each other state which it recognizes diplomatically an agent of its government called an ambassador or minister, and accepts at its seat of government similar diplomatic representatives of other states with which it is on friendly terms. The difference between an ambassador and a minister is merely one of rank. It was formerly the practice of major powers to send ambassadors to each other, but ministers to lesser countries, while the smaller countries sent only ministers. The present tendency is for almost all countries to exchange ambassadors. The ambassador or minister has a staff of helpers, the size of which varies with the importance of the country to which he is accredited. The head of this staff, called the secretary (or sometimes chancellor) of the embassy (or legation, if the chief diplomat is a minister), takes charge in the absence of the ambassador or minister, and is then known as a *chargé d'affairs.*

The ambassador or minister, having presented his credentials to the chief of state, may confer with officials of the government to which he is accredited (usually the foreign minister) and sometimes engages in the negotiation of treaties or other agreements. He presents and receives written communications on behalf of his government, and keeps his government informed of all developments that might influence the relations of the two governments. These diplomats enjoy what is called diplomatic immunity; they are never arrested or imprisoned for infractions of the law of the country where they are stationed. However, if a diplomat becomes objectionable to the government to which he is accredited, that government may request his recall, and this request is never refused.

States may also maintain consuls in foreign countries, several in each country, but these are concerned mainly with economic matters and are located in commercial centers. In recent decades, most countries, as matter of administrative efficiency, have combined their diplomatic and consular services into a foreign service.

In recent times, most important diplomacy is carried on through higher channels than the regular diplomats. International conferences are held, made up of special delegations of the participating countries. Special diplomats, sometimes called roving ambassadors, are sent on particular missions. Meetings of foreign ministers, in pairs or in larger groups, sometimes in connection with an international organization and sometimes on the invitation of one of them, are of frequent occurrence. Summit conferences, made up of heads of governments, are held from time to time. Through these various means, the government of a state tries to secure the cooperation of other states in the pursuit of policies it considers to be in the national interest of its country.

Treaties. A treaty is a formal contract between sovereign states. It may be bi-lateral, between two states, or multi-lateral, among several. A multi-lateral treaty is sometimes called a convention or a covenant. A treaty may cover any matter of international relations. It may settle disputes, end a war, transfer territory, or bind the parties to do certain things in the future. Treaties are made in the names of the chiefs of state of the participating countries, and formal ratifications are exchanged between or among these chiefs of state. Usually ratification must be preceded by approval by some constitutional agency, such as the Senate in the United States, but more commonly by the cabinet.

Treaties are binding at international law until or unless they are abrogated in accordance with their own terms or are cancelled by a declaration of war. In practice, they are usually ob-

served, though disputes sometimes arise as to their intent or the
meaning of their terms. If a government should refuse to be
bound by a treaty, there is no way to enforce compliance except
by resort to war.

Executive Agreements.   Less formal than treaties are executive agreements. These are agreements entered into between
or on behalf of heads of governments. They are often used to deal
with matters that are not considered important enough to justify
a formal treaty, and they are sometimes resorted to, when a
treaty would be in order, as a means of avoiding the delay and
difficulty that would be involved in securing approval of a
treaty. They sometimes raise questions of constitutionality, but
the general rule is that a head of government may agree with another head of government to do anything which the constitution
of his own country empowers him to do. An executive agreement
involving long range commitments might not be regarded as
binding by successors of the head of government who entered
into the agreement.

Indirect Diplomacy.   There are several varieties of indirect
diplomacy that are not new, but are much more in evidence today than in earlier times. One of the oldest is the state visit.
This means that the chief of state makes a formal ceremonial
visit to the government of another country to cultivate good
will or to smooth the way for diplomatic negotiations. Unless
the chief of state is also head of government, he can not actually engage in negotiations on such a visit, but he can sometimes create an atmosphere favorable to negotiations. Almost as
old a device is propaganda directed at another country. This is
intended to influence public opinion in the country to which it
is directed and so create pressure on the government of that
country to modify its policies. Two closely related devices that
have developed mainly since World War II are economic aid
and military assistance. Economic aid usually takes the form of
supplying capital goods and technical assistance to develop or

strengthen the economy of the recipient country. Military assistance usually stops short of sending combat forces and is limited to supplying weapons, munitions, military instructors, and military advisers. Both of these devices are aimed at wooing the friendship of the countries receiving aid, but they may also be aimed at putting the receiving country into a position to resist the infiltration of a hostile system such as Communism. The newest device of indirect diplomacy is the cultural exchange, in which two countries that are not on the best of terms arrange to exchange artists, entertainers, and technical observers with a view to generating more friendly understanding.

War. It is still true, despite great development of international law and international organization, that war is the court of last resort in international relations. The right to wage war is one of the inherent powers of sovereignty. When all other means of settling international disputes fail, any state may go to war to impose its will or uphold its policies. Perhaps a clarification of terms is in order. We usually think of war and military conflict as the same thing. They usually go together, but they are not the same. War is a legal condition, brought about by a declaration of war by whatever constitutional agency of the state has authority to declare war. Military conflict or "hostilities" is a physical situation which may sometimes take place, even on a large scale as in Korea or Viet Nam, without a declaration of war. On the other hand, a legal state of war continues after hostilities cease until it is ended by a peace treaty or some other legal action.

In earlier centuries, war was regarded as a normal means of pursuing national aims. As long as wars were fought by professional armies, with little disturbance of the civil populations, this was satisfactory. However, with the development of "total war," originated by the French revolutionists, advanced by the American Civil War, and becoming a world-wide concept in World War I, organized efforts for permanent peace began to appear. It was hoped that the League of Nations would insure peace, but it proved to be inadequate. In 1928, most of the nations of the world agreed, in the Kellogg-Briand Pact, to "renounce war as an instrument of national policy," but World War II showed the futility of such declarations. During and since World War II, especially with the development of atomic weapons and guided missiles, total war has become so horrible that the people of most nations have come to regard it as unthinkable. Limited wars will undoubtedly continue, but we may be reasonably sure that every effort will be made to avert a total atomic war. Even so, we can not be sure that one will not occur, since war remains the only final resort in international relations.

INTERNATIONAL LAW AND COURTS

Meaning of International Law.   International law, in the sense in which we use the word *law* within a country, exists only with regard to certain rules governing the conduct of individuals which are accepted internationally and which are enforced by the courts of individual states, such as rules against piracy or the slave trade. In its more commonly accepted sense of rules governing the conduct of states, international law is only a body of rules which are generally accepted and generally observed. Some of these rules grew out of custom and tradition (like Roman civil law and English common law) and were formulated in international arbitrations and court decisions. Other rules of international law have been agreed to by most states in multilateral treaties or conventions. For this reason, these rules are sometimes called "conventional" international law. These rules are just as binding as any other treaty, but no more so.

Enforcement.   Most states, most of the time, observe the rules on international law and settle their differences by negotiation, arbitration, or submission to a court. In the last analysis, though, there is no enforcement against a willful violator except resort to war. There are numerous means of international conciliation for settling disputes, including some international courts which apply the rules of international law, but these can operate only with the voluntary participation of all states concerned.

International Courts. Besides temporary bodies for arbitration set up from time to time, there are or have been so-called international courts. After World War II, international courts were set up for the trial of war criminals, such as the one in Munich which tried and condemned the Nazi leaders. These followed judicial procedure and applied rules of international law (as interpreted by the victorious countries), but they were imposed on the vanquished by the victors and did not become part of an international legal structure. From time to time, regional courts have been set up which were intended to be permanent, such as the one maintained by the Central American republics for several years (1907-1917). In 1899, the First Hague Conference established a "Permanent Court of Arbitration," usually called the Hague Tribunal. It consisted of a panel of arbitrators from which parties to a dispute could select members of an arbitration team. It settled several disputes, using the method of arbitration rather than judicial procedures, but had no compulsory jurisdiction.

After World War I, the first "World Court," the Permanent Court or International Justice, was established in connection with the League of Nations. The United Nations Charter established the second "World Court" (actually a continuation of the first with some improvement), called officially the International Court of Justice. The World Court follows judicial procedures and applies the rules of international law. The Charter provides that states may accept compulsory jurisdiction, and a number have done so. The United States attached so many reservations to its acceptance that the acceptance is almost meaningless. In a real showdown, though, it is doubtful whether even a state that has accepted compulsory jurisdiction could be compelled to appear in court to answer charges or to abide by a decision of the court.

INTERNATIONAL ORGANIZATION

Alliances. The oldest form of international organization is the alliance. Alliances among tribes existed even before historic times, and alliances among states have existed from the beginning of history. Their exact terms differ greatly, but usually they mean only that two or more states agree to assist each other in war. Sometimes this promise is conditioned on one of the allies being attacked by some other state. In modern times, alliances frequently go further and provide for the coordination of national policies and economic and cultural cooperation. Some alliances are strictly temporary (for the duration of a war or other crisis), some are for a fixed term of years, and others are intended to be permanent.

Confederations. A confederation goes beyond a mere alliance. Always intended to be permanent, it provides machinery for frequent consultation among the member states for coordinating policy and agreeing on cooperation. Each state, however, retains its full sovereignty. Some confederations have developed into federal unions, as in the case of Switzerland, the United States, and pre-World War I Germany. Most of them have disintegrated after a time. The more important international organizations of our time are really confederations.

Regional and Other Organizations. Since World War I, a number of important international organizations have appeared, most of which still survive. First was the League of Nations which was intended not only to be permanent, but eventually to include all the states of the world. The League got off to a bad start, failed to deal successfully wih the crises of the 1930's, and collapsed in World War II. Between World Wars, the British Commonwealth of Nations was formed when Great Britain acknowledged the independence of the dominions which then agreed to associate themselves with the mother country in a voluntary commonwealth. Two of the original members, Ireland and South Africa, have since withdrawn, but when, after World War II, Britain gave independence to most of her other colonies and dependencies, most of these joined the Commonwealth. Some of the member states acknowledged the Queen as their titular sovereign; the others accept her as Head of the Commonwealth. The only machinery consists of meetings of prime ministers (or sometimes of other ministers) from the member states. These meetings do not occur on a regular schedule, but are held at the call of any member. Despite the loose organization, members of the Commonwealth usually work in close cooperation.

Somewhat resembling the British Commonwealth, but with a geographic instead of a historic basis, is the Organization of American States, usually referred to as the OAS. All of the twenty-one republics of the Western Hemisphere are members, though Cuba under Castro has been barred temporarily from active participation. It grew out of the old Pan-American Union which was a loose association of Western Hemisphere countries which held periodic meetings, the Pan-American Congresses, to discuss common problems and to propose agreements on specific items. During World War II this developed into an alliance for the defense of the hemisphere, and at the Bogota Conference in 1948, the OAS was created. Along with its alliance features, the OAS Charter provides for economic and cultural cooperation. It has more elaborate machinery than the British Commonwealth with a permanent secretariat and a permanent council in Washington. Foreign ministers' conferences are held on call whenever a critical situation develops.

Another organization that has achieved prominence is the North Atlantic Treaty Organization, commonly called NATO. It was formed in 1949, primarily as a defense against communist expansion. It now consists of fifteen states: the United States, Canada, Iceland, Great Britain, France, Belgium, the Netherlands, Luxemburg, West Germany, Italy, Portugal, Norway, Denmark, Greece, and Turkey. It goes beyond an alliance by providing for unified military commands and a permanent council. Periodic meetings of heads of government and foreign and defense ministers are held for the coordination of policy. Other regional organizations that are primarily alliances are the Southeast Asia Treaty Organization (SEATO) and the Central Treaty Organization (CENTO) in the Middle East. The European Economic Community (the Common Market) is a loose confederation which is in the process of establishing a customs union.

The United Nations. The most important international organization of all is the United Nations or the U. N. Most of the states of the world (including a few quasi-states that are not fully sovereign) are members. The only important country that is not a member and has not sought membership is Switzerland, which has stayed out because of its unwillingness to vote on cold war issues. Neither Germany has been admitted because of the cold war situation. A clarification may be in order in regard to China. It is often said that Red China has been denied admission, but actually it is not a question of admission at all. China is a charter member and a permanent member of the Security Council. The Nationalist government held this membership before the Communists gained control of the Chinese mainland, and continues to hold it. A majority of the member states of the U. N. still regard the Nationalist government on Formosa as the legitimate government of China, and consider the Communist government in Peking merely a usurping regime. Whether or not this is right or desirable is a matter of opinion—and of the national policy of member states.

Since descriptions of the structure of the United Nations are so readily available, we shall not use space to describe it here. Its structure differs only in minor particulars from that of the former League of Nations, so we may wonder why the League was not revived after World War II. One reason, of course, was that the League was discredited, but equally important was the fact that, at that time, the leadership of any organization which should have a chance of being successful must be taken by the United States and the Soviet Union, neither of which was a member of the old League. That the United Nations has been more successful than the League ever was is beyond question and this is due to several significant reasons. The first of these is that, while there was never a time when all the major powers were members of the League, all of them (unless we include West Germany and Red China as major powers) are members of the U. N. Equally significant is the fact that, whereas the governments of the major countries did not appear to take the League seriously and did not carry their important differences to it for discussion, even the strongest countries today make participation in the U. N. a keystone of their foreign policy and carry even the most controversial issues to the organization for consideration. Still another reason is that the United Nations has had dynamic leadership in its successive Secretaries General, who have intervened actively in trouble spots all over the world. Finally we may note the fact that the smaller and newer nations regard the United Nations as their best defense and as their only means of having a voice in world affairs.

The United Nations, through its political organs and sometimes with the use of improvised armed forces, has been able to stop (at least temporarily) several armed conflicts such as the clash of India and Pakistan over Kashmir, the Palestine War, the British, French and Israeli invasion of Suez, and the Congo War. It has settled or contributed to the settlement of a number of serious international disputes, and has contributed greatly to keeping the cold war cold. Its affiliated specialized agencies have done excellent work in many fields.

There are some things that the U. N. has not been able to do, but this is understandable when we consider the nature of the organization. It is not a government and has no coercive power except the force of world public opinion which it can arouse. It is a confederation in which each member state retains full sovereignty. It can vote sanctions against aggressors, but only the member states can carry out these sanctions and they can not be compelled to do so. For a time there was much criticism of the big power veto in the Security Council. Not only was provision for the veto necessary to secure ratification of the Charter by the United States and the Soviet Union, but it would exist in fact, if not in form, whether provided for or not, since there is no means of coercing a great power except through total war.

WORLD POLITICS

Some Terms. World politics may be thought of as international relations in action. It is politics in the sense that governments are maneuvering and contending to achieve their aims and to carry out their policies in relation to other countries in the light of the world situation of the moment. It includes everything governments do in their dealings with foreign states. Another term we find used widely is *power politics*. This means world politics conducted on the basis of power. It always envisions the possibility of war and carries with it the implied threat to resort to force. Among other phases, it involves efforts to control localities that would be highly strategic in case of war. Practically all of the "hot spots" that have developed since World War II are to be explained in terms of power politics.

The Role of National Interest. Normally governments conduct their international relations with a view to serving the national interest of their respective countries. Perhaps it would be more accurate to say that governments seek to serve what policy-determining officials of the government, usually backed by the weight of public opinion, conceive to be the national interest. This national interest may be aggressive or defensive. It normally includes the desire to preserve peace, but not necessarily peace at any price. The risk of war may be considered necessary to protect the national interest. This is the case when resort is had to the type of diplomacy known as "brinkmanship"—pushing to the brink of war in the hope of outbluffing an opponent. National interest is usually influenced strongly by economic considerations. These may vary from a mere desire for favorable terms of foreign trade to the imperialistic desire to dominate other peoples for the economic advantage it is believed such dominance will bring. When a country is strongly committed to a particular ideology, such as democracy or communism, this will influence the concept of national interest, since it will be assumed that the advancement, or at least the preservation, of this ideology is necessary to the good of the nation.

Emotional Factors in National Interest.

While it is accepted as axiomatic that it is the duty of every government to strive for the national interest of its country, there are several emotional factors that may help to shape the idea of national interest in a particular country. One of these is nationalism. The feeling of nationalism may run the whole range from simple patriotism to the exaggerated form called "jingoism," but almost everywhere a strong feeling of nationalism is the keynote to a country's foreign policy. A century ago, this feeling of nationalism was apt, especially in the stronger countries, to spill over into one of the many forms of imperialism. Imperialism means a national policy of extending the sway of the state over alien peoples, particularly less advanced peoples. It could take the form of outright conquest, imposing some form of dependency by treaty, or merely securing special economic privileges in the country dominated. Today, outright imperialism has almost disappeared except in some of the Communist-ruled countries.

The Role of Power.

The more powerful states of the world, of necessity, conduct much of their international dealings on the basis of power, so that this part of their international relations becomes power politics. Power in this sense means primarily military power, but this in turn depends on other factors. Most important is power in being—the force that could be thrown into action immediately—but potential power and the ability to bring it into actual being quickly also figure in the picture.

Obviously the first element in power—even potential power—is population. To be powerful, a state must be able to put millions of men into its armed forces. Quality as well as size of population is important. The higher their living standard and level of education, the more readily young men can be turned into effective soldiers, sailors, or airmen. Then there must be in existence a well trained and disciplined armed force which can train and provide officers for recruits, and so be expanded into a top-strength force. A nation must also have economic strength to provide the equipment and sustenance for its armed forces and to sustain the civil population in time of crisis. The economic strength of the United States was the most important factor in changing defeat into victory for the anti-Axis allies in World War II. Finally, the people must have good morale: confidence in their country and its strength, faith in its aims, and willingness to sacrifice for the national interest.

How is power used in power politics? In an extreme situation, resort may be had to all-out use of force. However, now that total war has become so horrible most governments will seek by every feasible means to avoid the cataclysm of a third world war. But power also figures indirectly. It is axiomatic that bargaining power in international relations varies in almost exact ratio to power. Knowing that his opponent has military power equal to or excelling that of his own country, a negotiator is under strong pressure to make concessions and compromises in order not to provoke his opponent into the actual use of force. Even if force is resorted to in a local area, as in Korea in 1950, there may be a tacit agreement (never admitted openly) to localize the conflict and not permit it to expand into general war.

Balance of Power. A term much used in discussing power politics is *balance of power*. Presumably this means such an equilibrium between or among stronger states that, in a crisis, neither side will attack the other lest it risk defeat. Actually, each side in a controversy is seeking a preponderance of power in order to overawe its opponent. In bygone times, there was much talk of "redressing the balance of power," and in the eighteenth century wars were fought to "redress the balance of power." Supposedly this meant bringing power back into equilibrium when it had been tipped in favor of one side. Actually it meant that the weaker state or group of states was seeking to seize the preponderance from the opposing state or group of states.

Obviously this contest for preponderance of power can and does produce costly armament races which sometimes precipitate the very war they are intended to prevent. But it also affects diplomacy. States which consider that they have common interests group themselves into alliances in an effort to tip the balance of power in their favor. It also produces an effort on the part of each side in a critical situation, such as the "cold war" situation since World War II, to control geographic spots which would be of great military strategic importance in case of a major war. One or both of the opponents may use subversion and intrigue, or even force, to achieve this control. This was the basic consideration in the Korean conflict which began in 1950. All of Korea in the hands of one side in the cold war would constitute a serious military threat to the other. Hence, even though it meant a major military conflict, the Free World nations could not permit the Russians, first through the North Koreans and later through the Chinese Communists, to seize all of the peninsula. On the other hand, had we pushed the Chinese out (as General MacArthur wanted to do and was militarily capable of doing), the Russians would have felt compelled to enter the struggle directly, and that would have meant World War III. Hence, the only possible solution short of another world war was to end the conflict where it began, with a divided Korea. Much the same situation, which has not broken out into violence, explains the continued division of Germany. As already noted, almost all the "hot spots" that have developed since World War II may be explained by this aspect of power politics. To cite only one illustration, we may take the case of Trieste. The population of the city is mainly Italian, but that of the surrounding area is Yugoslav. Both countries claimed Trieste and its environs. Since Yugoslavia was then a dutiful satellite of Moscow, the Russians vigorously supported Yugoslav claims. Had these claims been conceded, the effect would have been to give the Soviet Union an air and sea base at the head of the Adriatic from which attacks could have been launched against Western Europe. For this reason, the United States, Britain, and France staunchly upheld Italy's claims. However, as the point neared at which open violence would become a serious threat, Marshal Tito (Broz) of Yugoslavia broke with the Kremlin and indicated a willingness to stand with the Western Powers. This changed the whole picture. Russia lost interest in Trieste. Now, in case of war, Italian and Yugoslavia troops would stand shoulder to shoulder at the head of the Adriatic, and this made it vital to the Western Powers that the Trieste controversy be settled amicably. Accordingly, they brought diplomatic pressure on both Italy and Yugoslavia to work out a compromise, and this was done.

Red China. The growing rift between the Soviet Union and Red China is one of several factors, and probably the most important one, in changing the pattern of power politics in recent times. Revolutions have a way of running their course and settling down to something different from what existed before the revolution but far less radical than what prevailed earlier when the extremists held sway. The Russians have now reached this settling-down point and are more interested in standard of living than in doctrines of Marxism-Leninism. The Chinese Reds are at the stage the Russians were in under Stalin. They are still frantically doctrinaire and aggressive, and appear willing to risk precipitating a world war. Beyond their ideological differences, there are many points of essential conflict of national interest between Russia and Red China, and the Soviet authorities are beginning to feel that Russia has more to fear from the Chinese than from the "capitalist" countries. This, along with the atomic "balance of power" and the decline of revolutionary zeal in Russia, has brought a decided thaw in the cold war. More and more cultural exchanges and cooperative projects are being arranged between the United States and the Soviet Union, and the threat of atomic war between these countries has diminished almost to the vanishing point. The way may be opening up for the settlement of such issues as arms limitation and the division of Germany. In all of the present "hot spots," it is the Chinese Reds rather than the Russians who are backing the aggressive elements.

Ideological Conflict. That the ideological conflict between what we usually call communism and democracy has been a major factor in the world tension of recent decades is a self-evident fact. However, as we have just noted, this conflict is wearing thin as between the Soviet Union and the United States. Even so, it is a mistake to regard this ideological conflict as the sole cause of the period of tension that followed World War II. That war destroyed the old power equilibrium. All but two of the pre-war great powers were reduced to helplessness or near-helplessness. Those two, the United States and the Soviet Union, emerged as super-powers, much stronger than when the war began. Between these, in addition to their ideological conflict, there were many clashes of national interest and national aims. Russia had always been aggressively expansionist, and so had constituted a threat to the peace and security of her neighbors. All through the nineteenth century, the "containment" of Russia had been a major policy of the countries of Western Europe. Britain and France fought the Crimean War for this purpose, and, in a great diplomatic crisis in 1878, Russia withdrew from penetration of the Balkans only when confronted with superior force. It was really Russian expansionism that precipitated World War I. This policy had to be abandoned at the time of the Bolshevik revolution, but after World War II, when they felt strong enough to do so, the Communists resumed where the Tsars had left off. This, along with Soviet demands for exorbitant war indemnity from Germany (which the United States would have had to pay indirectly) and other conflicts of interest, made a diplomatic conflict and an armaments race between the super-powers inevitable. This, in turn, was sure to bring into play all the maneuvers of power politics.

TEST-YOURSELF QUIZ

Without referring back to the text, check the answer or completion in each question that you think is right. Then turn to answers on page 236 and see how well you have done.

1. Which of these statements regarding the relations of component units of a federal union with each other is true:
( ) a. They may deal with each other only through the federal government.
( ) b. They may make agreements with each other, sometimes requiring consent of the federal government.
( ) c. They maintain diplomatic relations with each other.
( ) d. They may have no legal relations with each other at all.

2. Diplomacy is carried on in all but one of these ways. Which one?
( ) a. Direct military action.
( ) b. Exchange of ambassadors or ministers.
( ) c. International conferences.
( ) d. The United Nations.

3. The effectiveness of a treaty depends on:
( ) a. Enforcement by the World Court.
( ) b. Voluntary compliance.
( ) c. Enforcement by military action.
( ) d. Its compliance with international law.

4. Which of these statements about international law is correct.
( ) a. It is enacted by the United Nations.
( ) b. It consists of rules of international relations that either have been agreed to by treaty or are accepted as tradition.
( ) c. It is enforceable on all countries by the world court.
( ) d. It is proclaimed by a "great power."

5. The most closely knit, but least formal, of these international organizations is:
( ) a. The Organization of American States (OAS)

( ) b. The North Atlantic Treaty Organization (NATO).
( ) c. The British Commonwealth of Nations.
( ) d. The United Nations.

6. Which of these statements about the United Nations is correct?
( ) a. It is a government above national governments.
( ) b. It has power to enforce peace among the "great powers."
( ) c. It is only a debating society.
( ) d. It is a diplomatic organization of sovereign states.

7. Power politics means:
( ) a. The same as world politics.
( ) b. Any diplomatic relations among the "great powers."
( ) c. International relations conducted on the basis of power.
( ) d. The existence of a "balance of power."

8. The "cold war" was mainly the result of:
( ) a. Historic Russian expansionism.
( ) b. Ideological differences.
( ) c. Inadequacy of the United Nations.
( ) d. Atomic developments.

SUGGESTIONS FOR DISCUSSION

1. What relations may the government units within a country have with each other? What relations may they have with governments outside the country?
2. In the broadest sense, what is the meaning of diplomacy? What are the principal ways in which it is carried on?
3. What is the nature and what is the legal status of a treaty? How is an executive agreement different?
4. Why, and in what sense, is war "the court of last resort" in international relations?
5. How is international law different from law within a country? How and to what extent may international law be enforced?
6. What are the major types of international organization? Cite examples of each.
7. Describe the essential nature of the United Nations. Why has it been more successful than the League of Nations was?

8. Distinguish world politics and power politics. What are some of the ways in which they are carried on?

BIBLIOGRAPHY

Alting von Geusau, F. A. M., *European Organization and Foreign Relations of States* (Dobbs Ferry, N. Y., 1962).

American Academy of Political and Social Science, *The New Europe: Implications for the United States* (Philadelphia, 1963).

Bailey, S. D., *The United Nations* (New York, 1963).

Beloff, M., *The United States and the Unity of Europe* (Washington, D. C., 1963).

Bowett, D. W., *The Law of International Institutions* (New York, 1963).

Cohen, B. V., *The United Nations* (Cambridge, Mass., 1961).

Coyle, D. C., *The United Nations and How It Works* (New York, 1961).

Fawcett, J. E. S., *The British Commonwealth in International Law* (London, 1963).

Frankel, J., *International Relations* (Fair Lawn, N. J., 1964).

Friedman, W. G., *The Changing Structure of International Law* (New York, 1964).

Goldwin, R. A., and others, Eds., *Readings in World Politics* (Fair Lawn, N. J., 1959).

Greene, F., *Dynamics of International Relations* (New York, 1964).

Grosser, A., *The Federal Republic of Germany* (New York, 1964).

Hartman, F. H., *The Relations of Nations* (New York, 1962).

Herz, J. H., *International Politics in the Atomic Age* (New York, 1962).

Jennings, W. I., *Principles of Local Government Law* [*Britain*] (Mystic, Conn., 1964).

Knorr, K. E., and Verba, S., Eds., *The International System* (Princeton, N. J., 1961).

Korovin, E. A., and others, *International Law* (New York, 1961).

Larson, A., *When Nations Disagree* (Baton Rouge, La., 1961).

Larus, J., Ed., *Comparative World Politics* (Belmont, Cal., 1964).

McDougal, M. S., and others, *Studies in World Public Order* (New Haven, Conn., 1960).

McLellan, D. S., and others, *Theory and Practice of International Relations* (New York, 1959).

Nicholas, H. G., *The United Nations as a Political Institution* (Gloucester, Mass., 1964).

Peaslee, A. J., *International Institutions* (Clarkson, N. J., 1961).

Rambundo, B. A., *The [Soviet] Socialist Theory of International Law* (Washington, D. C., 1964).

Regala, R., *The Trends in Modern Diplomatic Practice* (Dobbs Ferry, N. Y., 1959).

Reuter, P., *International Relations* (New York, 1961).

Savage, K., *The Story of the United Nations* (London, 1964).

Schuschnigg, Kurt von, *International Law* (Milwaukee, Wis., 1959).

Stanger, R. J., Ed., *Essays on Espionage and International Law* (Columbus, O., 1963).

Stone, J., *Quest for Survival* (Cambridge, Mass., 1961).

Thomas, L., *Local Government [Britain]* (New York, 1964).

Webster, C. K., *The Art and Practice of Diplomacy* (New York, 1962).

Wood, J. M., and Garland, A., *Britain and the Commonwealth* (Toronto, 1958).

15

Summary

*In conclusion, it may be worth while to sum up
some of the high points of our subject. Political
science is the study or science of government.
There may be some question as to the propriety of
using this term, since the study of government
can not be an exact science like physics or chemistry, but it is established by long usage.*

It is possible to deduce a few general principles that apply to
certain phases of government, but for the most part we must be
content with descriptions of things as they are.

The State. The central theme of political science is the
state. We may think of a state as the people and territory of what
we commonly call a country, organized for purposes of government and possessing sovereignty. Sovereignty, in turn, means that
the state is legally independent of any authority outside itself,
though in practice its freedom of action may be restrained by such
outside factors as international law and its power relations with
other states. Treaty obligations are not regarded as infringing
sovereignty because treaties are entered into voluntarily by the
state. Sovereignty also implies that the state has full power to
regulate its own affairs through its constitution and government
and that it has the power, subject to the restrictions of its own
constitution, to order the lives of its citizens.

Ideology. Ideologies play a large part in political matters, using the term *political* in the broad sense of including everything pertaining to government. An ideology may be thought of as a group or system of widely held ideas or doctrines as to the form, character, and purposes of government. In remote times, the ideology of "divine right" monarchy held wide sway. In recent decades, the ideologies of democracy, fascism and communism have been most significant. Because it has emotional appeal, an ideology may not only shape the character of government within a country, but may be used as an instrument of propaganda or infiltration in international relations.

Constitutions. Every state has a constitution of some kind. It may not always be a written document like the Constitution of the United States. It may be only an accumulation of legal enactments, customs and traditions like the British constitution. Again, it may be a "constitutional system" combining both of these features. Whatever its character, the constitution prescribes the form and regulates the operation of government. It usually confers or restricts the powers of government and, normally, provides for the protection of the rights of citizens. A constitution may be observed rigidly, interpreted loosely, or largely ignored by the person or group in control of the government. Constitutions are always subject to change by formal amendment, by interpretation, by usurpation, or by revolutionary activity. A constitution is sometimes classified as flexible or rigid according to the ease or difficulty with which changes may be made.

Citizens and Rights. The people who make up the state are its citizens. Conversely, we may define a citizen as a full member of the body politic (the group of people who constitute the state) with all the rights and obligations that go with such membership. The population of the state may also include persons who are not citizens. Subjects are persons who are subject to the authority of the state without enjoying the status or full rights of citizenship. Thus, from 1898 to 1917, the Puerto Ricans were subjects of the United States. A denizen is a native-born inhabitant who is not directly subject to the authority of the state, but for whom the state is responsible; this was the status of the American Indians in the United States before they were given citizenship. Citizens, subjects and denizens are all "nationals" of the state. An alien is a person who is a national of another state than the one where he lives or happens to be. In general, he is subject to the authority of the state in which he is at the moment, though the government of his own state will give him diplomatic protection if he gets into trouble. Most citizens get their citizenship by birth, either by being born within the state (*jus soli*) or by being born of parents who are citizens (*jus sanguinis*), but most states permit aliens to acquire citizenship by naturalization.

Citizenship always suggests rights, though it also carries obligations. It is well to distinguish several kinds of "rights" that are often confused. The rights of the citizen, as such, are civil rights. They are conferred by law on all citizens, and sometimes on some non-citizens, and are enforceable in the courts. They include the ordinary personal liberties. Political rights are also conferred by law, but on a selective basis. Usually, but not necessarily, restricted to citizens, they are always subject to qualifications for voting or holding office such as age, residence, freedom from conviction of crime, and sometimes property holding or tax paying. Human rights are ideals of rights that should belong to all human beings. They are widely held and may be generally observed, but they have no legal standing until or unless they are made civil rights by being enacted into law.

GOVERNMENT

Kinds of Government. Every state has a government which makes and applies its laws and administers its affairs. No two governments are exactly alike, but groups of them do have enough features in common to classify them on several bases. At one time, the classification into monarchies and republics was important, but that classification has lost most of its meaning. The classification into authoritarian and popular coincides fairly well with what has become the most important classification for our time, totalitarian governments and "free" governments. In a totalitarian government the ruler or ruling group can be changed only by revolutionary means, since there are no free elections, and there are no adequate guarantees of civil rights. When a dictator dies, there is usually a struggle for power through intrigue or open violence. "Free" government has two distinguishing characteristics: it is responsible in that the voters may change the policy-making officials in free elections; it is limited in that its powers are limited by the constitution, and the civil rights of its citizens are enforceable in the courts. There are two main types of "free" government, with many variations. In the parliamentary or cabinet type there is a chief of state who performs ceremonial functions, but has little or no discretionary power. He acts only on the "advice" of his ministers. The executive power and the leadership in legislation are vested in a cabinet, headed by a prime minister who is the head of government. The prime minister and cabinet are appointed nominally by the chief of state, but are actually selected on the basis of political party representation in the legislative body. They may, as in Britain, also be members of Parliament and dominate its workings. Even where they are not members, they introduce most important bills and take part in parliamentary debates. They may be forced to resign by a vote of censure or "no confidence" in parliament or they may forestall this by "advising" the chief of state to dissolve parliament and call an election. In the presidential type, as found in the United States, the same person is both chief of state and head of government. The cabinet is responsible to him and can not be forced to resign by action of the legislative body. He may recommend or veto legislation but, except for the privilege of speaking before the legislative body, the head of government can take no part in the legislative process, and he can not dissolve the legislative body.

Powers and Functions of Government. The powers of a government are normally either conferred or restricted by the constitution. In an absolute monarchy or outright dictatorship, there are no constitutional restrictions, though in practice power may be restricted by custom or tradition. Totalitarian governments usually have restrictions in their constitutions, but these are ineffective in practice. In "free" governments, however, the restrictions are enforceable by the courts. A government of a state exercises whatever powers it has in full sovereignty; that is, with full authority. Among the powers that the governments of all states have are the powers to conduct relations with other states, to make and enforce laws, to administer public affairs, and to raise money by taxation to meet their expenses. Some governments also have other powers.

There are or have been various theories of the proper functions of government. In the early centuries of the modern era, the prevailing theory was mercantilism; that is, that the government should control the economic processes rigidly in the interest of the prosperity of the state. In the nineteenth century, the prevailing theory was *laissez faire:* the doctrine that the government should be little more than a policeman and protector of private rights, with almost no control over the economic processes. Today, the so-called "communist" countries hold to their own version of socialism which requires the government to operate all economic enterprise. In Free World countries, though, the prevailing theory is that of the "welfare state," which holds that, while preserving the major features of free enterprise, a government should do whatever is necessary to provide the maximum welfare of its citizens.

Branches of Government. It is usual to consider the structure of government to consist of three (some would say four) branches: legislative, executive, judicial, and (some would add) administrative. Except in absolute monarchies and outright dictatorships, the legislative functions are exercised by a representative body, sometimes unicameral but usually bicameral, which, with more or less participation by the executive, enacts laws, creates administrative machinery, and controls the finances. How truly representative this body is varies from country to country. The executive may be single or plural. In the single executive plan, all executive power is vested in a single individual (such as the President of the United States), with all other executive officers subordinate to and responsible to him. A plural executive may be either of the cabinet type, in which executive power belongs collectively to a cabinet which is responsible to the legislature, or the executive council type, as found in Switzerland, which differs from a cabinet in that the group is not responsible to the legislature. Some of the "states" of the United States have still a third type in which there are several separately elected executive officers who are independent of each other. The judicial branch consists of a pyramid of courts, with appeals from lower to higher courts, culminating in one or more courts at the top to which final appeals can be made and whose decisions can be overruled only by changing the laws which they have applied. In all "free" countries efforts are made, not always with complete success, to keep the courts independent of the political branches, the executive and the legislature. Administration means carrying on the governmental activities that are provided for by the constitution or laws. The administrative branch (sometimes considered a part of the executive branch) consists of the agencies and civil servants who carry on these activities. Agency officials with discretionary power are usually appointed by and responsible to the executive, but employees who perform the more routine tasks are usually selected under some kind of merit sysem.

Separation of Powers. The separation of powers doctrine holds that each of the three major branches of government should be sufficiently independent that it can not be controlled or dismissed by either or both of the other two. All "free" countries try to keep their courts independent, but, as between the executive and legislative branches, separation of powers does not exist in cabinet type government. Members of the cabinet participate directly in the legislative process. The legislature can force the resignation of the cabinet or the cabinet, subject to some restrictions, can bring about a "dissolution of parliament" and the calling of an election.

Separation of powers is usually applied in governments with a single executive or an executive council. In the United States, for example, the President may address Congress, and he can recommend or veto legislation, but neither he nor his cabinet may take a direct part in the legislative process. He can not dissolve Congress, nor can Congress force his resignation or that of his cabinet. Separation of powers is modified somewhat by what we call "checks and balances." Each branch of government may have some restraints on the other two. We have noted the presidential veto. Congress, in turn, may restrict the President by the laws it enacts and by its control of finances. The Senate, moreover, must approve his treaties and confirm his appointments to validate them. Congress provides for the structure of the courts and enacts the laws they apply. The President appoints the judges, with the approval of the Senate, but can not dismiss them. The Supreme Court can pass on the constitutionality of acts of both the President and Congress.

REPRESENTING THE PEOPLE

The Electorate. For the purpose of participating in government, the people are the electorate: those persons who are permitted to vote in elections. There are always qualifications for voting including citizenship, a minimum age (which varies from government to government), and a period of residence. Sometimes there are other qualifications such as property owning or tax paying, freedom from conviction of serious offenses, and mental soundness. Additional qualifications are sometimes imposed for holding certain offices. There is almost always a voters' list against which a person's name is checked when he offers to vote. Only in some of the "states" of the United States is responsibility put on the voter to register. In most countries, the lists are prepared by election officials, though the individual is usually given a chance to complain if he thinks his name has been omitted improperly.

Elections. Except in aboslute monarchies and outright dictatorships, there are elections, at least for choosing members of the legislative body. In totalitarian states, the elections are little more than a formality, since the voter has no freedom of choice. In all Free World countries, though, the voters may choose among the nominees of different political parties. In some countries, especially where proportional representation is used, the voter may vote only for the party and not for individual candidates. Nomination of candidates is made in different ways. Only in some of the "states" of the United States is the direct primary used. In most countries, nominations are made by party committees or other agencies in the party organization. In some countries, especially those with presidential type government, elections are held on a set schedule. In countries with cabinet type government, members of the legislative body are elected for maximum terms, but parliament may be dissolved and an election called at almost any time.

Political Parties. Except in referendum elections to vote on issues, in plebiscites to approve an act of the head of government, and in non-partisan elections in some small areas, the voters can express themselves only through political parties by voting for party candidates. Political parties of some sort exist almost everywhere. Even when they are forbidden by law, they usually exist "underground" and function as conspiracies. There are many kinds of parties. Some are formed to uphold definite principles or doctrines. Others represent some one of the wide variety of special interests. Others, as in the United States, have become institutional parties which are highly elastic on issues and doctrines, try to appeal to numerous interest groups, and are concerned chiefly with the success of the party as an organization. In organization, a political party is a pyramid of committees with a national committee or central committee at the top. Conventions (also called conferences or "congresses" in some countries) are held, either on a regular schedule or on call, to map party policy, sometimes to elect committees, and sometimes to nominate candidates. In totalitarian countries, where only one party is permitted, *the* party controls the government without the necessity of campaigning for election, since the voters have no choice. In two-party countries, the two parties compete for control by seeking to win elections. In multiple-party countries, no single party ever wins a complete victory, so administrations must be made up of coalitions of parties.

Public Opinion. Although the term defies simple definition, public opinion (or, more accurately, the weight of public opinion) is a major factor in the conduct of government almost everywhere, and even plays a significant part in international relations. In the Free World countries, public opinion expresses itself at the ballot box, but it may also operate between elections in the form of pressure politics. That public opinion is important even in totalitarian states is indicated by the great effort made by the government or ruling party to mold opinion by propaganda, censorship and sometimes even terror.

INTERGOVERNMENTAL RELATIONS

Governments Within a Country. Most governments have relations of one sort or another with other governments. Among local government units, which have no sovereign powers, these relations are either strictly informal or are carried on through agencies of the state of which the local government units are a part. Sometimes the state of which they are a part will authorize them by law to enter into specified cooperative agreements for the maintaining of services of which the separate units would be incapable or which they would find too expensive, such as regional schools, hospitals, or fire protection districts. Relations of local units to the state of which they are a part are regulated by the constitution and/or laws of the state. There may be constitutional safeguards for their limited autonomy, but they are always subject to a large measure of control by organs of the state government.

Component units of federal unions normally have no direct contact with the governments of foreign states. There are some limited exceptions. Union republics of the Soviet Union are permitted by the Soviet constitution (as of this writing) to conduct relations with foreign states. However, except that two of them are members of the United Nations (where they always mirror the stand of the Soviet government) none of them does so. "States" of the United States may, with the consent of Congress, enter into agreements with foreign states, but such agreements are always limited to such non-political matters as joining their highways at the boundary, building bridges over boundary rivers, and distributing impounded water for irrigation or water power. Units of federal unions usually have informal dealings with each other and enter into informal agreements. More formal agreements may or may not require approval of the federal authorities. In the United States they require the consent of Congress.

International Relations. The most important inter-governmental relations are those between sovereign states, usually called international relations. Each sovereign state has its "national" policies which it seeks to carry out through dealings with foreign states. These dealings are carried on mainly through various methods of diplomacy (which means, simply, formal dealings between governments) such as the work of regularly accredited diplomats, the use of special agents, meetings of foreign ministers, and summit conferences in which heads of governments meet and confer. Besides diplomacy, governments use other devices such as propaganda, foreign aid, and sometimes intrigue and subversion in the conduct of international relations.

International Organization. Most of the states of the world belong to one or more international organizations. These organizations are not super-governments and they have no real power over their member states. They are diplomatic groupings, sometimes with elaborate machinery, through which member states confer and seek to achieve agreement and cooperation in pursuit of the goals of the organization. The most important of these is the United Nations, to which most of the states of the world belong. Attached to the United Nations are a number of "Specialized Agency" organizations, with membership somewhat independent of U. N. membership, each carrying on a cooperative project. Among Free World countries there are the Organization of American States (OAS), the British Commonwealth of Nations, the North Atlantic Treaty Organization (NATO), the Southeast Asia Treaty Organization (SEATO), and the Central Treaty Organization (CENTO). The Communist countries have a separate set of organizations of their own. In addition, there are alliances, economic groupings like the Common Market, and still other types of international organization. A state joins one of these by treaty and gives up none of its sovereignty in doing so.

World Politics. When international relations are carried on with a view to influencing the course of world events, the process is called world politics. When, in this world setting, international dealings are conducted on the basis of power, as they usually are by the stronger countries, world politics becomes power politics. Some of the devices of power politics are: creation of alliances to checkmate the power of a rival; the building of great military forces; the implicit or explicit threat of force in negotiations; maneuvering for strategic positions; intrigue and subversion; actual use of force; and, in an extreme situation, resort to war. Each government seeks to serve what it regards as the national interests of its country. Inevitably, ideological conflicts play a large part in power politics.

This subject of world politics has become so large and so important in our time that it has become a separate field of study. In a general overview of political science it can be touched upon only lightly, but it can not be omitted because it has become one of the most vital aspects of government today.

ANSWERS TO TEST-YOURSELF QUIZZES

Chapter 1	Chapter 2	Chapter 3	Chapter 4
1. c	1. a	1. d	1. c
2. b	2. b	2. b	2. b
3. a	3. b	3. c	3. a
4. d	4. d	4. b	4. d
5. c	5. c	5. a	5. a
6. b	6. b	6. a	6. d
7. d	7. c	7. c	7. c
8. b	8. d	8. b	8. c

Chapter 5	Chapter 6	Chapter 7	Chapter 8
1. b	1. b	1. b	1. c
2. d	2. d	2. b	2. d
3. c	3. a	3. c	3. c
4. a	4. c	4. d	4. b
5. a	5. c	5. a	5. a
6. b	6. b	6. a	6. b
7. b	7. a	7. d	7. d
8. c	8. b	8. b	8. b

Chapter 9	Chapter 10	Chapter 11	Chapter 12
1. a	1. a	1. d	1. c
2. d	2. c	2. b	2. b
3. d	3. b	3. c	3. d
4. c	4. c	4. a	4. a
5. c	5. d	5. c	5. c
6. b	6. a	6. c	6. d
7. d	7. c	7. b	7. b
8. a	8. a	8. a	8. d

Chapter 13		Chapter 14	
1. d	5. b	1. b	5. c
2. c	6. b	2. a	6. d
3. c	7. d	3. b	7. c
4. a	8. b	4. b	8. a

Unitary and Federal States

UNITARY **FEDERAL**

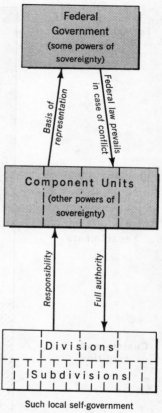

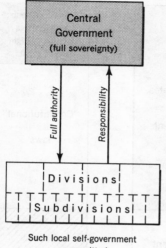

Central Government (full sovereignty)

Full authority

Responsibility

Divisions
Subdivisions

Such local self-government as permitted

Federal Government (some powers of sovereignty)

Basis of representation

Federal law prevails in case of conflict

Component Units (other powers of sovereignty)

Responsibility

Full authority

Divisions
Subdivisions

Such local self-government as permitted

CONFEDERATION

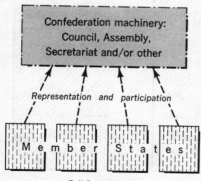

Confederation machinery:
Council, Assembly,
Secretariat and/or other

Representation and participation

Member States

Full Sovereignty

Working Constitutions

	UNITED STATES	GREAT BRITAIN
Formal documents	Constitution of the United States with Amendments	Basic documents: Magna Carta Petition of Right Bill of Rights
	Judicial interpretation	"Constitutional" laws
Statutory enactments	Constituent statutes	
Custom and tradition	The "unwritten constitution"	Custom and historic usage
Principles of legal system	Principles of common law	Principles of common law

Space given to each item indicates relative importance in the two countries. A comparable distribution of these items could be shown for many other countries.

Totalitarian and "Free" Governments

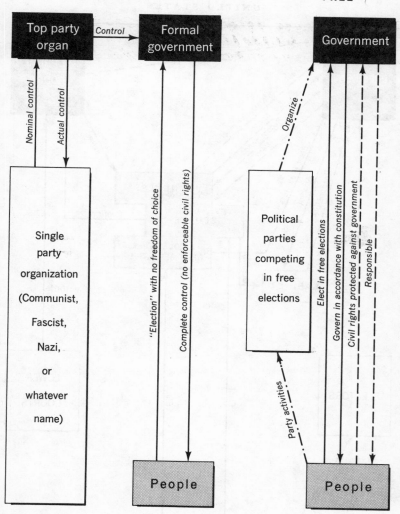

TOTALITARIAN   **"FREE"**

Top party organ — *Control* → Formal government   Government

Nominal control   *Actual control*

Organize

Single party organization (Communist, Fascist, Nazi, or whatever name)

"Election" with no freedom of choice   *Complete control (no enforceable civil rights)*

Political parties competing in free elections

Elect in free elections   *Govern in accordance with constitution*   *Civil rights protected against government*   *Responsible*

Party activities

People   People

Separation of Powers
(with Checks and Balances)

UNITED STATES

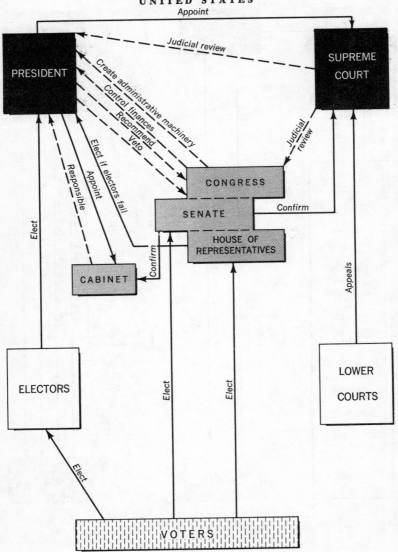

Cabinet System
(no Separation of Powers)

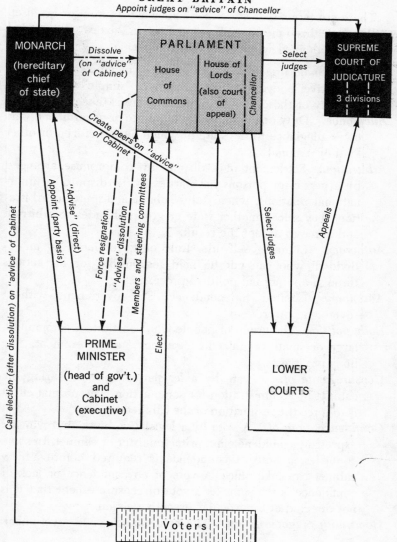

GREAT BRITAIN
Appoint judges on "advice" of Chancellor

MONARCH (hereditary chief of state)

Dissolve (on "advice" of Cabinet)

PARLIAMENT

House of Commons

House of Lords (also court of appeal)

Chancellor

Select judges

SUPREME COURT OF JUDICATURE

3 divisions

Create peers on "advice" of Cabinet

Call election (after dissolution) on "advice" of Cabinet

Appoint (party basis)

"Advise" (direct)

Force resignation

"Advise" dissolution

Members and steering committees

PRIME MINISTER (head of gov't.) and Cabinet (executive)

Elect

Select judges

Appeals

LOWER COURTS

Voters

Glossary

These are terms that are either somewhat unusual or are used with a specialized meaning. Terms defined in the text are included only if not defined where they first appear.

"Absolute" majority. A majority of all the members elected to a legislative body, as distinct from a "simple" majority—a majority of those present when the vote is taken.

Allegiance. Duty or responsibility to a state or government. One owes allegiance to the state of which he is a citizen or other kind of national.

Arbitration. Settlement of a dispute by compromise arranged by a person or persons not parties to the dispute. In international relations, when states submit a dispute to arbitration, they select another state or group of states to arbitrate and agree to accept the result.

Autocracy. Literally, self-rule. Rule or government by an individual who can not be held responsible for his actions through any normal political process.

Autonomy. Limited independence. Self-government without sovereign power.

Body politic. The group of people who constitute a community, large or small, organized for purposes of government. The body of citizens.

Censure, vote of. A vote by a legislative body censuring the cabinet or administration for some action. The normal effect is to force the resignation of the cabinet.

Confidence, vote of. A vote by a legislative body approving or expressing confidence in a prime minister or cabinet. In some countries, a vote of confidence is required before a new cabinet can take office. A vote of no confidence or lack of confidence is the same as a vote of censure except that it is not directed at a particular executive action.

Continuity of government. The continuance of a government, without interruption of its standing or authority, at the time of a change in political control or top personnel by regular or constitutional means. Continuity of government is broken by a revolutionary change.

Corporation. Sometimes defined as an artificial person. A group of persons empowered by an act of government, a law or a charter, to act with some of the legal rights and powers of an individual person. It may be a private business organization, a private non-business organization, a government corporation (owned entirely by the government), or a unit of local self-government.

Coup d'état. A French expression meaning literally "stroke of state." Seizure of power by an individual or group, normally with little or no violence. It is usually carried out by a military officer or group, or by a person or group of persons who already have some position in the government.

De facto. In fact. *De jure.* In law. A *de facto* government is one which is actually in control of a country, but which has not established its claim to be the legitimate government. A *de jure* government is the legitimate government. It has established its legitimacy by long continuance, by constitutional procedures, or by recognition by other states. In diplomacy, a government may give *de facto* recognition to a regime in another state, accepting the fact that it is in actual control, but not accepting it as legitimate or establishing diplomatic relations with it. When a government extends *de jure* recognition to a regime in another state, it accepts it as the legitimate government of that state and, normally, establishes diplomatic relations with it.

Dissolution. A dissolution of a legislative body ends the tenure of all of its members and is, normally, the occasion for the calling of an election for new members. In most cabinet-governed countries, the chief of state may decree a dissolution of parliament on advice of the prime minister or cabinet. If the legislative body is bicameral, only the more directly elected chamber is usually subject to dissolution.

Divine right. The doctrine that the ruler is selected by the Deity through the process of inheritance and rules by God's authority.

Election at large. Election of all the members of a legislative body from the whole country as distinct from election from single-member or multiple-member districts. In a federal union, it means that all members of a federal legislative body from a component unit of the union are elected by the entire unit.

Elite. The element or group in a population which enjoys superior status or special privileges.

Equity. Literally, fairness. In common law countries, a body of legal rules developed from "writs" or orders issued in the later middle ages by the chancellor of England. These writs were intended to do justice in situations where the rules or procedures of common law might fail to do so. In general, equity undertook to prevent wrongs where common law only provided remedies for wrongs already committed. In some common law countries, and in some of the "states" of the United States, equity is administered by separate courts called courts of chancery.

Ex officio. Literally, from an office. Usually translated, by virtue of an office. A person who holds one office automatically holds another. Thus, the Vice President of the United States is *ex officio* President of the Senate.

Free elections. Elections in which voters have some real freedom of choice between or among candidates or parties.

Free enterprise. Private ownership and management of business, with or without government regulation.

Free World. A term applied to those countries which have "responsible" governments. Members of their legislative bodies (at least of one chamber) are chosen in free elections, the executive is elected directly or indirectly, and personal liberties are enforced as civil rights.

Habeas corpus. A procedure in common law countries for preventing arbitrary arrest and imprisonment. An arrested person may secure a writ from a judge ordering him to be brought before a magistrate for a preliminary hearing to determine whether he is accused of a punishable offense and whether there is enough presumptive evidence to justify holding him for trial. If there is not a specific accusation supported by presumptive evidence, he is released. The name comes from the opening words of the old Latin writ, "have the person . . . [brought into court]."

Ideological totalitarianism. Totalitarianism based on an ideology, such as Fascism, Nazism, or Communism.

Impeachment. Formal accusation of a public official by the lower house of a legislative body, charging misconduct in office. Traditionally, the impeached official is tried by the upper house, acting as a court. In the United States federal government, any executive or judicial officer may be impeached by the House of Representatives and is tried by the Senate. In Britain, he may be impeached by the House of Commons and is tried by the House of Lords. Some of the "states" of the United States and a few national governments have substituted trial by a judicial panel. Upon conviction, the official is removed from office. If his offense was a crime at law, he may then be tried by a court and given appropriate punishment.

Indictment. Formal accusation of a person by a grand jury, charging a punishable crime. The indicted person is then put on trial in a trial court.

Interest appeal. Having appeal to the special interests of a person or group.

International. Used in such terms as international relations or international law, international means among sovereign states, rather than among nations as such.

Irresponsible government. Government which can not be made to answer for its acts by the voters in free elections.

Jingoism. Exaggerated or blustering nationalism; chauvinism; belief in an overaggressive foreign policy.

Judicial procedure. Procedure such as a court would use, based on some kind of law. Used in contrast with such procedures for settling disputes as arbitration and conciliation.

Junta. A Spanish word (pronounced *hunta*) which means, literally, council. Often used to mean a small group, usually of military officers, which seizes power in a *coup d'état* and carries on an irresponsible government.

Laissez faire (or **laisser faire**). Literally, leave be or let alone. The doctrine that government should limit its activities to the protection of life and property and take no part in the economic processes.

Legitimate government. Government which has established its *de jure* right to govern a country.

Martial law. Rule of a country or part of a country set up in time of crisis, suspending the civil authorities and governing under military authority. In some cases, only the criminal jurisdiction of the courts is suspended with military courts (which operate without juries) set up to replace the regular courts for criminal cases. Something very much like martial law is called "state of seige" in some countries.

Monopoly. Control of all the production or sale of a commodity by a single person or business group. Complete monopoly rarely exists except when it is created by government action. In economics, monopoly is used to mean control of enough of a commodity to be able to set prices arbitrarily.

Municipality. A community, such as a city, town, or county, which possesses a large measure of self-government under a charter or special laws. It is legally a corporation with the corporate rights of holding property, making contracts, and suing and being sued in court. The adjective *municipal* means pertaining to such a community.

Oligarchy. Government by a few. A regime in which all political power is held by a relatively small group, usually self-appointed. The term is applied both to such a government and to the group holding power.

Patronage. The privilege of a political party organization or party leader of directing the appointment of public officials or employees as rewards for support in political campaigns. It easily degenerates into a spoils system.

Plebiscite. A special election in which an unauthorized act of government or seizure of power in a *coup d'état* is referred to the voters for approval. Similar to, but not identical with, a referendum.

Power relations. Relations among sovereign states based on power. Also used to mean the relative power of states involved in an international situation.

Pressure politics. The efforts of organized groups (pressure groups), other than political parties, to influence legislation or executive policy in the interest of the group or its members. Pressure politics involves the use of such devices as lobbying, petition, propaganda, and support of candidates favorable to the interests of the group.

Private enterprise. Essentially the same as free enterprise, but with emphasis on private ownership rather than on freedom in management.

Protest vote. The vote of an individual (or group) for a party or candidate he does not really favor to express dissatisfaction with alternative choices.

Referendum. General meaning, the referring of a question, such as a tax increase, a bond issue or a constitutional amendment, to the voters for decision directly by their votes. In some of the "states" of the United States (and in a few European countries), referendum has the specific meaning of a procedure by which, upon petition signed by a required number of voters, an act passed by the legislative body is referred to the voters for approval or disapproval.

Responsible government. A government which is responsible for its acts to the voters in free elections.

Sacrosanct. Literally, sacred or holy. Applied to any custom, institution or person that is considered inviolable and entitled to the highest respect.

Secretariat. The whole group of secretaries and civil servants who conduct the routine business of an international organization, such as the United Nations.

Sovereign state. A state that is legally independent of all authority outside itself. The term is really tautological, since a state is sovereign by definition, but it is often used for emphasis.

Special interest group. A coherent group with special interests which it seeks to have government serve. When such a group is organized and uses the methods of pressure politics to attain its ends, it is called a pressure group.

Subpoena. A writ or order commanding a person to appear in court, usually as a witness, under penalties for disobedience of the order.

Summons. Similar to a subpoena, but directed to the person who is ordered to appear in court as defendant in a suit, rather than as a witness.

Titular. Having a title which implies authority, but with little or no discretion in the exercise of authority. Thus, the Queen of Great Britain is the titular ruler; in the United States, a defeated candidate for President is the titular head of his political party.

Trial examiner. An officer of a regulatory board or commission, but not a member of the board, who is employed to conduct hearings on behalf of the agency.

Underground. A term used figuratively to describe a political group which operates secretly or as a conspiracy in defiance of law or government authority.

Governments of the Major Powers

FRANCE (THE FRENCH REPUBLIC). A unitary republic with considerable centralization of administration. The Fifth Republic was established in 1958, upon the virtual breakdown of the government of the Fourth Republic with its multiple-party cabinet system, over the Algerian crisis. The constitution was drafted under the personal guidance of General Charles de Gaulle, was approved by the last Council of Ministers of the Fourth Republic, and was ratified in a plebiscite. The constitution, as amended later, provides for a French Community, similar to the British Commonwealth of Nations. Most of the former French colonies and dependencies are now members of this Community. The government combines features of both the presidential and cabinet systems. The President appoints and controls the prime minister and cabinet, may dissolve the Assembly, may submit constitutional amendments (Parliament may also submit them), and may, in certain circumstances, assume the power to rule by decree. The prime minister and cabinet (called the "government") are nominally responsible to the Assembly, but can be overthrown only if the prime minister voluntarily submits to a confidence vote, and then an absolute majority vote of the Assembly is required. The Parliament is bicameral. The Senate consists of one Senator for each 300,000 population, and shares powers almost equally with the Assembly. The Senators are elected by a large electoral college consisting of members of the Assembly and local officials. Originally, this same electoral college also elected the President, but a constitutional amendment adopted in 1962 provides for direct popular election. Members of the Assembly, the larger chamber, are elected in single-member districts by universal adult suffrage. There is a Constitutional Council, whose members are appointed by the President, which, at the request of the President, passes on the constitutionality of laws and has some other special powers. Parliament, with the approval of the Constitutional Council, may enact "organic laws," which are similar to our constituent statutes. *Departments* (the main divisions of the country) and communes have some self-government through popularly elected councils, but are subject to a large degree of control by the central government.

GERMANY, FEDERAL REPUBLIC OF (West Germany). A quasi-federal republic consisting of eleven *Länder* (lands) or "states." The regime was established in 1949, with the approval of the occupying powers, over the American, British and French occupation zones. In 1955, all occupational authority was withdrawn and the country became fully independent. The President, who is chief of state only, is elected by a special assembly made up of members of the *Bundestag* and delegates from the *Land* parliaments. All real executive power centers in the Chancellor, who is elected by the *Bundestag* and formally appointed by the President. The Chancellor appoints the cabinet members, who are responsible to him alone. He, himself, is nominally responsible to the *Bundestag*, but a no-confidence vote to remove him must be accompanied by the election of a new Chancellor, a thing that is almost impossible with the multiple-party situation. The Chancellor may introduce bills into the *Bundestag* and these may become law even if rejected by the *Bundesrat*. He may have the President dissolve the *Bundestag* and call an election. He may authorize expenditures if Parliament fails to pass his budget and, if one of his important bills fails to pass the *Bundestag*, he may declare a "legislative emergency" and declare the law enacted if passed by the *Bundesrat* alone. Parliament is bi-cameral. Members of the "upper house" or *Bundesrat* (Council of the Union) are chosen by the *Land* cabinets from among their own membership. Members of the more important "lower house" or *Bundestag* (Diet of the Union) are elected by universal adult suffrage, one half from single-member districts and one half under proportional representation. Each *Land* has a *Landtag* or "state legislature," unicameral except in Bavaria. Each *Landtag* elects a minister-president, who is a combination of governor and prime minister, and a council of ministers, each of whom heads an administrative department. The *Landtag* can legislate on almost any matter, so long as its acts do not conflict with national law, but the central government has concurrent authority and can overrule almost any legislative or administrative act of the *Land* government. The *Landtag* can direct its representatives in the *Bundestag* how to vote on national legislation. Superficially, the government of East Germany (THE DEMOCRATIC REPUBLIC OF GERMANY) is similar, but one-party Communist control makes it a dictatorship.

GREAT BRITAIN AND NORTHERN IRELAND, UNITED KINGDOM OF.   A unitary constitutional monarchy. The monarch is strictly a ceremonial chief of state. The head of government is the Prime Minister, nominally appointed by the monarch, but always the official leader of the political party holding a majority of seats in the House of Commons and chosen by the parliamentary party. There is a large ministry, its members selected by the Prime Minister and formally appointed by the monarch, a varying number of whom constitute the cabinet which is a plural executive and a steering committee of Parliament. Cabinet ministers must be members of Parliament, introduce all important bills, and dominate the procedure of Parliament. Rejection of a major "government" bill by the House of Commons is regarded as a "no confidence" vote and calls for either a resignation of the ministry or a dissolution of Parliament (which applies only to the House of Commons) and the calling of an election. The bi-cameral parliament consists of the House of Lords and the House of Commons. Some of the peers (lords) are hereditary and some are appointed for life. Women may now sit in the House of Lords and a lord may resign his peerage (for his own lifetime only) to run for membership in the House of Commons. Since hereditary peers seldom attend sessions and the Lords can only delay, but not block, the passage of an important bill, the House of Lords has become a sort of consultative body of elder statesmen. It is also a supreme court for certain cases, but when it acts in this capacity, only the Lord Chancellor, a member of the ministry who always presides over the Lords and chief law officer of the Kingdom, and the "law lords," appointed for life for this purpose and taking part in no other proceedings of the Lords, participate in the judicial proceedings. All real legislative power belongs to the House of Commons. Its members, who receive a salary, are elected for a maximum term of seven years in single-member districts, by universal adult suffrage. Although the historic nations of the Kingdom, England, Scotland, Wales and Northern Ireland, have no separate governments (except Northern Ireland) Parliament may legislate for them separately. Judges of all higher courts are selected by the Lord Chancellor and are formally appointed for life by the monarch.

ITALY (The Italian Republic). A unitary republic with some quasi-federal features. The primary divisions of the country are provinces, similar to the French *departments,* but the constitution provides for grouping provinces into autonomous regions. Most of these regions have not been fully organized. The President, elected for a seven-year term by the two houses of Parliament meeting in joint session, is a ceremonial chief of state, but may exercise some discretion in deciding which party leader to call upon to try to form a coalition cabinet. Members of the cabinet (always a coalition), appointed formally by the President, are selected by the Prime Minister on the basis of political party arrangements. The Prime Minister and other ministers are members of Parliament, may introduce bills, and take part in parliamentary procedure, but do not dominate Parliament as in Great Britain. The bi-cameral Parliament consists of a Senate and a Chamber of Deputies which have equal power. A vote of censure or a vote of confidence must pass both houses, and a dissolution applies to both. The Senators, one for each 200,000 population, are elected in groups from the regions for six-year terms, and voters must be twenty-five years of age. There are five Senators-at-large appointed by the President in recognition of cultural achievement, and all ex-Presidents are Senators for life. Deputies are elected under proportional representation by universal adult suffrage with compulsory voting. Initiative and referendum are provided for in certain situations. The multiple-party situation makes cabinet crises frequent and difficult to resolve. The Fascist Party is outlawed, but the Communist Party is legal and comparatively strong. Dissolutions of Parliament are possible, but rarely occur.

THE UNION OF SOVIET SOCIALIST REPUBLICS (the Soviet Union). Formally, a federal union of fifteen Union Republics. The largest of these, the Russian Soviet Socialist Republic, which contains over half the population and over half the territory of the country, is in turn organized on a federal basis, consisting of autonomous republics, autonomous regions and national regions. The formal government structure of each Union Republic consists of a pyramid of soviets (councils), with a legislative body at each level which elects members of the council. At the lowest level, the legislative body is a primary assembly or mass meeting of the voters. Members of higher councils are elected by the voters. At the top republic level, the council designates ministers for administrative departments. Over all is the Supreme Soviet of the Union, which nominally has supreme authority. It consists of two chambers, the Soviet of the Union, elected on the basis of one deputy for each 300,000 population, and the Soviet of Nationalities, made up of twenty-five deputies from each Union Republic, eleven from each autonomous republic, five from each autonomous region, and one from each national district. The Supreme Soviet, which has around two thousand members, meets twice a year in brief sessions of three or four days each. The two chambers meet jointly to elect the ministers, higher military officers, members of the Supreme Court, and the Presidium, and to amend the constitution. For all other purposes, the chambers meet and vote separately. In its brief sessions, the Supreme Soviet merely ratifies decisions of the ministers and acts of the Presidium. Voting is by acclamation. The Presidium of the Supreme Soviet is a body of thirty-three members, which performs the routine functions of a legislature between sessions of the Supreme Soviet. The President of the Presidium performs the formal functions of a chief of state, but is not a chief of state in the Western sense. All real policy-making power is held by the Presidium of the Communist Party (not to be confused with the Presidium of the Supreme Soviet). The ministers are nominally responsible to the Supreme Soviet, but their real responsibility is to the party presidium. All citizens over eighteen years of age may vote by secret ballot. However, since all candidates must be approved by the Communist Party and there is usually only one candidate for each office, the voters have little (if any) freedom of choice and have no means of shaping policy or holding officials responsible. The Communist Party, with a very restricted membership, is the only legal political party, and membership carries an elite status with special privileges. The constitution may be amended, or a completely new one adopted, by the Supreme Soviet (which means, in effect, the Party Presidium) with no form of ratification required. The present constitution contains the equivalent of a bill of rights but, since no means of enforcement is provided, the Party oligarchy can violate civil rights with impunity. Day to day direction of government is by the First Secretary of the Communist Party and the Prime Minister, usually (but not as of this writing) the same man.

THE UNITED STATES OF AMERICA. A federal Republic consisting of fifty "states" and the District of Columbia. Each "state" may make and amend its own constitution without federal consent, so long as it includes nothing which conflicts with the Constitution of the United States. The federal government is of the presidential type, based on the principle of separation of powers. Formally, the President is elected by electors, apportioned among the "states" according to the "state's" representation in Congress and chosen in any manner the state legislature directs (all have "directed" election by popular vote). Under the "unwritten constitution," the political parties nominate candidates in national conventions, and the voters choose between these candidates. The President holds supreme executive power and cabinet members are responsible to him alone. He may address Congress, recommend legislation, and veto bills, but neither he nor his cabinet members take any part in the procedures of Congress. The bicameral Congress has the legislative powers conferred by the Constitution, including complete control of finances. The Senate must also approve treaties before they can be ratified, and confirm the President's appointments to higher offices. Senators are elected for six-year terms (one third each biennial election), two from each "state." Members of the House of Representatives, now set at 435 and apportioned among the "states" according to population, are elected for two-year terms. Suffrage is determined by the laws of each "state," but in general and with some limitations, there is universal adult suffrage. The federal government and the "states" have separate systems of courts, and appeals from state to federal courts are possible only on matters over which the Constitution of the United States gives the federal courts jurisdiction. Judges of the state courts are chosen in different ways in different "states," but all federal judges are appointed for life by the President with the approval of the Senate. All courts, but especially the Supreme Court of the United States, exercise the power of judicial review of legislation on questions of constitutionality, but only in deciding cases brought before them. By interpreting the Constitution and laws, the Supreme Court, in effect, legislates. Civil rights are enforceable in the courts.

Thumbnail Sketches of Sixty Governments

Note. The governments of the major powers are discussed in a separate section of this appendix. A number of very small or remote countries are omitted because of their relative unimportance. Most of the newly independent countries of Africa are excluded because they have not yet developed definite forms of government; many of them are operating under provisional dictatorships. Several other countries in the Middle East or Southeast Asia are omitted because they are in the throes of revolutionary change.

AFGHANISTAN, KINGDOM OF. A unitary constitutional monarchy. The bicameral parliament consists of a Senate of 50 members, appointed for life by the sovereign, and a National Assembly of 171 members elected by restricted suffrage. The Prime Minister and Cabinet, appointed by the King, are nominally responsible to the National Assembly, but the King still exercises major executive control.

ALBANIA, PEOPLE'S REPUBLIC OF. Except that it is unitary instead of federal, the Albanian government follows the Soviet model closely. Nominally, supreme power is vested in a unicameral National Assembly which operates through a Presidium when not in session. The Chairman of the Presidium acts as chief of state. The Prime Minister and Cabinet are elected by the Assembly and are responsible to it. The Albanian Labor (Communist) Party maintains complete control through Soviet type elections, so that the Secretary General of the Party, Enver Hoxha, is virtual dictator.

ARGENTINA (THE ARGENTINE REPUBLIC). A quasi-federal republic, modeled on the United States of America. The Federal District (Buenos Aires), like the District of Columbia, is under direct national control. Each of the 22 provinces has its own constitution, with an elected governor and legislature, but in emergencies the President may suspend a provincial government and put the province under a "federal interventor." The President and Vice President are elected by an electoral college for six-year terms. The Vice President presides over the Senate. Congress is bicameral; members of both houses are chosen for six-year terms with one third of each house renewed every two years. The 46 Senators are chosen by the provincial legislatures; members of the Chamber of Deputies are elected by direct popular vote with universal adult suffrage. For nearly half a century prior to 1916, Argentina maintained political stability under her democratic constitution. Since then, the constitutional order has been interrupted several times by dictatorships and military seizures of power.

AUSTRALIA, COMMONWEALTH OF. A federal union of six "states," and member of the British Commonwealth of Nations. The British monarch is recognized as titular sovereign and is represented by a Governor General for the union and a Governor for each state. These are appointed on nomination by the cabinet of the union or the state, and have only the formal duties of a chief of state. Supreme power is exercised by a bicameral Parliament, members of both houses of which are elected by direct popular vote with universal adult suffrage. The 60 Senators are apportioned equally among the states, are elected for six-year terms, and one half are renewed every three years. The 124 members of the House of Representatives are apportioned according to population and are elected for three-year terms, subject to an earlier dissolution. The cabinet system of government follows the British model closely.

AUSTRIA, REPUBLIC OF. A federal union of nine provinces, one of which is the capital city of Vienna. The central government has much greater powers than the provincial governments. The President, a mere ceremonial chief of state, is elected directly for a six-year term. The *Bundesrat* has 50 members chosen by the provincial legislatures. The 165 members of the *Nationalrat* are popularly elected in single member districts for four-year terms. Under a permanent coalition of the two major parties, the Chancellor is the leader of the majority party in the *Nationalrat* and the Cabinet is apportioned between the parties. They are technically responsible to the *Nationalrat* but, because of the coalition arrangement, there is never a no-confidence vote or a dissolution.

BELGIUM, KINGDOM OF. A unitary constitutional monarchy with some autonomy for the nine provinces. The Senate, with limited powers, is elected partly directly and partly indirectly. Members of the Chamber of Deputies are elected directly for four-year terms under proportional representation. Citizens who do not vote are fined. The King, little more than a ceremonial chief of state, appoints the Prime Minister, but must select a party leader who can form a coalition cabinet. Prime Minister and Cabinet are responsible to the Chamber of Deputies and must resign on a no-confidence vote. Dissolutions are possible but rarely occur.

BOLIVIA (THE BOLIVIAN REPUBLIC). A unitary republic with a presidential type of government. The President and members of both houses of Congress are elected directly, Senators for six-year terms, President and Deputies for four-year terms. The Cabinet is appointed by and responsible to the President alone. All persons who have reached the age of 20 can vote. Disturbances of the constitutional order and military dictatorships have been frequent.

BRAZIL, THE UNITED STATES OF. A federal union of 20 "states," with five territories and a federal district. The President is elected directly for a five-year term and may not succeed himself. Senators are elected for eight year terms, Deputies for four-year terms, both under proportional representation. The government is normally of the presidential type, but in 1961 the constitution was amended to transfer most of the executive power to a Prime Minister elected by Congress. Each "state"

has its own constitution with an elective governor and a bicameral legislature.

BULGARIA, PEOPLE'S REPUBLIC OF. In most respects, the government follows the Russian pattern. Nominally, supreme power
is vested in a unicameral National Assembly whose members
are elected for four-year terms by universal suffrage. Voting
age is 18. The Assembly elects a Presidium, consisting of a
chairman, two vice-chairmen and 15 members, which performs the usual functions of a legislature between the brief
meetings of the Assembly. The Chairman of the Presidium
acts as chief of state. The Presidium also appoints the ministers, interprets the laws, calls elections, ratifies treaties, and
appoints civil, military and diplomatic officials. Actual power
is exercised by the Presidium or Politburo of the Communist Party.

BURMA, REPUBLIC OF. A unitary republic with cabinet-type
government. Members of both houses of Parliament, the
Chamber of Deputies and the Chamber of Nationalities, are
elected for four-year terms. The President, a mere ceremonial
chief of state, is elected by Parliament. The Prime Minister
and Cabinet, formally appointed by the President, are nomi-
nated by and are responsible to the Chamber of Deputies.

CANADA, DOMINION OF. A federal union of ten provinces, a
member of the British Commonwealth of Nations. The British
monarch is recognized as titular sovereign of Canada and is
represented by a Governor General (usually a Canadian) appointed on nomination of the Canadian Cabinet. Each province has a Lieutenant Governor appointed on nomination of its
own cabinet. Parliament consists of a Senate with very limited
powers, whose members are appointed for life, and a House
of Commons whose members are apportioned according to
population and are elected from single member districts for
maximum five-year terms. There is usually a dissolution before
the end of the five years. Except Quebec, the provinces have
unicameral legislatures. The cabinet-type government, both of
the Dominion and of each province, follows the British model
very closely.

CEYLON, REPUBLIC OF. A unitary republic, member of the British Commonwealth of Nations. For several years after independence, Ceylon was a dominion with a governor general appointed by the British monarch on nomination of Singhalese Cabinet. The country has now declared itself a republic and substituted an elected president for the governor general. The House of Representatives is popularly elected, but half of the Senators are appointed (by the President on nomination of the Cabinet) and the other half are elected by the House of Representatives. The Prime Minister and Cabinet are responsible to the House of Representatives.

CHILE, REPUBLIC OF. A unitary republic with presidential-type government. The President is elected directly every six years. Senators are elected for eight-year terms, with one half renewed every four years, and Deputies are all elected every four years. All literate Chileans over 21 years of age may vote. The Cabinet is responsible to the President alone. Chile is one of the few Latin American countries where democracy usually works smoothly and disruptions of the constitutional order are rare.

CHINA (NATIONALIST). THE REPUBLIC OF CHINA. Although it claims to be the legitimate government of all China, and is so recognized by the United States, the Nationalist government has actual control only of the Island of Formosa or Taiwan. It appoints the provincial governor of Formosa, but there is an elective provincial legislature. The Nationalist government itself is little more than a skeleton. It consists of the President, who is declared to have supreme power, and five *yuan* or councils. The Executive Yuan, equivalent to a ministry or cabinet, is appointed by and responsible to the President. The Legislative Yuan and the Control Yuan (censorship and internal security) are, according to the constitution, elected for three-year terms, but it has been impossible to hold elections in mainland China. The Judicial Yuan (supreme court) and Examination Yuan (civil service board) are appointed by the President.

CHINA (COMMUNIST). PEOPLE'S REPUBLIC OF CHINA. All power is vested in a Government Council which consists of a chairman (usually referred to as President of the country), six vice chairmen, and 56 members. Actually self-perpetuating, the Government Council is nominally elected by the People's Political Consultative Conference (the nearest thing to a parliament) which represents Communist and collaborating groups. The Government Council appoints the State Administration Council (the Premier and ministries, which are mostly committees), the Military Council, the Supreme Court, and the Procurator General. So far, there has been no pretense of a nationwide election.

COLOMBIA, REPUBLIC OF. A unitary republic, with some autonomy for the provinces. The government is of the presidential type. An amendment adopted in 1957, to operate for 12 years, provides for equal representation of the two major political parties in both houses of Congress, regional legislatures, municipal councils, and most other organs of government. The President, elected directly for a four-year term and not eligible for reelection, alternates between the two parties. The arrangement appears to be working well. All citizens over 21 may vote.

COSTA RICA, REPUBLIC OF. A unitary republic with presidential-type government. The President and members of the unicameral Congress are popularly elected for four-year terms. There is no army. Since 1882, with two brief intervals, Costa Rica has maintained orderly constitutional government. Elections are free and all citizens over 21 may vote.

CUBA, REPUBLIC OF. Before Castro's seizure of power in 1959, Cuba was a unitary republic with a presidential-type of government and a bicameral Congress. True, presidents sometimes turned into dictators, but at least the forms of democratic self government were preserved. Once in control, Castro nullified the constitution by dissolving Congress, filling all government posts with his own followers, and refusing to call an election. Today, he is the government, with the title of Prime Minister. He has set up a puppet President, but that official has no real authority. Castro has declared himself to be a "Marxist-Leninist," and maintains close ties with Moscow.

CZECHOSLOVAKIA (THE CZECHOSLOVAK REPUBLIC). In form, a unitary republic with a cabinet-type government. The Constitution gives supreme power to the unicameral Parliament which elects a President for a seven-year term. The President formally appoints the Prime Minister and Cabinet, but these are responsible to Parliament. Actually, they are selected by the central committee of the Communist Party. By the use of Soviet-type elections, the Communists and a small group of collaborationist parties maintain solid control of Parliament. Between world wars, Czechoslovakia was a true parliamentary democracy.

DENMARK, KINGDOM OF. A unitary constitutional monarchy with cabinet-type government. Both houses of Parliament are chosen according to proportional representation. Members of the lower house are elected directly by voters over 25 years of age. One fourth of each new upper house is chosen by the outgoing upper house; the others are elected indirectly, through electoral colleges, by voters over 35 years of age. The Prime Minister and Cabinet are appointed formally by the King, but they are selected on the basis of a parliamentary majority. They are responsible to the lower house.

DOMINICAN REPUBLIC. A unitary republic with presidential-type government. The President and members of both houses of Congress are elected directly for five-year terms. In certain circumstances, specified in the constitution, the President may rule by decree without congressional action. The country has been afflicted with dictators, such as the late Rafael Trujillo, who sometimes hold the presidency and sometimes install a puppet President, but hold the command of the armed forces.

ECUADOR (REPUBLIC OF THE EQUATOR). A unitary republic with presidential-type government. There is a bicameral Congress. The President is elected for a four-year term and can not be reelected until an intervening term has elapsed. The country has been plagued by military seizures of power.

EGYPT (THE UNITED ARAB REPUBLIC). Virtually a dictatorship, Egypt was formerly a unitary republic with cabinet-type government. In 1954, Gamal Abdel Nasser seized power in a military *coup d'état*. In 1958, Syria was united with Egypt and the name became United Arab Republic. Syria has since seceded, but the name United Arab Republic is retained by Egypt. Nasser has abolished the elective parliament and substituted a "Council of the Nation," whose members he appoints. Political parties are prohibited. The President rules by decree. The ministers are responsible to him alone. Nasser's provisional constitution was approved in a plebiscite.

FINLAND, REPUBLIC OF. A unitary republic with presidential-type government. The President is elected indirectly through an electoral college for a six-year term. He appoints the Cabinet, which is responsible to him. Members of the unicameral Diet are elected for three-year terms by proportional representation.

GREECE, KINGDOM OF. A unitary constitutional monarchy with cabinet-type government. The popularly elected parliament is unicameral. The King is a mere ceremonial chief of state.

HAITI, REPUBLIC OF. A unitary republic with presidential-type government. Senators are elected for six-year terms, Deputies for four-year terms. More often than not, elections have been controlled by a dictator-president. The President is elected nominally by a two-thirds vote of the National Assembly, the two houses of parliament meeting jointly for the purpose. In practice, most presidents have seized power by a *coup d'état* and have then been confirmed by a subservient Assembly.

HONDURAS, REPUBLIC OF. A unitary republic with presidential-type government. The President and members of the unicameral Congress are popularly elected for six-year terms, and the President can not be reelected. The country has been characterized by political instability and internal disorder.

HUNGARY, REPUBLIC OF. Government follows Russian pattern in many respects. Formally, supreme power rests in a National Assembly of 298 members elected from 20 districts on single lists. A presidium exercises the functions of the Assembly between its brief sessions. In form, the Assembly enacts legislation and appoints and dismisses the ministers. The presidium, called the Presidential Council, consists of a President (who also acts as ceremonial chief of state), two vice presidents, and 17 members. The ministers, who are hand picked by the central committee of the Communist Party and can not be members of the Presidential Council, exercise all real power.

ICELAND, REPUBLIC OF. A unitary republic with cabinet-type government. The President, popularly elected for a four-year term, is only ceremonial chief of state. Members of the parliament, called the *Althing*, are elected under proportional representation, without indication of the house in which they are to serve. After the election, the members choose one third of their number as an upper house, the remaining members constituting the lower house. The Prime Minister and Cabinet, appointed formally by the President, are selected on the basis of a parliamentary majority and are responsible to the *Althing*. Elections occur when the Cabinet orders a dissolution of parliament.

INDIA, REPUBLIC OF. A quasi-federal republic of 28 component "states." The "states" are grouped into three classes. Classes A and B have considerable self government with elected legislatures and responsible ministries. Their governors, however, are appointed by the President (on nomination of the Prime Minister) and represent the central government, exercising a number of powers independently of their ministries; they may also reserve local laws for approval of the central government. India is a member of the British Commonwealth of Nations, recognizing the British monarch as "head of the Commonwealth," but not as sovereign of India. The President, a mere ceremonial chief of state, is elected for a five-year term by an electoral college consisting of all members of both houses of the National Parliament and all members of the state legislatures. The upper house of Parliament, called the Council of States, has 250 members who serve for six years, one third retiring every two years. Twelve are appointed by the President in recognition of preeminence in literature, the arts, science or business. The others are elected by an electoral college made up of members of the state legislatures. Members of the lower house, called the House of the People, are elected for five-year terms by universal suffrage. The government is of the cabinet type. The Prime Minister is formally appointed by the President, but is the leader of the political party with a majority in the House of the People. He chooses his own cabinet colleagues on a party basis and they are formally appointed by the President. In time of emergency, the central government may take over the rule of class A and B states. Class C states are governed regularly by representatives of the central government.

INDONESIA, REPUBLIC OF. In form, a unitary republic with a government that is a combination of cabinet and presidential types. Members of the unicameral parliament, called the House of Representatives, are elected under proportional representation for four-year terms. All persons over 18 years of age may vote. The Prime Minister and Cabinet are constitutionally responsible to the House of Representatives. However, the President is permitted by the constitution to dissolve the House, suspend the constitution and govern by decree. President Sukarno has done this so that, for the time being, Indonesia is a dictatorship.

IRAN, KINGDOM OF (*formerly* PERSIA). A unitary constitutional monarchy with cabinet-type government. Members of the lower house of the bicameral parliament are elected. One half of the Senators are elected and the other half are appointed by the Shah. The Prime Minister and Cabinet are responsible to parliament and may request the Shah to dissolve the lower house. The Shah (king) exercises more discretionary power than is usual in parliamentary monarchies.

IRELAND, REPUBLIC OF. A unitary republic with cabinet-type government. The President, a mere ceremonial chief of state, is directly elected for a seven-year term. The Prime Minister, who selects his own Cabinet, is appointed by the President on nomination of the *Dail Eireann* (lower house of Parliament) and is responsible to the *Dail*. He may "advise" the President to dissolve the *Dail* and call an election. Members of the *Dail* are popularly elected under proportional representation for maximum five-year terms. Of the sixty members of the Senate,

which has very limited powers, eleven are designated by the
Prime Minister, six by the universities, and forty-three by vocational groups. Ireland has withdrawn from the British Commonwealth of Nations, but still enjoys privileged relations
with Great Britain.

ISRAEL, REPUBLIC OF. A unitary republic with cabinet-type
government. The unicameral parliament, *the Knesset,* elects
the President for a five-year term. All citizens over 21 years
of age vote for members of the *Knesset.* The Prime Minister
and Cabinet, who are responsible to the *Knesset,* are selected
on the basis of party strength in parliament and are appointed
formally by the President.

JAPAN (NIPPON), EMPIRE OF. A unitary constitutional monarchy with some federal features (the prefectures now elect
their own officers and enjoy a large measure of local self-government). The Emperor has been reduced to a mere ceremonial chief of state. Members of the House of Councillors
are elected, 100 at large and 150 from the prefectures. The
powers of this house are limited in a manner similar to the
British House of Lords. Members of the House of Representatives are elected for four-year terms from small multi-member
districts in which the voter votes for one candidate only. This
provides a semblance of proportional representation. This bicameral Diet or parliament has complete legislative power except that, as in the United States, the Supreme Court can
declare its laws unconstitutional. The Diet nominates the
Prime Minister (one of its own members) who is formally
appointed by the Emperor, and who then selects the members
of his own Cabinet, a majority of whom must also be members of one house or other of the Diet. The ministers are
jointly responsible to the House of Representatives. On failure
to get a vote of confidence, they must either resign or have
the Emperor dissolve the House and call an election. All citizens over 20 years of age can vote.

LIBERIA, REPUBLIC OF. A unitary republic with presidential
type of government modeled consciously on that of the United
States. The President and Vice President are elected directly

for initial eight-year terms. They may be reelected indefinitely for four-year terms. Members of the House of Representatives are elected for four years, Senators for six years. Voters must be citizens 21 years of age, belong to the Negro race, and pay a small tax. Some tribal chiefs from the interior are *ex officio* members of the House of Representatives.

LIBYA, KINGDOM OF. A federal constitutional monarchy with three self-governing provinces. Half of the Senators are named by the King, half by the provincial legislatures. Members of the House of Representatives are elected on the basis of one for each 20,000 inhabitants. The Prime Minister and Cabinet are responsible to Parliament.

MEXICO (THE UNITED MEXICAN STATES). A federal republic with presidential type of government. Each of the 29 member states has its own constitution, with elective governor, legislature and courts. The President is elected directly for a six-year term, and may not succeed himself. The Federal Congress is bicameral. The Senators, two from each state and the Federal District, are elected for six-year terms. Members of the lower house are elected for three-year terms. Married men over 18, and women and unmarried men over 21, may vote. Since the revolution of 1910-1920, Mexico has maintained political stability and made great economic progress.

MOROCCO, KINGDOM OF. Instead of an adopted constitution, Morocco has a charter granted by the King. It provides for a Deliberative Assembly, whose members are elected by the rural and municipal councils, which shares legislative power with the King. The rural and municipal councils are popularly elected under a restricted suffrage and have limited powers of local self-government. The King also acts as prime minister, and the ministers are responsible to him alone.

NETHERLANDS, KINGDOM OF. A unitary constitutional monarchy with some traces of its former federal character. The upper house of Parliament, whose members are elected for six-year terms by the provincial assemblies, can not introduce bills or amend those passed by the lower house; it can only approve or reject them. Members of the lower house are elected directly in single-member districts for four-year terms. The Premier and Cabinet can not be members of Parliament, but may speak in either house. They are appointed formally by the monarch, but are selected on the basis of party strength in the lower house of Parliament, and are responsible to the lower house. The provinces have legislative assemblies with limited power.

NICARAGUA, REPUBLIC OF. A unitary republic with presidential-type of government. The President and members of both houses of Congress are elected for six-year terms. Former Presidents are *ex officio* Senators for life. Seizures of power by *coup d'état* have occurred on a number of occasions.

NORWAY, KINGDOM OF. A constitutional monarchy with modified cabinet-type government. The parliament, called the *Shorthing*, has 150 members elected under proportional representation. On political and financial matters, it meets and votes as a single body. For other legislative business, it divides into two houses: the *Lagsthing*, with 38 members, and the *Odelsthing* with 112 members. All legislation must originate in the larger body. If the upper house rejects a bill, it may be repassed by the lower. If it is then rejected again by the *Lagsthing*, the two groups meet as a single body to act on it; a two-thirds majority is then necessary for passage. The Prime Minister and Cabinet are selected in the usual way in cabinet-type governments, and are responsible to the *Shorthing*. They can not, however, have the King dissolve parliament. Voting age is 23.

PAKISTAN, REPUBLIC OF. For several years, Pakistan has been ruled by a dictatorship under a President who seized power in a military *coup d'état*. He has promised to write a new constitution and restore constitutional government in the near future. Under the old constitution there was a unicameral National Assembly whose members, equally divided between East and West Pakistan, were popularly elected for five-year terms. The President was elected for a five-year term by members of the National Assembly and the provincial legislatures. The government was of the cabinet type, with the Prime

Minister and Cabinet responsible to the National Assembly. East and West Pakistan are nearly equal in population, but differ greatly in area. They are separated by territory of India. Pakistan is a member of the British Commonwealth of Nations.

PANAMA, REPUBLIC OF. A unitary republic with presidential-type government. The President is elected directly for a four-year term and may not succeed himself. The two vice presidents and members of the unicameral National Assembly are also elected directly for four-year terms. All citizens over 21 years of age may vote.

PARAGUAY, REPUBLIC OF. A unitary republic with presidential-type government. The President is elected by direct popular vote for a five-year term. There is an elective Congress or lower house, and a Council of State, whose members are designated by the President. The Cabinet is appointed by the President and is responsible to him alone. The President and Cabinet may legislate by decree, merely informing the Congress and the Council of State of their actions. Most presidents have seized power by *coup d'état* and had their positions confirmed in controlled elections.

PERU, REPUBLIC OF. A unitary republic with a presidential-type government. According to the constitution, the President, two Vice Presidents, and members of both houses of Congress are elected by popular vote for six-year terms. The President may not succeed himself. The Cabinet, though headed by a Prime Minister, is appointed by and responsible to the President. In practice, most presidents have been deposed by military uprisings and new presidents "proclaimed" by the military *junta*.

PHILIPPINES, REPUBLIC OF THE. Except that it is unitary instead of federal, the government of the Philippines is modeled closely on that of the United States. The President, Vice President, and members of both the Senate and the House of Representatives are elected directly under universal adult suffrage. The courts follow the American model closely. As in the United States, the Cabinet is responsible to the President alone and has no direct contact with Congress. The powers of the President and Congress in relation to each other are almost exactly the same as in the United States.

POLAND, PEOPLE'S REPUBLIC OF. Government arrangements, in general, follow the model of the Soviet Union. In form, supreme power is vested in a unicameral assembly, the *Sejm*, whose members are elected for four-year terms by the vote of all citizens over 18 years of age. Soviet-type elections insure solid Communist control. A Council of State, equivalent to the Presidium of the Supreme Soviet in the Soviet Union, exercises legislative power between the brief sessions of the *Sejm*, and its Chairman acts as ceremonial chief of state. The Prime Minister and other ministers are officially designated by the *Sejm* and are responsible to it. In practice, the central committee of the Communist Party dictates to all organs of government. The head of this committee, Wladyslaw Gomulka, is virtual dictator. He has managed to maintain more independence of Russian control than the rulers of most of the satellite states.

PORTUGAL (THE PORTUGUESE REPUBLIC). In form, a constitutional republic, but actually a dictatorship under Premier Salazar. The parliament consists of a National Assembly, with members popularly elected for four-year terms, and a Corporative Chamber which represents economic groupings. The Premier, who selects his own Cabinet which is not responsible to Parliament, is nominally appointed by the President. The President is elected for a seven-year term by an electoral college which consists of members of both chambers of Parliament and representatives of the metropolitan districts. Salazar controls all elections by finding devious ways of eliminating all candidates opposed to his followers. Thus he hand picks the President, who becomes a mere figurehead and ceremonial chief of state.

RUMANIA, PEOPLE'S REPUBLIC OF. Rumania has the government arrangements that are usual in the Russian satellite states. Nominally, supreme power is vested in a popularly elected National Assembly, but single candidate elections insure solid

Communist control. The functions of the Assembly are exercised by a Presidium between its brief sessions, and the Chairman of the Presidium acts as ceremonial chief of state. The Prime Minister and Cabinet are formally elected by the Assembly and are technically responsible to it. In reality, though, they are puppets of the central committee of the Communist Party which holds all real power and dictates to all organs of government.

SALVADOR, EL, REPUBLIC OF. A unitary republic with presidential-type government. The constitution provides that the President be elected for a six-year term by direct popular vote and be ineligible to succeed himself, and that members of the unicameral legislature be popularly elected for two-year terms. In practice, the constitution is seldom followed. Most presidents have seized power by military force and been deposed in the same manner. They usually suspend the legislature, along with the constitutional guarantees, and rule as dictators.

SAUDI ARABIA, KINGDOM OF. One of the few remaining absolute monarchies. The King legislates by decree. He appoints the Prime Minister and Council of Ministers, who are responsible to him alone. There is no legislature and there are no elections.

SOUTH AFRICA, REPUBLIC OF. A quasi-federal republic of four provinces. Until 1961, it was a member of the British Commonwealth of Nations under the name of Union of South Africa. It had as its titular chief of state a Governor General representing the British monarch. At that time, it withdrew from the Commonwealth, declared itself a republic, and substituted a President, chosen by the Parliament, for the Governor General. The provinces have their own constitutions and legislatures, but their acts can be overridden by the central government. Government at both levels is of the cabinet type, the ministers being members of Parliament and responsible to it. Formally, the Prime Minister and Cabinet are appointed by the President, but, as in Great Britain, the Prime Minister is the parliamentary leader of the majority party in Parliament and selects his own cabinet colleagues. Members of both houses of the bicameral Parliament are popularly elected by the white citizens; Senators for a maximum ten-year term and members of the House of Assembly for maximum five-year terms. A dissolution of parliament applies to both houses.

SPAIN. Nominally a kingless kingdom, but actually a dictatorship with Fascistic background under Francisco Franco. Franco has the tile of *Caudillo* (leader) and combines the roles of chief of state, prime minister, and head of the Falange Party, the only political party permitted by law. He appoints the Cabinet, which is responsible to him alone. He may legislate by decree. A unicameral *Cortes* or parliament, elected under a restricted suffrage in controlled elections, may formulate legislation, but the *Caudillo* has an absolute veto on its acts. Under a succession law, drafted by Franco and approved in a plebiscite, a Council of the Realm is to be set up at Franco's death or complete incapacity, which is to elect a king, but Franco reserves the right to designate his own successor.

SWEDEN, KINGDOM OF. A unitary constitutional monarchy which a recent King called a "crowned republic." Government is of the cabinet type, with the King a mere ceremonial chief of state. The parliament, called the *Riksdag*, is bicameral, the two houses having essentially the same powers. All standing committees are joint committees of the two houses. The members of the upper house are elected by the provincial assemblies for eight-year terms, rotated so that one eighth are elected each year. The members of the lower house are elected directly under proportional representation for four-year terms. Voters in elections of the provincial assemblies must be 27 years of age and own a small amount of property. All citizens 23 years of age or over may vote in electing members of the lower house. The Prime Minister and Cabinet, appointed formally by the King but selected on the party basis that is usual in cabinet-governed countries, are responsible to both houses of the *Riksdag* equally. However, because of a permanent coalition of the two major parties, Socialist and Agrarian, no-confidence votes forcing a resignation of the Cabinet are rare and dissolutions of parliament, though permissible, never occur.

SWITZERLAND (THE SWISS CONFEDERATION). A true federal union of 25 cantons, each with its own constitution and government. Some of the smaller cantons are direct democracies, with the functions of a legislature performed by a meeting of citizens. Another feature of direct democracy at all levels of government is the initiative and referendum. Members of the Council of States, the upper house of the bicameral parliament, are apportioned two to each canton (like United States Senators) and are elected in such manner and for such terms as the canton constitution provides. Members of the lower chamber, or National Council, are elected under proportional representation for four-year terms. All male citizens over 20 years of age may vote. Switzerland is one of the few remaining countries where women may not vote. The executive is a board of seven members, elected by a joint session of the two chambers after each general election, called the Federal Council. It is not responsible to parliament in the sense of having to resign if no-confidence is voted. It may dissolve the National Council, but almost never does. The Federal Council elects its own chairman, who has the title President of the Swiss Confederation and acts as ceremonial chief of state. He has no individual discretionary powers. The Federal Council apportions ministries among its own members. There is no position that really corresponds to a prime minister.

TUNISIA, REPUBLIC OF. A unitary republic with presidential-type government. The President is popularly elected for a five-year term and may be reelected for two additional terms. The unicameral National Assembly is elected by universal adult suffrage. The President appoints the Cabinet, which is responsible to him alone.

TURKEY, REPUBLIC OF. A unitary republic with cabinet-type government. In 1960, a military *coup d'état* suspended the constitution and set up a provisional regime, but the country is now in the process of returning to constitutional government. According to the constitution, supreme power rests in a unicameral Grand National Assembly whose members are elected for four-year terms by all citizens over 21 years of age. The Assembly elects one of its members as President for a four-year term. The Prime Minister, who is the real chief executive, is appointed by the President and confirmed by the Assembly. He in turn appoints the other ministers who, along with him, are jointly and individually responsible to the Assembly. A Council of State, whose members are designated by the Prime Minister, replaces the Cabinet as the advisory body on matters of general national policy. A "High Tribunal" of fifteen members, drawn from the Court of Cassation (Supreme Court) and the Council of State, may be set up to try impeachments.

URUGUAY, REPUBLIC EAST OF THE. A unitary republic with its government modeled on the Swiss. This little country has long been noted for political, social and economic experimentation. It was one of the first countries to establish bipartisan government on a permanent basis. One of its peculiarities is that it permits a foreigner to become a naturalized Uruguayan citizen without giving up his former citizenship. For many decades, it had elected presidents, but too many of them seized dictatorial power. To end this possibility, the present constitution vests the executive power in a National Council of nine members, six from the majority party and three from the minority party, elected for simultaneous four-year terms by the two houses of Congress meeting in joint session. The Presidency is rotated annually among the majority party members of the Council. As in Switzerland, the President presides over the Council and acts as ceremonial chief of state, but has no individual discretionary powers. The Council members allot the ministries among themselves; there is no separate Cabinet, and the Council is not responsible to Congress in the sense of having to resign if denied a vote of confidence. Members of the Senate and Chamber of Deputies are elected by direct popular vote for four-year terms. Congress appoints a special tribunal of five members to arbitrate disputes between the National Council and Congress.

VENEZUELA, REPUBLIC OF. A unitary republic with presidential-type government. The President is directly elected for a five-year term. He appoints the Cabinet which is responsible to him alone. Members of both houses of Congress are elected directly by universal suffrage. For many decades, the country alternated between periods of dictatorship and disorder. More recently, despite an occasional *coup d'état*, constitutional government appears to be working more smoothly.

YUGOSLAVIA (FEDERAL UNION OF YUGOSLAV REPUBLICS). Officially, a federal republic of six "states," though in practice Communist Party control negates true federalism. Legislative power, in most matters, is vested in a Federal Council of 352 members: 282 elected by universal suffrage, and 70 chosen by the councils of the member "states." On legislation affecting federal relations, these 70 act separately as a Council of Nationalities. There is a second chamber, the Producers Council, representing occupational groups, but its powers are limited. An Executive Council of 37, headed by the President of the Republic, is elected by, and is nominally responsible to, the Federal Council. It has full executive powers. Administration is organized into five secretariats without cabinet status. In practice, President Josip Broz (Tito), as head of the Communist Party, controls all organs of government and so is a virtual dictator. In elections, opposition candidates are permitted, but seldom appear. Although Communist, Tito has been able to achieve independence of Russian control, so that Yugoslavia is not regarded as one of the satellite states.

The Declaration of Independence[†]

In Congress, July 4, 1776

THE UNANIMOUS DECLARATION OF THE THIRTEEN UNITED STATES OF AMERICA

When, in the Course of human events, it becomes necessary for one people to dissolve the political bands which have connected them with another, and to assume among the powers of the earth, the separate and equal station to which the Laws of Nature and of Nature's God entitle them, a decent respect to the opinions of mankind requires that they should declare the causes which impel them to the separation.

We hold these truths to be self-evident, that all men are created equal, that they are endowed by their Creator with certain unalienable Rights, that among these, are Life, Liberty, and the pursuit of Happiness. That, to secure these rights, Governments are instituted among Men, deriving their just powers from the consent of the governed, that, whenever any Form of Government becomes destructive of these ends, it is the Right of the People to alter or to abolish it, and to institute new Government, laying its foundation on such principles, and organizing its powers in such form, as to them shall seem most likely to effect their Safety and Happiness. Prudence, indeed, will dictate that Governments long established, should not be changed for light and transient causes; and, accordingly, all experience hath shewn, that mankind are more disposed to suffer, while evils are sufferable, than to right themselves by abolishing the forms to which they are accustomed. But, when a long train of abuses and usurpations, pursuing invariably the same Object, evinces a design to reduce them under absolute Despotism, it is their right, it is their duty, to throw off such Government and to provide new Guards for their future security.—Such has been the patient sufferance of these Colonies; and such is now the necessity which constrains them to alter their former Systems of Government. The history of the present King of Great Britain is a history of repeated injuries and usurpations, all having in direct object the estab-

---

† *Spelling and capitalization follow the parchment copy.*

lishment of an absolute Tyranny over these States. To prove this, let Facts be submitted to a candid world.—

He has refused his Assent to Laws the most wholesome and necessary for the public good.

He has forbidden his Governors to pass Laws of immediate and pressing importance, unless suspended in their operation till his Assent should be obtained; and when so suspended, he has utterly neglected to attend to them.

He has refused to pass other laws for the accommodation of large districts of people, unless those people would relinquish the right of Representation in the Legislature; a right inestimable to them and formidable to tyrants only.

He has called together legislative bodies at places unusual, uncomfortable, and distant from the depository of their public Records, for the sole purpose of fatiguing them into compliance with his measures.

He has dissolved Representative Houses repeatedly, for opposing with manly firmness his invasions on the rights of the people.

He has refused for a long time, after such dissolutions, to cause others to be elected; whereby the Legislative powers, incapable of Annihilation, have returned to the People at large for their exercise; the State remaining, in the meantime, exposed to all the dangers of invasion from without, and convulsions within.

He has endeavored to prevent the population of these States; for that purpose, obstructing the Laws for Naturalization of Foreigners; refusing to pass others to encourage their migrations hither, and raising the conditions of new Appropriations of Lands.

He has obstructed the Administration of Justice, by refusing his Assent to Laws for establishing Judiciary powers.

He has made Judges dependent on his Will alone, for the tenure of their offices, and the amount and payment of their salaries.

He has erected a multitude of New Offices, and sent hither swarms of Officers to harass our people, and eat out their substance.

He has kept among us, in times of peace, Standing Armies, without the Consent of our legislatures.

He has affected to render the Military independent of, and superior to, the Civil power.

He has combined, with others, to subject us to a jurisdiction foreign to our constitution, and unacknowledged by our laws; giving his Assent to their Acts of pretended Legislation:

For quartering large bodies of armed troops among us:

For protecting them by a mock Trial, from punishment, for any Murders which they should commit on the Inhabitants of these States:

For cutting off our Trade with all parts of the world:

For imposing Taxes on us without our Consent:

For depriving us, in many cases, of the benefits of Trial by Jury:

For transporting us beyond Seas to be tried for pretended offenses:

For abolishing the free System of English Laws in a neighboring Province, establishing therein an Arbitrary government, and enlarging its Boundaries, so as to render it at once an example and fit instrument for introducing the same absolute rule into these Colonies:

For taking away our Charters, abolishing our most valuable Laws, and altering, fundamentally, the Forms of our Governments:

For suspending our own Legislatures, and declaring themselves invested with power to legislate for us in all cases whatsoever.

He has abdicated Government here, by declaring us out of his Protection, and waging War against us.

He has plundered our seas, ravaged our Coasts, burnt our towns, and destroyed the lives our our people.

He is, at this time, transporting large Armies of foreign Mercenaries to compleat the works of death, desolation, and tyranny, already begun with circumstances of Cruelty & perfidy scarcely paralleled in the most barbarous ages, and totally unworthy the Head of a civilized nation.

He has constrained our fellow Citizens, taken Captive on the high Seas, to bear Arms against their Country, to become the executioners of their friends and Brethren, or to fall themselves by their Hands.

He has excited domestic insurrections amongst us, and has endeavored to bring on the inhabitants of our frontiers, the merciless Indian Savages, whose known rule of warfare, is an undistinguished destruction of all ages, sexes and conditions.

In every stage of these Oppressions, We have Petitioned for Redress, in the most humble terms; our repeated Petitions have been answered only by repeated injury. A Prince, whose character is thus marked by every act which may define a Tyrant, is unfit to be the ruler of a free people.

Nor have we been wanting in attentions to our British brethren. We have warned them, from time to time, of attempts made by their legislature to extend an unwarrantable jurisdiction over us. We have reminded them of the circumstances of our emigration and settlement here. We have appealed to their native justice and magnanimity, and we have conjured them by the ties of our common kindred to disavow these usurpations, which would inevitably interrupt our connections and correspondence. They too have been deaf to the voice of justice and of consanguinity. We must, therefore, acquiesce in the necessity, which denounces our Separation, and hold them, as we hold the rest of mankind, Enemies in War, in Peace Friends.

We, therefore, the Representatives of the united States of America, in General Congress, Assembled, appealing to the Supreme Judge of the world for the rectitude of our intentions, do, in the Name, and by Authority of the good People of these Colonies, solemnly publish and declare, That these United Colonies are, and of Right ought to be, Free and Independent States; that they are Absolved from all Allegiance to the British Crown, and that all political connection between them and the State of Great Britain is, and ought to be, totally dissolved: and that, as Free and Independent States, they have full Power to levy War, conclude Peace, contract Alliances, establish Commerce, and to do all other Acts and Things which Independent States may of right do. And, for the support of this Declaration, with a firm reliance on the protection of divine Providence, we mutually pledge to each other our Lives, our Fortunes, and our sacred Honor.

The foregoing Declaration was, by order of Congress, engrossed, and signed by the following members:

John Hancock

NEW HAMPSHIRE
  Josiah Bartlett
  William Whipple
  Matthew Thornton
MASSACHUSETTS BAY
  Samuel Adams
  John Adams
  Robert Treat Paine
  Elbridge Gerry
RHODE ISLAND
  Stephen Hopkins
  William Ellery
CONNECTICUT
  Roger Sherman
  Samuel Huntington
  William Williams
  Oliver Wolcott
NEW YORK
  William Floyd
  Philip Livingston
  Francis Lewis
  Lewis Morris
NEW JERSEY
  Richard Stockton
  John Witherspoon

  Francis Hopkinson
  John Hart
  Abraham Clark
PENNSYLVANIA
  Robert Morris
  Benjamin Rush
  Benjamin Franklin
  John Morton
  George Clymer
  James Smith
  George Taylor
  James Wilson
  George Ross
DELAWARE
  Caesar Rodney
  George Read
  Thomas M'Kean
MARYLAND
  Samuel Chase
  William Paca
  Thomas Stone
  Charles Carroll, of Carrollton
VIRGINIA
  George Wythe
  Richard Henry Lee

Thomas Jefferson
Benjamin Harrison
Thomas Nelson, Jr.
Francis Lightfoot Lee
Carter Braxton
NORTH CAROLINA
William Hooper
Joseph Hewes
John Penn

SOUTH CAROLINA
Edward Rutledge
Thomas Heyward, Jr.
Thomas Lynch, Jr.
Arthur Middleton
GEORGIA
Button Gwinnett
Lyman Hall
George Walton

RESOLVED, That copies of the Declaration be sent to the several assemblies, conventions, and committees, or councils of safety, and to the several commanding officers of the continental troops; that it be proclaimed in each of the united States, at the head of the army.

The Constitution of the United States[†]

We the People of the United States, in Order to form a more perfect Union, establish Justice, insure domestic Tranquility, provide for the common defence, promote the general Welfare, and secure the Blessings of Liberty to ourselves and our Posterity, do ordain and establish this CONSTITUTION for the United States of America.

ARTICLE. I.

Section. 1. All legislative Powers herein granted shall be vested in a Congress of the United States, which shall consist of a Senate and House of Representatives.

Section. 2. The House of Representatives shall be composed of Members chosen every second Year by the People of the several States, and the Electors in each State shall have the Qualifications requisite for Electors of the most numerous Branch of the State Legislature.

No Person shall be a Representative who shall not have attained to the Age of twenty-five Years, and been seven Years a Citizen of the United States, and who shall not, when elected, be an Inhabitant of that State in which he shall be chosen.

[Representatives and direct Taxes shall be apportioned among the several States which may be included within this Union, according to their respective Numbers, which shall be determined by adding to the whole Number of free Persons, including those bound to Service for a Term of Years, and excluding Indians not taxed, three fifths of all other Persons.] [‡] The actual Enumeration shall be made within three Years after the first Meeting of the Congress of the United States, and within every subsequent Term of ten Years, in such Manner as they shall by Law direct. The Number of Representatives shall not exceed one for every thirty Thousand, but each State shall have at Least one Representa-

---

[†] *This text of the Constitution follows the engrossed copy signed by Gen. Washington and the deputies from 12 States. The superior number preceding the paragraphs designates the number of the clause; it was not in the original.*

[‡] *Changed by section 2 of the 14th Amendment.*

281

tive; and until such enumeration shall be made, the State of New Hampshire shall be entitled to chuse three, Massachusetts eight, Rhode-Island and Providence Plantations one, Connecticut five, New-York six, New Jersey four, Pennsylvania eight, Delaware one, Maryland six, Virginia ten, North Carolina five, South Carolina five, and Georgia three.

When vacancies happen in the Representation from any State, the Executive Authority thereof shall issue Writs of Election to fill such Vacancies.

The House of Representatives shall chuse their Speaker and other Officers; and shall have the sole Power of Impeachment.

Section. 3. The Senate of the United States shall be composed of two Senators from each State, [chosen by the Legislature thereof,] † for six Years; and each Senator shall have one Vote.

Immediately after they shall be assembled in Consequence of the first Election, they shall be divided as equally as may be into three Classes. The Seats of the Senators of the first Class shall be vacated at the Expiration of the second Year, of the second Class at the Expiration of the fourth Year, and of the third Class at the Expiration of the sixth Year, so that one-third may be chosen every second Year; [and if Vacancies happen by Resignation, or otherwise, during the Recess of the Legislature of any State, the Executive thereof may make temporary Appointments until the next Meeting of the Legislature, which shall then fill such Vacancies].‡

No Person shall be a Senator who shall not have attained to the Age of thirty Years, and been nine Years a Citizen of the United States, and who shall not, when elected, be an Inhabitant of that State for which he shall be chosen.

The Vice President of the United States shall be President of the Senate, but shall have no vote, unless they be equally divided.

The Senate shall chuse their other Officers, and also a President pro tempore, in the absence of the Vice President, or when he shall exercise the Office of President of the United States.

The Senate shall have the sole Power to try all Impeachments. When sitting for that purpose, they shall be on Oath or Affirmation. When the President of the United States is tried, the Chief Justice shall preside: And no person shall be convicted without the Concurrence of two thirds of the Members present.

Judgment in Cases of Impeachment shall not extend further than to removal from Office, and disqualification to hold and enjoy any Office of honor, Trust, or Profit under the United States: but the Party convicted shall nevertheless be liable and subject to Indictment, Trial, Judgment, and Punishment, according to Law.

Section. 4. The Times, Places and Manner of holding Elections for Senators and Representatives, shall be prescribed in each State by the Legislature thereof;

---

† *Changed by section 1 of the 17th Amendment.*
‡ *Changed by clause 2 of the 17th Amendment.*

but the Congress may at any time by Law make or alter such Regulations; except as to the Places of Chusing Senators.

The Congress shall assemble at least once in every Year, and such Meeting shall [be on the first Monday in December,] † unless they shall by Law appoint a different Day.

Section. 5. Each House shall be the Judge of the Elections, Returns and Qualifications of its own Members, and a Majority of each shall constitute a Quorum to do Business; but a small number may adjourn from day to day, and may be authorized to compel the Attendance of absent Members, in such Manner, and under such Penalties, as each House may provide.

Each House may determine the Rules of its Proceedings, punish its Members for disorderly Behavior, and, with the Concurrence of two thirds, expel a Member.

Each House shall keep a Journal of its Proceedings, and from time to time publish the same, excepting such Parts as may in their Judgment require Secrecy; and the Yeas and Nays of the Members of either House on any question shall, at the Desire of one fifth of those Present, be entered on the Journal.

Neither House, during the Session of Congress, shall, without the Consent of the other, adjourn for more than three days, nor to any other Place than that in which the two Houses shall be sitting.

Section. 6. The Senators and Representatives shall receive a Compensation for their Services, to be ascertained by Law, and paid out of the Treasury of the United States. They shall in all Cases, except Treason, Felony, and Breach of the Peace, be privileged from Arrest during their Attendance at the Session of their respective Houses, and in going to and returning from the same; and for any Speech or Debate in either House, they shall not be questioned in any other Place.

No Senator or Representative shall, during the Time for which he was elected, be appointed to any civil Office under the Authority of the United States, which shall have been created, or the Emoluments whereof shall have been increased, during such time; and no Person holding any Office under the United States shall be a Member of either House during his continuance in Office.

Section. 7. All Bills for raising Revenue shall originate in the House of Representatives; but the Senate may propose or concur with Amendments on other bills.

Every Bill which shall have passed the House of Representatives and the Senate, shall, before it become a law, be presented to the President of the United States; If he approve he shall sign it, but if not he shall return it, with his Objections, to that House in which it shall have originated, who shall enter the Objections at large on their Journal, and proceed to reconsider it. If after such Reconsideration two thirds of that House shall agree to pass the bill, it shall be sent, together with the objections, to the other House, by which it shall likewise be reconsidered, and if approved by two thirds of that House, it shall become a

† *Changed by section 2 of the 20th Amendment.*

Law. But in all such Cases the Votes of both Houses shall be determined by Yeas and Nays, and the Names of the Persons voting for and against the Bill shall be entered on the Journal of each House respectively. If any Bill shall not be returned by the President within ten Days (Sundays excepted) after it shall have been presented to him, the Same shall be a Law, in like Manner as if he had signed it, unless the Congress by their Adjournment prevent its Return, in which Case it shall not be a Law.

Every Order, Resolution, or Vote to which the Concurrence of the Senate and House of Representatives may be necessary (except on a question of Adjournment) shall be presented to the President of the United States; and before the Same shall take Effect, shall be approved by him, or being disapproved by him, shall be repassed by two thirds of the senate and House of Representatives, according to the Rules and Limitations prescribed in the Case of a Bill.

Section. 8. The Congress shall have Power To lay and collect Taxes, Duties, Imposts and Excises, to pay the Debts and provide for the common Defence and general Welfare of the United States; but all Duties, Imposts and Excises shall be uniform throughout the United States;

To borrow money on the credit of the United States;

To regulate Commerce with foreign Nations, and among the several States, and with the Indian Tribes;

To establish an uniform Rule of Naturalization, and uniform Laws on the subject of Bankruptcies throughout the United States;

To coin Money, regulate the Value thereof, and of foreign Coin, and fix the Standard of Weights and Measures;

To provide for the Punishment of counterfeiting the Securities and current Coin of the United States;

To establish Post Offices and post Roads;

To promote the Progress of Science and useful Arts, by securing for limited Times to Authors and Inventors the exclusive Right to their respective Writings and Discoveries;

To constitute Tribunals inferior to the Supreme Court;

To define and punish Piracies and Felonies committed on the high Seas, and Offenses against the Law of Nation ,

To declare War, grant Letters of Marque and Reprisal, and make Rules concerning Captures on Land and Water;

To raise and support Armies, but no Appropriation of Money to that Use shall be for a longer Term than two Years;

To provide and maintain a Navy;

To make Rules for the Government and Regulation of the land and naval forces;

To provide for calling forth the Militia to execute the Laws of the Union, suppress Insurrections and repel Invasions;

To provide for organizing, arming, and disciplining the Militia, and for governing such Part of them as may be employed in the Service of the United States, reserving to the States respectively, the Appointment of the Officers, and the Authority of training the Militia according to the discipline prescribed by Congress;

To exercise exclusive Legislation in all Cases whatsoever, over such District (not exceeding ten Miles square) as may, by Cession of particular States, and the acceptance of Congress, become the Seat of the Government of the United States, and to exercise like Authority over all Places purchased by the Consent of the Legislature of the State in which the Same shall be, for the Erection of Forts, Magazines, Arsenals, dock-Yards, and other needful Buildings;—And

To make all Laws which shall be necessary and proper for carrying into Execution the foregoing Powers, and all other Powers vested by this Constitution in the Government of the United States, or in any Department or Officer thereof.

Section. 9. The Migration or Importation of such Persons as any of the States now existing shall think proper to admit, shall not be prohibited by the Congress prior to the Year one thousand eight hundred and eight, but a tax or duty may be imposed on such Importation, not exceeding ten dollars for each Person.

The privilege of the Writ of Habeas Corpus shall not be suspended, unless when in Cases of Rebellion or Invasion the public Safety may require it.

No Bill of Attainder or ex post facto Law shall be passed.

† No capitation, or other direct, Tax shall be laid unless in Proportion to the Census or Enumeration herein before directed to be taken.

No Tax or Duty shall be laid on Articles exported from any State.

No Preference shall be given by any Regulation of Commerce or Revenue to the Ports of one State over those of another: nor shall Vessels bound to, or from, one State, be obliged to enter, clear, or pay Duties in another.

No Money shall be drawn from the Treasury, but in Consequence of Appropriations made by Law; and a regular Statement and Account of the Receipts and Expenditures of all public Money shall be published from time to time.

No Title of Nobility shall be granted by the United States: And no Person holding any Office of Profit or Trust under them, shall, without the Consent of the Congress, accept of any present, Emolument, Office, or Title, of any kind whatever, from any King, Prince, or foreign State.

Section. 10. No State shall enter into any Treaty, Alliance, or Confederation; grant Letters of Marque and Reprisal; coin Money; emit Bills of Credit; make any Thing but gold and silver Coin or Tender in Payment of Debts; pass any Bill of Attainder, ex post facto Law, or Law impairing the Obligation of Contracts, or grant any Title of Nobility.

No State shall, without the Consent of the Congress, lay any Imposts or Duties on Imports or Exports, except what may be absolutely necessary for executing its

† *See also the 16th Amendment.*

inspection Laws: and the net Produce of all Duties and Imposts, laid by any State on Imports or Exports, shall be for the Use of the Treasury of the United States; and all such Laws shall be subject to the Revision and Control of the Congress.

No State shall, without the Consent of Congress, lay any duty of Tonnage, keep Troops, or Ships of War in time of Peace, enter into any Agreement or Compact with another State, or with a foreign Power, or engage in War, unless actually invaded, or in such imminent Danger as will not admit of delay.

ARTICLE. II.

Section. 1. The executive Power shall be vested in a President of the United States of America. He shall hold his Office during the Term of four years, and, together with the Vice-President, chosen for the same Term, be elected, as follows:

Each State shall appoint, in such Manner as the Legislature thereof may direct, a Number of Electors, equal to the whole Number of Senators and Representatives to which the State may be entitled in the Congress: but no Senator or Representative, or Person holding an Office of Trust or Profit under the United States, shall be appointed an Elector.

[The Electors shall meet in their respective States, and vote by Ballot for two persons, of whom one at least shall not be an Inhabitant of the same State with themselves. And they shall make a List of all the Persons voted for, and of the Number of Votes for each; which List they shall sign and certify, and transmit sealed to the Seat of the Government of the United States, directed to the President of the Senate. The President of the Senate shall, in the Presence of the Senate and House of Representatives, open all the Certificates, and the Votes shall then be counted. The Person having the greatest Number of Votes shall be the President, if such Number be a Majority of the whole Number of Electors appointed; and if there be more than one who have such Majority, and have an equal Number of Votes, then the House of Representatives shall immediately chuse by Ballot one of them for President; and if no Person have a Majority, then from the five highest on the List the said House shall in like Manner chuse the President. But in chusing the President, the Votes shall be taken by States, the Representation from each State having one Vote; a quorum for this Purpose shall consist of a Member or Members from two-thirds of the States, and a Majority of all the States shall be necessary to a Choice. In every Case, after the Choice of the President, the Person having the greatest Number of Votes of the Electors shall be the Vice President. But if there should remain two or more who have equal votes, the Senate shall chuse from them by Ballot the Vice-President.] †

The Congress may determine the Time of chusing the Electors, and the Day

---

† *Superseded by the 12th Amendment.*

on which they shall give their Votes; which Day shall be the same throughout the United States.

No person except a natural-born Citizen, or a Citizen of the United States, at the time of the Adoption of this Constitution, shall be eligible to the Office of President; neither shall any Person be eligible to that Office who shall not have attained to the Age of thirty-five years, and been fourteen Years a Resident within the United States.

In Case of the Removal of the President from Office, or of his Death, Resignation, or Inability to discharge the Powers and Duties of the said Office, the same shall devolve on the Vice President, and the Congress may by Law provide for the Case of Removal, Death, Resignation, or Inability, both of the President and Vice President, declaring what Officer shall then act as President, and such Officer shall act accordingly, until the disability be removed, or a President shall be elected.

The President shall, at stated Times, receive for his Services a Compensation, which shall neither be increased nor diminished during the Period for which he shall have been elected, and he shall not receive within that Period any other Emolument from the United States, or any of them.

Before he enter on the execution of his Office, he shall take the following Oath or Affirmation:—"I do solemnly swear (or affirm) that I will faithfully execute the Office of President of the United States, and will, to the best of my Ability, preserve, protect, and defend the Constitution of the United States."

Section. 2. The President shall be Commander in Chief of the Army and Navy of the United States, and of the Militia of the several States, when called into the actual Service of the United States; he may require the Opinion, in writing, of the principal Officer in each of the executive Departments, upon any subject relating to the Duties of their respective Offices, and he shall have Power to Grant Reprieves and Pardons for Offenses against the United States, except in Cases of Impeachment.

He shall have Power, by and with the Advice and Consent of the Senate, to make Treaties, provided two thirds of the Senators present concur; and he shall nominate, and by and with the Advice and Consent of the Senate, shall appoint Ambassadors, other public Ministers and Consuls, Judges of the supreme Court, and all other Officers of the United States, whose Appointments are not herein otherwise provided for, and which shall be established by Law: but the Congress may by Law vest the Appointment of such inferior Officers, as they think proper, in the President alone, in the Courts of Law, or in the Heads of Departments.

The President shall have Power to fill up all Vacancies that may happen during the Recess of the Senate, by granting Commissions which shall expire at the End of their next Session.

Section. 3. He shall from time to time give to the Congress Information of the State of the Union, and recommend to their Consideration such Measures as he shall judge necessary and expedient; he may, on extraordinary occasions, convene both Houses, or either of them, and in Case of Disagreement between them, with respect to the Time of Adjournment, he may adjourn them to such Time as he shall think proper; he shall receive Ambassadors and other public Ministers; he shall take Care that the Laws be faithfully executed, and shall Commission all the Officers of the United States.

Section. 4. The President, Vice President and all civil Officers of the United States, shall be removed from Office on Impeachment for, and Conviction of, Treason, Bribery, or other high Crimes and Misdemeanors.

ARTICLE. III.

Section. 1. The judicial Power of the United States, shall be vested in one supreme Court, and in such inferior Courts as the Congress may from time to time ordain and establish. The Judges, both of the supreme and inferior Courts, shall hold their Offices during good Behaviour, and shall, at stated Times, receive for their Services, a Compensation, which shall not be diminished during their Continuance in Office.

Section. 2. The judicial Power shall extend to all Cases, in Law and Equity, arising under this Constitution, the Laws of the United States, and Treaties made, or which shall be made, under their Authority;—to all Cases affecting ambassadors, other public ministers and consuls;—to all cases of admiralty and maritime Jurisdiction;—to Controversies to which the United States shall be a Party;—to Controversies between two or more States; between a State and Citizens of another State;†—between Citizens of different States,—between Citizens of the same State claiming Lands under Grants of different States, and between a State, or the Citizens thereof, and foreign States, Citizens or Subjects.

In all Cases affecting Ambassadors, other public Ministers and Consuls, and those in which a State shall be Party, the supreme Court shall have original Jurisdiction. In all the other Cases before mentioned, the supreme Court shall have appellate Jurisdiction, both as to Law and Fact, with such Exceptions, and under such Regulations as the Congress shall make.

The trial of all Crimes, except in Cases of Impeachment, shall be by Jury; and such Trial shall be held in the State where the said Crimes shall have been committed; but when not committed within any State, the Trial shall be at such Place or Places as the Congress may by Law have directed.

Section. 3. Treason against the United States, shall consist only in levying War against them, or in adhering to their Enemies, giving them Aid and Comfort. No Person shall be convicted of Treason unless on the Testimony of two Witnesses to the same overt Act, or on Confession in open Court.

The Congress shall have power to declare the Punishment of Treason, but

† *Restricted by the 11th Amendment.*

no Attainder of Treason shall work Corruption of Blood, or Forfeiture except during the Life of the Person attainted.

Article. IV.

Section. 1. Full Faith and Credit shall be given in each State to the public Acts, Records, and judicial Proceedings of every other State. And the Congress may by general Laws prescribe the Manner in which such Acts, Records and Proceedings shall be proved, and the Effect thereof.

Section. 2. The Citizens of each State shall be entitled to all Privileges and Immunities of Citizens in the several States.

A Person charged in any State with Treason, Felony, or other Crime, who shall flee from Justice, and be found in another State, shall on demand of the executive Authority of the State from which he fled, be delivered up, to be removed to the State having Jurisdiction of the crime.

[No Person held to Service or Labour in one State, under the Laws thereof, escaping into another, shall, in Consequence of any Law or Regulation therein, be discharged from such Service or Labour, but shall be delivered up on Claim of the Party to whom such Service or Labour may be due.] †

Section. 3. New States may be admitted by the Congress into this Union; but no new State shall be formed or erected within the Jurisdiction of any other State; nor any State be Formed by the Junction of two or more States, or parts of States, without the Consent of the Legislatures of the States concerned as well as of the Congress.

The Congress shall have Power to dispose of and make all needful Rules and Regulations respecting the Territory or other Property belonging to the United States; and nothing in this Constitution shall be so construed as to Prejudice any Claims of the United States, or of any particular State.

Section. 4. The United States shall guarantee to every State in this Union a Republican Form of Government, and shall protect each of them against invasion; and on Application of the Legislature, or of the Executive (when the Legislature cannot be convened) against domestic Violence.

Article. V.

The Congress, whenever two-thirds of both Houses shall deem it necessary, shall propose Amendments to this Constitution, or, on the Application of the Legislatures of two-thirds of the several States, shall call a Convention for proposing Amendments, which, in either Case, shall be valid to all Intents and Purposes, as part of this Constitution, when ratified by the Legislatures of three-

† *Superseded by the 13th Amendment.*

fourths of the several States, or by Conventions in three-fourths thereof, as the one or the other Mode of Ratification may be proposed by the Congress; Provided, [that no Amendment which may be made prior to the Year One thousand eight hundred and eight shall in any Manner affect the first and fourth Clauses in the Ninth Section of the first Article; and] † that no State, without its Consent, shall be deprived of its equal Suffrage in the Senate.

ARTICLE. VI.

All Debts contracted and Engagements entered into, before the Adoption of this Constitution, shall be as valid against the United States under this Constitution, as under the Confederation. This Constitution, and the Laws of the United States which shall be made in Pursuance thereof; and all Treaties made, or which shall be made, under the Authority of the United States, shall be the supreme Law of the Land; and the Judges in every State shall be bound thereby, any Thing in the Constitution or Laws of any State to the Contrary notwithstanding.

The Senators and Representatives before mentioned, and the Members of the several State Legislatures, and all executive and judicial officers, both of the United States and of the several States, shall be bound by Oath or Affirmation to support this Constitution; but no religious Test shall ever be required as a qualification to any Office or public Trust under the United States.

ARTICLE. VII.

The Ratification of the Conventions of nine States shall be sufficient for the Establishment of this Constitution between the States so ratifying the same.

Done in Convention by the Unanimous Consent of the States present the Seventeenth Day of September in the Year of our Lord one thousand seven hundred and Eighty seven, and of the Independence of the United States of America the Twelfth. In Witness whereof We have hereunto subscribed our Names.

---

† *Obsolete.*

Articles in Addition to, and Amendment of, the Constitution of the United states of America, Proposed by Congress, and Ratified by the Legislatures of the Several States, Pursuant to the Fifth Article of the Original Constitution†

ARTICLE [I] ‡

Congress shall make no law respecting an establishment of religion, or prohibiting the free exercise thereof; or abridging the freedom of speech, or of the press; or the right of the people peaceably to assemble, and to petition the Government for a redress of grievances.

ARTICLE [II]

A well regulated Militia, being necessary to the security of a free State, the right of the people to keep and bear Arms shall not be infringed.

ARTICLE [III]

No Soldier, shall, in time of peace, be quartered in any house, without the consent of the Owner, nor in time of war, but in a manner to be prescribed by law.

ARTICLE [IV]

The right of the people to be secure in their persons, houses, papers, and effects, against unreasonable searches and seizures, shall not be violated, and no Warrants shall issue, but upon probable cause, supported by Oath or affirmation, and particularly describing the place to be searched, and the persons or things to be seized.

ARTICLE [V]

No person shall be held to answer for a capital or otherwise infamous crime, unless on a presentment or indictment of a Grand Jury, except in cases arising in the land or naval forces, or in the Militia, when in actual service in time of War or public danger; nor shall any person be subject for the same offence to

---

† *This heading appears only in the joint resolution submitting the first ten amendments.*
‡ *Only the 13th, 14th, 15th, and 16th articles of amendment had numbers assigned to them at the time of ratification.*

be twice put in jeopardy of life or limb; nor shall be compelled in any criminal case to be a witness against himself, nor be deprived of life, liberty, or property, without due process of law; nor shall private property be taken for public use, without just compensation.

ARTICLE [VI]

In all criminal prosecutions, the accused shall enjoy the right to a speedy and public trial, by an impartial jury of the State and district wherein the crime shall have been committed, which district shall have been previously ascertained by law, and to be informed of the nature and cause of the accusations; to be confronted with the witnesses against him; to have compulsory process for obtaining witnesses in his favor, and to have the Assistance of Counsel for his defence.

ARTICLE [VII]

In suits at common law, where the value in controversy shall exceed twenty dollars, the right of trial by jury shall be preserved, and no fact tried by a jury, shall be otherwise reexamined in any Court of the United States, than according to the rules of the common law.

ARTICLE [VIII]

Excessive bail shall not be required, nor excessive fines imposed, nor cruel and unusual punishments inflicted.

ARTICLE [IX]

The enumeration in the Constitution, of certain rights, shall not be construed to deny or disparage others retained by the people.

ARTICLE [X]

The powers not delegated to the United States by the Constitution, nor prohibited by it to the States, are reserved to the States respectively, or to the people.

(Amendments I–X, in force 1791.)

ARTICLE [XI] †

The Judicial power of the United States shall not be construed to extend to any suit in law or equity, commenced or prosecuted against one of the

† *Adopted in 1798.*

United States by Citizens of another State, or by Citizens or Subjects of any Foreign State.

Article [XII] †

The Electors shall meet in their respective States and vote by ballot for President and Vice-President, one of whom, at least, shall not be an inhabitant of the same State with themselves; they shall name in their ballots the person voted for as President, and in distinct ballots the person voted for as Vice-President, and they shall make distinct lists of all persons voted for as President, and of all persons voted for as Vice-President, and of the number of votes for each, which lists they shall sign and certify, and transmit sealed to the seat of the government of the United States, directed to the President of the Senate;—The President of the Senate shall, in the presence of the Senate and House of Representatives, open all the certificates and the votes shall then be counted;—The person having the greatest number of votes for President, shall be the President, if such number be a majority of the whole number of Electors appointed; and of no person have such majority, then from the persons having the highest numbers not exceeding three on the list of those voted for as President, the House of Representatives shall choose immediately, by ballot, the President. But in choosing the President, the votes shall be taken by states, the representation from each state having one vote; a quorum for this purpose shall consist of a member or members from two-thirds of the states, and a majority of all the states shall be necessary to a choice. [And if the House of Representatives shall not choose a President whenever the right of choice shall devolve upon them, before the fourth day of March next following, then the Vice-President shall act as President, as in the case of the death or other constitutional disability of the President.] ‡ The person having the greatest number of votes as Vice-President, shall be the Vice-President, if such number be a majority of the whole number of Electors appointed, and if no person have a majority, then from the two highest numbers on the list, the Senate shall choose the Vice-President; a quorum for the purpose shall consist of two-thirds of the whole number of Senators, and a majority of the whole number shall be necessary to a choice. But no person constitutionally ineligible to the office of President shall be eligible to that of Vice-President of the United States.

Article XIII *

Section 1. Neither slavery nor involuntary servitude, except as a punishment for crime whereof the party shall have been duly convicted, shall exist within the United States, or any place subject to their jurisdiction.

† *Adopted in 1804.*
‡ *Superseded by section 3 of the 20th Amendment.*
* *Adopted in 1865.*

Section 2. Congress shall have power to enforce this article by appropriate legislation.

Article XIV †

Section 1. All persons born or naturalized in the United States, and subject to the jurisdiction thereof, are citizens of the United States and of the State wherein they reside. No State shall make or enforce any law which shall abridge the privileges or immunities of citizens of the United States; nor shall any State deprive any person of life, liberty, or property, without due process of law; nor deny to any person within its jurisdiction the equal protection of the laws.

Section 2. Representatives shall be apportioned among the several States according to their respective numbers, counting the whole number of persons in each State, excluding Indians not taxed. But when the right to vote at any election for the choice of electors for President and Vice-President of the United States, Representatives in Congress, the Executive and Judicial officers of a State, or the members of the Legislature thereof, is denied to any of the male inhabitants of such State, being twenty-one years of age, and citizens of the United States, or in any way abridged, except for participation in rebellion, or other crime, the basis of representation therein shall be reduced in the proportion which the number of such male citizens shall bear to the whole number of male citizens twenty-one years of age in such State.

Section 3. No person shall be a Senator or Representative in Congress, or elector of President and Vice-President, or hold any office, civil or military, under the United States, or under any State, who, having previously taken an oath, as a member of Congress, or as an officer of the United States, or as a member of any State legislature, or as an executive or judicial officer of any State, to support the Constitution of the United States, shall have engaged in insurrection or rebellion against the same, or given aid or comfort to the enemies thereof. But Congress may by a vote of two-thirds of each House, remove such disability.

Section 4. The validity of the public debt of the United States, authorized by law, including debts incurred for payment of pensions and bounties for services in suppressing insurrection or rebellion, shall not be questioned. But neither the United States nor any State shall assume or pay any debt or obligation incurred in aid of insurrection or rebellion against the United States, or any claim for the loss or emancipation of any slave; but all such debts, obligations, and claims shall be held illegal and void.

Section 5. The Congress shall have the power to enforce, by appropriate legislation, the provisions of this article.

---

† *Adopted in 1868.*

ARTICLE XV †

Section 1. The right of citizens of the United States to vote shall not be denied or abridged by the United States or by any State on account of race, color, or previous condition of servitude—

Section 2. The Congress shall have power to enforce this article by appropriate legislation.

ARTICLE XVI ‡

The Congress shall have power to lay and collect taxes on incomes, from whatever source derived, without apportionment among the several States, and without regard to any census or enumeration.

ARTICLE [XVII] *

The Senate of the United States shall be composed of two senators from each State, elected by the people thereof, for six years; and each senator shall have one vote. The electors in each State shall have the qualifications requisite for electors of the most numerous branch of the State legislature.

When vacancies happen in the representation of any State in the Senate, the executive authority of such State shall issue writs of election to fill such vacancies: *Provided,* That the legislature of any State may empower the executive thereof to make temporary appointments until the people fill the vacancies by election as the legislature may direct.

This amendment shall not be so construed as to affect the election or term of any Senator chosen before it becomes valid as part of the Constitution.

[ARTICLE [XVIII] **

[*Section 1.* After one year from the ratification of this article, the manufacture, sale, or transportation of intoxicating liquors within, the importation thereof into, or the exportation thereof from the United States and all territory subject to the jurisdiction thereof for beverage purposes is hereby prohibited.

[*Section 2.* The Congress and the several States shall have concurrent power to enforce this article by appropriate legislation.

[*Section 3.* This article shall be inoperative unless it shall have been ratified as an amendment to the Constitution by the legislatures of the several States, as

---

† *Proclaimed March 30, 1870.*
‡ *Adopted in 1913.*
* *Adopted in 1913.*
** *Adopted in 1919.*

provided in the Constitution, within seven years from the date of the submission hereof to the States by the Congress.] †

ARTICLE [XIX] ‡

The right of citizens of the United States to vote shall not be denied or abridged by the United States or by any State on account of sex.

Congress shall have power to enforce this article by appropriate legislation.

ARTICLE [XX] *

Section 1. The terms of the President and Vice President shall end at noon on the 20th day of January, and the terms of Senators and Representatives at noon on the 3d day of January, of the years in which such terms would have ended if this article had not been ratified; and the terms of their successors shall then begin.

Section 2. The Congress shall assemble at least once in every year, and such meeting shall begin at noon on the 3d day of January, unless they shall by law appoint a different day.

Section 3. If, at the time fixed for the beginning of the term of the President, the President elect shall have died, the Vice President elect shall become President. If a President shall not have been chosen before the time fixed for the beginning of his term, or if the President elect shall have failed to qualify, then the Vice President elect shall act as President until a President shall have qualified; and the Congress may by law provide for the case wherein neither a President elect nor a Vice President elect shall have qualified, declaring who shall then act as President, or the manner in which one who is to act shall be selected, and such person shall act accordingly until a President or Vice President shall have qualified.

Section 4. The Congress may by law provide for the case of the death of any of the persons from which the House of Representatives may choose a President whenever the right of choice shall have devolved upon them, and for the case of the death of any of the persons from whom the Senate may choose a Vice President whenever the right of choice shall have devolved upon them.

Section 5. Sections 1 and 2 shall take effect on the 15th day of October following the ratification of this article.

Section 6. This article shall be inoperative unless it shall have been ratified as an amendment to the Constitution by the legislatures of three-fourths of the several States within seven years from the date of its submission.

---

† *Repealed by section 1 of the 21st Amendment.*
‡ *Adopted in 1920.*
* *Adopted in 1933.*

Article [XXI] †

Section 1. The Eighteenth Article of amendment to the Constitution of the United States is hereby repealed.

Section 2. The transportation or importation into any State, Territory, or possession of the United States for delivery or use therein of intoxicating liquors in violation of the laws thereof, is hereby prohibited.

Section 3. This article shall be inoperative unless it shall have been ratified as an amendment to the Constitution by conventions in the several States, as provided in the Constitution, within seven years from the date of the submission thereof to the States by the Congress.

Article [XXII] ‡

Section 1. No person shall be elected to the office of the President more than twice, and no person who has held the office of President, or acted as President, for more than two years of a term to which some other person was elected President shall be elected to the office of the President more than once. But this article shall not apply to any person holding the office of President when this Article was proposed by the Congress, and shall not prevent any person who may be holding the office of President, or acting as President, during the term within which this Article becomes operative from holding the office of President or acting as President during the remainder of such term.

Section 2. This article shall be inoperative unless it shall have been ratified as an amendment to the Constitution by the legislatures of three-fourths of the several States within seven years from the date of its submission to the States by the Congress.

Article [XXIII] *

Section 1. The District constituting the seat of Government of the United States shall appoint in such manner as the Congress may direct:

A number of electors of President and Vice President equal to the whole number of Senators and Representatives in Congress to which the District would be entitled if it were a State, but in no event more than the least populous State; they shall be in addition to those appointed by the States, but they shall be considered, for the purposes of the election of President and Vice President, to be electors appointed by a State; and they shall meet in the District and perform such duties as provided by the twelfth article of amendment.

Section 2. The Congress shall have power to enforce this article by appropriate legislation.

---

† *Adopted in 1933.*
‡ *Adopted in 1951.*
* *Adopted in 1961.*

General Bibliography

Appadorai, A., *The Substance of Politics* (Fair Lawn, N. J., 1961).

Arnold, T. W., *The Symbols of Government* (New York, 1962).

Ashirvatham, E., *Political Theory* (Lucknow, India, 8th ed.).

Blackham, H. J., *Political Discipline in a Free Society* (New York, 1963).

Cantril, H., *Human Nature and Political Systems* (New Brunswick, N. J., 1961).

Carter, G. M., and Herz, J. H., *Government and Politics in the Twentieth Century* (New York, 1961).

Dahl, R. A., *Modern Political Analysis* (Englewood Cliffs, N. J., 1963).

Ebenstein, W., *Political Thought in Perspective* (New York, 1963).

Eckstein, H. H., and Apter, D. E., Eds., *Comparative Politics* (New York, 1963).

Field, G. C., *Political Theory* (London, 1963).

Finer, H., *The Major Governments of Europe* (Evanston, Ill., 1960).

Finer, H., *The Theory and Practice of Modern Government* (London, 1961).

Hacker, A., *The Study of Politics* (New York, 1963).

Hamilton, H. D., Ed., *Political Institutions* (Boston, 1962).

Hitchner, D. G., and Harbold, W. H., *Modern Government* (New York, 1962).

Lasswell, H. D., *The Future of Political Science* (Englewood Cliffs, N. J., 1963).

Merriam, C. E., *Political Power* (New York, 1964).

Miller, J. D. B., *The Nature of Politics* (London, 1964).

Pennock, J. R., and Smith, D. G., *Political Science* (New York, 1964).

Rienow, R., *Introduction to Government* (New York, 3rd ed., 1964).

Schmandt, H. J., and Steinbicker, P. G., *Fundamentals of Government* (Milwaukee, 1963).

Suggestions for Further Study

CHAPTER 1

Appadorai, A., *The Substance of Politics*. Quite thorough treatise on all aspects of political science by an Indian scholar. Especially useful for reference. Oxford University Press, London, 6th ed. 1952. 524 pp.

Brown, Delbert F., *The Growth of Democratic Government*. Describes government, democratic or otherwise, as it operates in several countries, pointing out flaws and failures. Intended as a warning. Public Affairs Press, Washington, D. C., 1959. 117 pp.

Burgess, John W., *The Foundations of Political Science*. An old "classic" on political science, still valuable for considerations of theory. Columbia University Press, New York, 1933. 158 pp.

Field, G. C., *Political Theory*. A survey of major aspects of political science with considerable discussion of the "pros" and "cons" of democracy. The author was a British professor of philosophy. Methuen & Co., London, 1956. 297 pp.

Garner, James W., *Introduction to Political Science*. One of the early textbooks on general political science. Still valid and useful. American Book Co., New York, 1910. 616 pp.

Garner, James W., *Political Science and Government*. A somewhat later revision and enlargement of the author's *Introduction to Political Science*. American Book Co., New York, 1928. 821 pp.

Gettell, Raymond G., *Political Science*. An old but thorough treatise on the field of political science in general. Still valid and useful. Grimm & Co., Boston & New York, 1933. 488 pp.

Neumann, Robert G., *European and Comparative Government*. An advanced comparative government text of the traditional type. Contains much information that is useful in illustrating many points of political science. Some of the material on particular governments is outdated. McGraw-Hill Book Co., New York and London, 1955. 818 pp.

Pennock, J. Roland, and Smith, David G., *Political Science: An Intro-*

duction. An advanced college textbook covering most phases of the subject, but does not include structural forms of government. Macmillan Co., New York, 1964. 707 pp.

CHAPTER 2

Laski, Harold J., *Politics.* A handbook, by an eminent British political scientist of a generation ago, covering four aspects of the state: its nature, its place in society, its organization, and its relation to other states. J. B. Lippincott Co., Philadelphia, 1961. 160 pp.

Jouvenel, Bertrand de (translated by J. F. Huntington), *Sovereignty: An Inquiry into the Political Good.* A scholarly study of the nature and operation of authority and its relation to the concept of sovereignty. Heavy reading, but rewarding. University of Chicago Press, Chicago, 1957. 320 pp.

Jouvenel, Bertrand de (translated by J. F. Huntington), *On Power.* An elaborate analytical and somewhat philosophical study of the numerous aspects of power, and of its operation within and among states. The Viking Press, New York, 1949. 421 pp.

Schermerhorn, Richard A., *Society and Power.* A sociological analysis of the structure and operation of power within a society. Random House, New York, 4th printing, 1964. Paperback. 114 pp.

CHAPTER 3

Arendt, Hannah, *The Origins of Totalitarianism.* The historical development, nature and operations of totalitarianism as a menace to the Free World. Harcourt, Brace & Co., New York, 1951. 477 pp.

Barbu, Zevedei, *Democracy and Dictatorship: Their Psychology and Patterns of Life.* Psychological and sociological analysis of democracy, Nazism and Communism. Grove Press, New York, 1956. 275 pp.

Burns, Edward McNall, *Ideas in Conflict: The Political Theories of the Contemporary World.* Description and analysis of present-day ideologies and political theories. W. W. Norton & Co., New York, 1960. 587 pp.

Dallin, Alexander, Ed., *Diversity in International Communism 1961-1963.* Prepared for the Research Institute on Communist Affairs, Columbia University. Traces and analyzes the disruptive forces operating within the Communist movement, including the Soviet-Chinese break, relations of the Soviet Union and its satellites, and developments in Communist parties in the Western World. Columbia University Press, New York, 1963. 867 pp.

Daniels, Robert V., *The Nature of Communism*. Discusses various aspects of Communism, its recent role in the world, and its future prospects. Quite up-to-date. Random House, New York, 1962. 398 pp.

Ebenstein, William, *Today's Isms: Communism, Fascism, Capitalism, Socialism*. Description and critical examination of each of these ideologies. Prentice-Hall, New York, 1954. 191 pp.

Ebenstein, William, *Totalitarianism: New Perspectives*. Good brief study of totalitarianism: kinds, characteristics, background. Holt, Rinehart and Winston, New York, 1962. Paperback. 80 pp.

Hoover, J. Edgar, *A Study of Communism*. The head of the F. B. I. looks into Communist activity everywhere, but stresses its subversive efforts in the United States. Holt, Rinehart and Winston, New York, 1962. 212 pp.

Lane, Robert E., *Political Ideology: Why the American Common Man Believes What He Does*. A defense of American ideology rather than an objective study, but provides some good analysis. Macmillan Co., New York, 1962. 509 pp.

Rossiter, Clinton, *Conservatism in America: The Thankless Persuasion*. Traces the history of conservatism in America and defends its role in shaping American institutions. Alfred A. Knopf, New York, 2nd ed. 1962. 308 pp.

Schmandt, Henry J., *A History of Political Philosophy*. Sketches the history of political thought from earliest times. Especially useful is Part VII (chapters 19-23) on present-day ideologies. Bruce Publishing Co., Milwaukee, 1960. 499 pp.

Schumpeter, Joseph A., *Capitalism, Socialism and Democracy*. Scholarly but pro-Socialist analysis of the conflict of socialist and capitalist viewpoints in relation to democracy. Stresses mainly economic aspects, especially in relation to the United States. Harper & Brothers, New York, 3d edition 1950. 431 pp.

CHAPTER 4

Jennings, W. Ivor, *The British Constitution*. A good, clear description of the structure and operation of the major features of the British constitutional system. Cambridge University Press, London, 1941. 232 pp.

McIlwain, Charles Howard, *Constitutionalism Ancient and Modern.* Traces the historic development of constitutionalism from ancient to modern times. Cornell University Press, Ithaca, N. Y., 1940. 162 pp.

Spiro, Herbert J., *Government by Constitution: The Political Systems of Democracy.* A general text on political science. Discusses various aspects of democratic government and describes governments of several individual countries. Random House, New York, 1959. 496 pp.

Strong, C. F., *Modern Political Constitutions: An Introduction to the Comparative Study of Their History and Existing Form.* Analytical and historical discussion of constitutionalism and of different types of constitutions and constitutional institutions. Rather old, but still useful. G. P. Putnam's Sons, New York and London, 1930. 385 pp.

Wilson, Woodrow, *Constitutional Government in the United States.* After an opening essay on constitutional government in general, this book describes the government of the United States as a constitutional system. Columbia University Press, New York, 1921. 236 pp.

CHAPTER 5

Appleby, Paul H., *Citizens as Sovereigns.* A commentary on the freedom of citizens and the political process in the United States. Syracuse University Press, Syracuse, N. Y., 1962. 200 pp.

Brogan, D. W., *America in the Modern World.* A Cambridge University professor of political science evaluates American society and institutions in the setting of the present-day world. Rutgers University Press, New Brunswick, N. J., 1960. 117 pp.

Brogan, D. W., *Citizenship Today.* Three lectures on problems of citizenship, one each in England, France and the United States. University of North Carolina Press, Chapel Hill, N. C., 1960. 116 pp.

Douglas, William O., *The Anatomy of Liberty: The Rights of Man Without Force.* Stimulating discussion by a Supreme Court justice of the protection of liberty through law in the United States, the United Nations, and other international organizations. Trident Press, New York, 1963. 194 pp.

Hayek, F. A., *The Constitution of Liberty.* An evaluation of liberty under law, noting the pitfalls. Part III is concerned with the economics of the welfare state. University of Chicago Press, Chicago, 1960. 570 pp.

Muller, Herbert J., *Issues of Freedom: Paradoxes and Promises*. Author describes as "a philosophical essay." Analyzes the nature and basis of freedom and its relation to various institutions and ideals. Harper & Brothers, New York, 1960. 170 pp.

CHAPTER 6

Arnold, Thurman W., *The Symbols of Government*. Despite its title, the book is devoted mainly to law as an aspect of government. It also touches on political philosophy. Yale University Press, New Haven, Conn., 1935. 278 pp.

Berman, Harold J., *The Russians in Focus*. Most of the book is a sociological description of various phases of Russian life under Stalin, but the last three chapters (10-12) describe certain features of Soviet government: Soviet law, the Communist party, and the discipline of terror. Little, Brown & Co., Boston, 1953. 209 pp.

Brogan, D. W., and Verney, Douglas V., *Political Patterns in Today's World*. Compares and contrasts government structures and political systems in the Free World and the Communist World. Very stimulating. Harcourt, Brace & World, New York, 1962. 274 pp.

Buell, Raymond Leslie, and others, *New Governments in Europe*. Descriptions of the totalitarian regimes that were in full sway when the book appeared. A publication of the Foreign Policy Association. Thomas Nelson and Sons, New York, 1935. 444 pp.

Cantril, Hadley, *Soviet Leaders and Mastery Over Man*. Explains how and why the Soviet leaders manipulate people to maintain their system. Rutgers University Press, New Brunswick, N. J., 1960. 273 pp.

Fine, Sidney, *Laizzez Faire and the General-Welfare State*. Analysis of the conflict of these two viewpoints. University of Michigan Press, Ann Arbor, Mich., 1956. 468 pp.

Godfrey, E. Drexel, Jr., *The Government of France*. Describes the government of France under the Fifth Republic with some discussion of historical background, national characteristics and problems. Thomas Y. Crowell Co., New York, 1961. 186 pp.

Harris, Richard, *Independence and After: Revolution in Underdevel-*

oped Countries. An examination of the factors in recent revolutions in former colonial areas with an assessment of the Communist threat. Issued under the auspices of the London Institute of Race Relations. Oxford University Press, London, 1962. Paperback. 69 pp.

Heidenheimer, Arnold J., *The Governments of Germany*. Handbook describing and contrasting the governments and social and economic structures of West and East Germany. Thomas Y. Crowell Co., New York. Second printing 1962. Paperback. 224 pp.

Loewenstein, Karl, *Political Power and the Governmental Process*. Treats most aspects of government in general with particular emphasis on controls over government. A somewhat different approach. University of Chicago Press, Chicago, 1956. 442 pp.

Morstein-Marx, Fritz, and others, *Foreign Governments: The Dynamics of Politics Abroad*. Chapters by different authors on various aspects of general political science and comparative government. Some of the descriptions of governments are outdated. Prentice-Hall, New York, 1949. 713 pp.

Neumann, Robert G., *European and Comparative Government*. An advanced comparative government textbook of the traditional type. Much information that is useful in illustrating many points of political science. McGraw-Hill Book Co., New York and London, 1955. 818 pp.

Rossiter, Clinton L., *Constitutional Dictatorship: Crisis Government in Modern Democracies*. Describes regimes, devised within a constitutional framework, to cope with major crises in Germany, France, Britain and the United States. Discusses the value and importance of crisis government. Princeton University Press, Princeton, N. J., 1948. 322 pp.

Verney, Douglas V., *The Analysis of Political Systems*. A comparison of the structure and operation of the principal types of "free" government. The Free Press, Chicago, 1959. 239 pp.

CHAPTER 7

Binkley, Wilfred E., *President and Congress*. A historical sketch and evaluation of the relations of the President and Congress in the United States. Random House, New York, 3rd ed. 1962. 404 pp. (Also cited under Chapter VIII)

Haskins, George L., *The Growth of English Representative Govern-*

ment. A historical sketch of the medieval beginnings and development of Parliament with stress on the growth of its representative character. University of Pennsylvania Press, Philadelphia, 1948. 131 pp.

Wheare, K. C., *Legislatures*. A comparison of the organization and operation of legislative bodies with some evaluation of their effectiveness. Oxford University Press, London, 1963. 247 pp.

Young, Roland, *The British Parliament*. A rather elaborate description of Parliament and its operations. Northwestern University Press, Evanston, Ill., 1962. 259 pp.

CHAPTER 8

Binkley, Wilfred E., *The Man in the White House: His Powers and Duties*. A clear and concise analysis of the United States presidency in its numerous aspects. Johns Hopkins Press, Baltimore, Md., 1958. 310 pp.

Binkley, Wilfred E., *President and Congress*. A historical sketch and evaluation of the relations of the President and Congress in the United States. Random House, New York, 3rd ed. 1962. 404 pp. (Also cited under Chapter VII)

Carter, Byrum E., *The Office of Prime Minister*. A good description of all major aspects of the office of Prime Minister of Great Britain. Faber and Faber, London, 1956. 362 pp.

Daalder, Hans, *Cabinet Reform in Britain 1914-1963*. A discussion of developments and changes in the British cabinet system during the years indicated. The author is a Dutch scholar. Stanford University Press, Stanford, Cal., 1963. 381 pp.

Jennings, Sir Ivor, *Cabinet Government*. A rather full description and explanation of various aspects of the British cabinet system. Cambridge University Press, Cambridge, Eng., 1959. 587 pp.

Laski, Harold J., *The American Presidency*. Written by a British political scientist with Labor Party leanings to interpret the American presidency to British readers. Harper & Brothers, New York and London, 1940. 278 pp.

CHAPTER 9

Berman, Harold J., *Justice in Russia: An Interpretation of Soviet Law*. Describes Soviet law, courts and judicial procedures before some recent reforms. Harvard University Press, Cambridge, Mass., 1950. 322 pp.

Hazard, John N., *Settling Disputes in Soviet Society*. The development and operation of the Soviet judicial system and court procedures. Columbia University Press, New York, 1960. 554 pp.

Jackson, R. M., *The Machinery of Justice in England*. A very full, but non-technical description of the legal system, judicial system and individual courts in England by an eminent English lawyer. Cambridge University Press, Cambridge, Eng., 1940. 342 pp.

McWhinney, Edward, *Judicial Review in the English-Speaking World*. A comparison of judicial review features in the various common law countries. The author is concerned primarily with Canada. University of Toronto Press, Toronto, Canada, 1956. 201 pp.

CHAPTER 10

Dawson, Robert MacGregor, *The Civil Service in Canada*. A sketch of the historical development and description of present arrangements on the Canadian civil service. Oxford University Press, London, 1929. 266 pp.

Dimock, Marshall E., *Modern Politics and Administration: A Study of the Creative State*. Included here for Part II, "Administration," which explains most of the major features of governmental administration, specifically in the United States, but of general application. American Book Co., New York, 1937. 440 pp.

Gladden, E. N., *An Introduction to Public Administration*. A good sketch of public administration and the civil service in Great Britain. Staples Press, London, 2nd ed. 1948. 174 pp.

Kilpatrick, Franklin P., Cummings, Milton C., and Jennings, M. Kent, *The Image of the Federal Service*. A description and evaluation of the civil service and administration in the United States federal government. The Brookings Institution, Washington, D. C., 1964. 301 pp.

CHAPTER 11

Banfield, Edward C., *Political Influence*. A study of irregular political influence in the Chicago area, but Parts II and III (chapters 8-12) give an insight into the nature and operation of such political influences in general. Free Press of Glencoe (Crowell Collier), New York, 1961. 354 pp.

Birke, Wolfgang, *European Elections by Direct Suffrage*. Thesis submitted to the Council of Europe, Strasbourg, in fulfillment of a

Research Fellowship. "A comparative study of electoral systems used in western Europe and their utility for the direct election of a European parliament." A. W. Sythoff, Leyden, 1961. 124 pp.

Brogan, D. W., *Politics in America.* A Cambridge University professor describes and interprets American politics and political problems, primarily for British readers. Harper & Brothers, New York, 1954. 467 pp.

Butler, D. E., Ed., *Elections Abroad.* Studies by different authors of a particular election in each of four countries: France, Poland, Ireland and South Africa. Macmillan, London, 1959. 280 pp.

Merriam, Charles Edward, *New Aspects of Politics.* A discussion of new trends and influences in politics as of the mid-1920's. For the most part, these trends and influences still continue. The author was an eminent political scientist. University of Chicago Press, Chicago, 1925. 253 pp.

Mosca, Gaetano (edited and revised by Arthur Livingston, translated by Hannah D. Kahn), *The Ruling Class.* An elaborate study of numerous aspects of the role of a ruling class in politics. McGraw-Hill Book Co., New York, 1939. Paperback. 514 pp.

Snyder, Richard C., and Wilson, H. Hubert, *Roots of Political Behavior: Introduction to Government and Politics.* A large collection of essays by prominent authorities on almost all aspects of politics and the relation of politics to other activities. American Book Co., 1949. 694 pp.

Williamson, Chilton, *American Suffrage: From Property to Democracy, 1760-1860.* A history of the expansion of suffrage in America during the century indicated. Princeton University Press, Princeton, N. J., 1960. 306 pp.

CHAPTER 12

Alford, Robert R., *Party and Society: The Anglo-American Democracies.* A study of the relation of social class to party politics in Great Britain, Australia, the United States and Canada. Rand McNally & Co., Chicago, 1963. 396 pp.

Bailey, Sidney D., Ed., *Political Parties and the Party System in Britain.* A symposium of studies by various authors concerning the historical development of parties, discussion of individual parties, and analysis of political operations in Britain. Frederick A. Praeger, New York, 1952. 63 pp.

Barron, Richard, *Parties and Politics in Modern France*. A description of French politics and individual parties during the Fouth Republic. Public Affairs Press, Washington, D. C., 1959. 213 pp.

Duverger, Maurice (translated by Barbara and Robert North), *Political Parties: Their Organization and Activity in the Modern State*. An analytical study of the structure and operation of parties and party systems, with emphasis on Europe. Methuen & Co., London, 1954. 439 pp.

Michels, Robert (translated from the Italian by Eden and Cedar Paul), *Political Parties: A Sociological Study of the Oligarchical Tendencies of Modern Democracy*. Although old and a bit heavy, this book brings out significant, but often overlooked, features of party politics. Jarrold & Sons, London. 1915. 454 pp.

CHAPTER 13

Berdes, G. R., *Up From Ashes: An American Journalist Reports from Germany*. An optimistic appraisal of developments in West Germany, with some insight into German public opinion on political issues. Marquette University Institute of German Affairs, Milwaukee, Wis., 1964. 58 pp.

Key, V. O., Jr., *Public Opinion and American Democracy*. An analytical study of the factors involved in public opinion and the channels through which it operates to influence government. It applies to the United States specifically, but much of it is valid for other countries as well. Alfred A. Knopf, New York, 1964. 586 pp.

La Polombara, Joseph, *Interest Groups in Italian Politics*. A study, made under a Social Science Research Council grant, of various aspects of pressure politics in Italy. Princeton University Press, Princeton, N. J., 1964. 452 pp.

Wilson, Francis Graham, *A Theory of Public Opinion*. A study of the characteristics of public opinion from a philosophical rather than an analytical point of view. Henry Regnery Co., Chicago, 1962. 308 pp.

Zeigler, Harmon, *Interest Groups in American Society*. A good discussion of pressure groups and pressure politics in the United States. It would be interesting to compare this with La Polombara's *Interest Groups in Italian Politics*. Prentice-Hall, Englewood Cliffs, N. J., 1964. 343 pp.

CHAPTER 14

Bowett, D. W., *Self-Defense in International Law*. A legalistic treatment of the portions of international law which deal with defense, neutrality, aggression and related topics. Recommended only as a sampling of the character and operation of international law. Frederick A. Praeger, New York, 1958. 294 pp.

Cantril, Hadley, Ed., *Tensions that Cause Wars*. Statements and individual papers brought together by UNESCO. University of Illinois Press, Urbana, Ill., 1950. 303 pp.

Chase, Eugene P., *The United Nations in Action*. Story of the background and establishment, and description of the organizational structure of the United Nations. Written when the United Nations was just getting into operation. McGraw-Hill Book Co., New York, 1950. 464 pp.

Cohen, Benjamin V., *The United Nations: Constitutional Developments, Growth, and Possibilities*. Three lectures delivered at Harvard University Law School. Discusses powers under the Charter, responsibilities of member nations, and future prospects. Harvard University Press, Cambridge, Mass., 1961. 106 pp.

Dallin, Alexander, Ed., *Soviet Conduct in World Affairs: A Selection of Readings*. A collection of essays, by especially qualified writers, on the character and explanation of Soviet foreign policy, especially under Stalin. Columbia University Press, New York, 1960. 318 pp.

Frankel, Joseph, *International Relations*. A good handbook on the conduct of international relations. Oxford University Press, New York, 1964. 227 pp.

Herz, John H., International Politics in the Atomic Age. Describes major features of international relations and discusses the impact of atomic weapons on world politics. Columbia University Press, New York, 1959. 360 pp.

Knorr, Klaus, *The War Potential of Nations*. An analysis of the elements that enter into military strength. Issued by Center for International Studies, Princeton University. Princeton University Press, Princeton, N. J., 1956. 310 pp.

Larson, Arthur, *When Nations Disagree: A Handbook on Peace Through Law*. A descriptive analysis of international law and its operation, with evaluation of the influence of international law in the maintenance of peace. Louisiana State University Press, Baton Rouge, La., 1961. 251 pp.

Larus, Joel, Ed., *Comparative World Politics*. A collection of essays by different authors discussing the state system, the role of power, diplomacy, and international law, as well as some ethical and philosophical questions in international relations. Wadsworth Publishing Co., Belmont, Cal., 1964. 274 pp.

MacIver, R. M., *An Abiding Peace*. Discusses ways of building abiding peace through equitable international settlements and the development of international law. These are the views of an eminent sociologist. Macmillan, New York, 1943. 195 pp.

Nicholas, H. G., *The United Nations as a Political Institution*. An analytical description of the United Nations and its major organs. Oxford University Press, London, 1959. 222 pp.

Peaslee, Amos J., *United Nations Government*. A discussion of the making of the United Nations Charter and of features of the Charter itself, written while the drafting of the Charter was still in its final stages. G. P. Putnam's Sons, New York, 1945. 183 pp.

Webster, Sir Charles, *The Art and Practice of Diplomacy*. A collection of lectures, some of which throw considerable light on British diplomacy (and diplomacy in general) and on British foreign policy. Barnes & Noble, New York, 1962. 246 pp.

Index

311

NOTES

NOTES

NOTES

NOTES

NOTES

NOTES

NOTES

NOTES